Advances in Management Research

Edited by

Debasis Chanda
Dean – Academic and Professor, MDI Murshidabad

Amrita Sengupta
Assistant Professor, MDI Murshidabad

Debaditya Mohanti
Assistant Professor, MDI Murshidabad

Advances in Management Research

Emerging Challenges and Trends

Edited by

Debasis Chanda
Amrita Sengupta
Debaditya Mohanti

Routledge
Taylor & Francis Group
London   New York

First published 2023
by Routledge
4 Park Square, Milton Park, Abingdon, Oxon OX14 4RN

and by Routledge
605 Third Avenue, New York, NY 10158

Routledge is an imprint of the Taylor & Francis Group, an Informa business

© 2023 Management Development Institute, Murshidabad, India

ISBN: 9781032387147 (pbk)
ISBN: 9781003366638 (eBook)
DOI: 10.4324/9781003366638

Typeset in Sabon LT Std
by HBK Digital

Contents

List of figures

List of tables

Foreword

MDIM's vision is to be an internationally excellent B-school known for academic excellence towards creating a sustainable future for both business and society globally. We are highly focused to create an ethical and knowledge centric culture that values outstanding academic excellence, training, research and consultancy. We follow a three pronged approach- connect, nurture and grow, with open doors at all levels.

The purpose of the present edited book 'Advances in Management Research: Emerging Challenges and Trends' is to provide a wide range of paradigmatic and theoretical substantive research articles in management research. The book covers a wide range of current, comprehensive, state-of-the-art articles in review of management research. The chapters in this book reviews the literature, offer a critical commentary, develop an innovative framework, and discuss future developments, as well as present specific empirical studies. I shall feel amply rewarded if the book proves helpful in the development of result-oriented management research studies.

Wish you the very best.

Prof. (Dr.) Atmanand
Director, MDI Murshidabad

1 Progress of financial inclusion in India – A comprehensive index

Priyanka Roy[1] *and Binoti Patro*[2] *

[1]Research Scholar, Department of Management Studies, National Institute of Technology Silchar, India

[2]Assistant Professor, Department of Management Studies, National Institute of Technology Silchar, India

*Corresponding author: binotipatro@mba.nits.ac.in

Abstract

The importance of financial inclusion in promoting sustainable economic growth has been emphasised in growing literatures. This paper endeavours to construct an index of financial inclusion in India to track progress over a period of fourteen years. The index incorporates indicators for determining financial inclusion and applies endogenous weighting methodology with a two-step principal component analysis. The results indicate that the level of financial inclusion has increased over the years from 2005–2018. The dimension indices however reveal that India has progressed well in terms of 'access' to formal financial services after 2014 but the 'usage' of financial services has not been consistent.

Keywords: Dimensions; financial inclusion; formal financial services; index; indicators; principal component analysis

Introduction

Financial inclusion is one of the topmost priorities in different economies around the globe. An inclusive financial system is believed to provide equitable growth and aids in poverty reduction especially in low income and developing countries. In a broad approach, financial inclusion can be described as the provision of financial services to poorer sections of an economy at a convenient and affordable manner. As defined by the World Bank, 'Financial inclusion means that individuals and businesses have access to useful and affordable financial products and services that meet their needs – transactions, payments, savings, credit and insurance – delivered in a responsible and sustainable way.'

An inclusive financial system is instrumental in efficiently allocating productive resources, improving routine management of finances and facilitating reduction of informal finances (Sarma, 2010). The World Bank Global Findex data shows that there are still 1.7 billion adults globally who are unbanked and are not a part of a formal financial system. The policymakers across the globe are thus giving priority to framing of various policies in building a more inclusive financial system. Financial inclusion has also been placed prominently as an enabling factor for the achievement of developmental goals featuring it as a target in eight (out of 17) sustainable development goals (SDG) of 2030 by the United Nations.

Not only framing policies for financial inclusion are important, but also keeping a track of its implementation and subsequent progress is equally significant. This makes it imperative to measure financial inclusion over time using different indicators explaining the dimensions of financial inclusion. A handful of literatures have proposed financial inclusion indices considering different indicators. While there is no consensus on the dimensions and indicators chosen for measuring financial inclusion, a majority of the studies have focused on bank related indicators. This paper has attempted to include different possible dimensions significant in the construction of financial inclusion index for India over a period of 14 years as per data availability. The measure is thus expected to be comprehensive in terms of indicators used as well as in terms of tracking progress over time.

Literature review

Financial inclusion has gained priority at a global level for sustainable growth and has enticed interest in the academic community. Various studies have shown the importance of financial inclusion enabling growth and reducing poverty and inequality (Abor et al., 2018; Agyemang-badu et al., 2018; Allen et al., 2014; and Park and Mercado, 2015; Sharma, 2016). Demirgüç-Kunt and Klapper (2013) have viewed an inclusive financial system to be beneficial to the economically disadvantaged groups. Sarma and Pais (2008) used the financial inclusion index developed by Sarma (2008) in a cross country analysis, and ascertained a positive connection between financial inclusion and development. Demirguc-Kunt et al. (2017) stressed on the formal financial services being beneficial for the consumers and the usage of different financial products being a contributor to inclusive and sustainable economic growth. To realise the importance of financial inclusion, it is equally important to understand financial exclusion (Demirguc-Kunt et al., 2015). The reasons of financial exclusion have been segregated into different supply side and demand side barriers (Barboni et al., 2017; Soedarmono and Prasetyantoko, 2017). Mialou and Amidzic (2017) mentioned insufficient income, excessive lending risk profile and government failures to be the causes of involuntary financial exclusion.

The importance of financial inclusion has resulted in continuous iterations made to identify measures in determining the extent of financial inclusion in different economies. However different studies have differed in their approach either in terms of selecting different indicators or changes in the methodology. The approaches proposed in different literatures include a variety of financial inclusion dimensions. Honohan (2008) estimated the accessibility of formal financial services of a proportion of households for 160 countries. However his study has been criticised on the grounds of failing to justify differences across countries over time. Sarma (2008) presented a multidimensional index by giving equal importance to all the dimensions defining financial inclusion. Chakravarty and Pal (2010) also constructed index for financial inclusion but demonstrated an axiomatic approach for its measurement. Arora (2010) followed the arithmetic average method to measure financial inclusion index by including dimensions like ease and cost for advanced and developing economies. Goel andSharma (2017) through their index measured the level of financial inclusion in India by including insurance indicators along with banking indicators. Gupte et al. (2012) used the geometric mean and incorporated comprehensive dimensions to build financial inclusion for India. Few others have also assessed financial inclusion for specific states in India (Kumar and Mishra, 2009; Ambarkhane et al., 2016; Mehrotra et al., 2009). A study by Amidzic et al. (2014) identified and assigned different weights to financial inclusion dimensions using factor analysis and developed the index of financial inclusion.

Contribution of this study

The earlier studies have attempted to construct indices of financial inclusion using select dimensions which is evident from analysing different literatures. One of the earlier measures has been developed by Sarma (2008). The gradual development in the study has been done by Sarma (2010, 2012, 2015) by bringing in changes like addition of indicators under certain dimension or modifying the methodology to calculate financial inclusion but lacked in incorporating weights to different indicators of financial inclusion. Certain other studies followed the same methodology and incorporated the index of financial inclusion (Kuri and Laha, 2011; Yorulmaz, 2013; Sethy, 2016). Few others have applied arithmetic average or geometric average for calculating the financial inclusion index (Arora, 2010; Chakravarty and Pal, 2010; Gupte et al., 2012; Amidzic et al., 2014). The attempt of objective weights assignment to the indicators and dimensions have been considered by only a few studies (Amidzic et al., 2014; Cámara and Tuesta, 2017; Park and Mercado, 2018). In terms of dimensions and indicators chosen, there is no particular consensus among the studies. While most of the earlier studies have considered only bank related indicators using dimensions of financial inclusion classified into three categories: penetration, availability, and usage of financial services. However, collating the definitions of different studies, it is observed that the dimensions of penetration and availability are often used synonymously. While some studies have combined these two dimensions as "outreach" dimension, others have used the term "access" to define availability or penetration dimension (Ngo, 2019; Wang and Guan, 2017).

Examining the variables taken by different studies, the present study has tried to incorporate maximum dimensions possible as per data availability for the Indian context. It incorporates banking indicators as well as indicators from other financial services like insurance and credit cooperatives. Credit unions have a potential to enhance financial inclusion among the poor as they can pool their savings and take loans at lower interest rates. In the areas where financial inclusion is hindered because of lower penetration of banking services, credit unions can play a role in advancing greater financial inclusion. The earlier studies have not incorporated this indicator in measuring India's financial inclusion. IMF Financial Access Survey data and reports of Insurance Regulatory Development Authority of India (IRDAI) have been used for the required data[1]. The indicators under outreach, availability, or penetration dimension have not been considered separately but combined into 'access' dimension. So our study uses different indicators under two main dimensions, access and usage as shown in Table 1.1.

---

[1]The geographic and demographic indicators for insurance were not available directly and have been imputed from the estimated adult population figures from World Development Indicators (World Bank) and geographical area (in sq kms) from Census 2011.

Table 1.1 Indicators used for measuring financial inclusion in the current study

Access indicators	Number of deposit accounts with commercial banks per 1,000 adults
	Number of loan accounts with commercial banks per 1,000 adults
	Demographic outreach of bank branches
	Geographic outreach of bank branches
	Demographic outreach of ATMs
	Geographic outreach of ATMs
	Demographic outreach of credit union and credit cooperative branches
	Geographic outreach of credit union and credit cooperative branches
	Demographic outreach of Life Insurance Offices
	Geographic outreach of Life Insurance Offices
	Demographic outreach of life insurance agents
	Geographic outreach of life insurance agents
Usage indicators	Outstanding deposits with commercial banks (% of GDP)
	Outstanding deposits with credit unions and credit cooperatives (% of GDP)
	Outstanding loans from commercial banks (% of GDP)
	Outstanding loans from credit unions and credit cooperatives (% of GDP)
	Insurance penetration
	Insurance density

Source: By Authors
(The definition of the indicators, except the insurance indicators have been taken from IMF Financial Access Survey data)

However, quality or barriers dimension is not considered in the study because of problems with data availability. The detailed explanation of these indicators has been given in section 3.1.

In terms of methodology, the study has attempted to construct an index of financial inclusion following Camara and Tuesta (2017) by incorporating principal component analysis (PCA) for endogenous weights assignment to dimensions and indicators. The earlier studies incorporating this methodology are cross country studies and it has not been studied in analysing the progress of financial inclusion in the Indian context. The studies on the Indian context are also only for a limited time period. This study considers a period of 14 years which makes it a broader study for analysing progress over the years. The study assesses the extent of enhancement of financial inclusion since it was formally initiated (2005) up to 2018 (the most recently available data[2]). This represents an updated study and allows reflecting upon the initiatives by policy makers over these years.

---

[2]The most recent data from IMF FAS is that of 2019. Due to unavailability of data on few indicators of insurance for the year 2019, we have considered data up to 2018 as the most recently available data for all the indicators to avoid discarding the indicators.

Methodology

The computation of the index follows a three-step methodology:

- The identification of dimensions and their indicators to be used for the financial inclusion measurement
- The calculation of dimension indices
- The calculation of the index of financial inclusion of India from 2005–2018

Dimensions and Indicators to measure financial inclusion

The dimensions are selected based on the definition of financial inclusion as maximization of access and usage of financial services. In addition to access to financial services which accounts for supply side of financial inclusion, usage of financial services accounting for demand side of financial inclusion is equally important. For instance, mere access to a bank account will not benefit the economy unless the bank account is used for transactions which will lead to capital formation by channelizing the funds into productive resources. Thus having an increased number of accounts in the bank will be of little significance if the accounts lay dormant. So, two dimensions- access and usage- have been considered for the current study.

We have considered twelve indicators for the access dimension (Table 1.1). These pertain to bank related indicators as well as other financial services indicators like insurance and credit unions and cooperatives. As banks are the backbone of any financial system and the initial definition of financial inclusion accounted for the access to bank accounts by the poor, we have divided the access dimension into 'access to banking services' and 'access to other financial services'. In the usage dimension, we have considered six indicators pertaining to bank as well as non-bank indicators.

The dimension 'accesses to banking services' includes six indicators:

- Number of deposit accounts with commercial banks per 1,000 adults (d_1)
- Number of loan accounts with commercial banks per 1,000 adults (d_2)
- Demographic outreach of bank branches (d_3)
- Geographic outreach of bank branches (d_4)
- Demographic outreach of ATMs (d_5)
- Geographic outreach of ATMs (d_6)

The first two indicators can be considered as proxies for the size of banked population which is reflective of the penetration of banking services to its users. The demographic branch and ATM outreach is defined by the number of commercial bank branches per lakh adults and number of ATMs per lakh adults respectively. The geographic branch and ATM penetration is defined by the number of commercial bank branches and ATMs, respectively, per thousand square kilometres. This reflects the intensity of branches and ATMs in geographic and demographic terms and a higher value of these indicators reflects higher possibilities of access opportunities of banking services by households.

'Access to other financial services' also includes six indicators reflecting the geographic and demographic penetration of credit cooperatives and insurance services like life insurance offices and agents[3] :

- Demographic outreach of credit union and credit cooperative branches defined by number of credit union and credit cooperative branches per 100,000 adults (d_7)
- Geographic outreach of credit union and credit cooperative branches defined by number of credit union and credit cooperative branches per 1,000 square km (d_8)
- Demographic outreach of life insurance offices defined by number of insurance offices (life) per thousand adults (d_9)
- Geographic outreach of life insurance offices defined by number of insurance offices (life) per 1000 square km (d_{10})
- Demographic outreach of life insurance agents – number of agents per lakh adults (d_{11})
- Geographic outreach of life insurance agents – number of agents per 1000 square km (d_{12})
- The 'usage of financial services' includes six indicators:
- Outstanding deposits with commercial banks (% of GDP) (d_{13})
- Outstanding deposits with credit unions and credit cooperatives (% of GDP) (d_{14})
- Outstanding loans from commercial banks (% of GDP) (d_{15})
- Outstanding loans from credit unions and credit cooperatives (% of GDP) (d_{16})
- Insurance penetration (d_{17})
- Insurance density (d_{18})

Deposit and credit to the gross domestic product (GDP) can be seen as the indicator of participation of banks and other financial services in a country's economy. The usage of financial services will contribute to GDP growth by channelizing resources to productive uses. The insurance penetration is defined as the ratio of yearly premium underwritten to the GDP whereas insurance density measures the ratio of yearly premium underwritten to the total number of population. Both these measures are reflective of the growth of the insurance sector in an economy due to an increase in the premium collection which is possible with the usage of the insurance products and services. The descriptive statistics of the different indicators in measuring access and usage dimensions are depicted in Table 1.2.

Calculation of financial inclusion index: two-step PCA.

The present study computes the index of financial inclusion (IF) for India using a two-step PCA following the method used by Camara and Tuesta (2017). The method incorporates calculation of dimension indices in the first step and then the

---

[3]We have not considered non-life insurance data due to unavailability of data on number of non life insurance offices and agents. While number of non- life insurance offices data is available after 2010, the data for non-life sector agents are not available for any year.

overall financial inclusion is calculated using the values of the dimension indices. This method allows for the estimation of endogenous weights to the indicators and the dimensions which is critical because there should not be subjective bias towards a particular indicator while constructing an index. Using PCA helps in determining the best weighted combination of indicators defining the underlying latent structure in computing the index.

The financial inclusion for each year is considered to be a latent variable which is linearly determined as:

$$FI_t = w_1 D_t^{ba} + w_2 D_t^{fsa} + w_3 D_t^{u} \tag{1}$$

Here t denotes the years while, D_t^{ba}, D_t^{fsa}, D_t^{u} are the dimensions of access to banking services, access to other financial services and usage of financial services respectively.

The three dimensions also can be expressed as a linear combination of indicators in the following set of equations:

$$D_t^{ba} = \alpha_1 d_1 + \alpha_2 d_2 + \alpha_3 d_3 + \alpha_4 d_4 + \alpha_5 d_5 + \alpha_6 d_6 \tag{2}$$

$$D_t^{fsa} = \beta_1 d_7 + \beta_2 d_8 + \beta_3 d_9 + \beta_4 d_{10} + \beta_5 d_{11} + \beta_6 d_{12} \tag{3}$$

$$D_t^{u} = \gamma_1 d_{13} + \gamma_2 d_{14} + \gamma_3 d_{15} + \gamma_4 d_{16} + \gamma_5 d_{17} + \gamma_6 d_{18} \tag{4}$$

Here α, β, γ, are the unknown parameters and $d_i (i = 1,2,3,...,18)$ are the indicators of different dimensions as defined in previous sections. These indicators are aggregated to dimension indices using the first stage PCA. So, the dimensions of bank access, access to other financial services, and usage are sub- indices estimated as linear functions using principal components.

Assume a p dimensional matrix R_p *(pxp)* as the correlation matrix of standardised indicators of each dimension. The jth Eigen value of j principal components is denoted by λ_j where $j = 1,2,...,p$; p being the number of indicators. So, there are p principal components for p number of variables and p Eigen values for each component. ϕj is a column vector of p dimension *(px1)* which is the Eigen vector of the correlation matrix. Assuming $\lambda_1 > \lambda_2 > ... \lambda_p$, the kth principal component is denoted by P_k *(k = 1,2,...,p)*.

The estimators for dimension indices are obtained from the weighted averages of principal components:

$$D_t^{ba} = \frac{\sum_{j,k=1}^{p} \lambda_j^{ba} P_{kt}^{ba}}{\sum_{j=1}^{p} \lambda_j^{ba}} \tag{5}$$

$$D_t^{fsa} = \frac{\sum_{j,k=1}^{p} \lambda_j^{fsa} P_{kt}^{fsa}}{\sum_{j=1}^{p} \lambda_j^{fsa}} \tag{6}$$

Table 1.2 Descriptive statistics of the indicators

Indicators	Mean	Median	Std. deviation	Min	Max
Number of deposit accounts with commercial banks per 1,000 adults	1,124.47	974.62	477.86	604.74	1,937.29
Number of loan accounts with commercial banks per 1,000 adults	143.77	140.43	26.43	99.95	199.63
Number of commercial bank branches per 100,000 adults	11.32	10.81	2.20	8.86	14.51
Number of commercial bank branches per 1,000 sqkm	33.95	31.94	9.23	23.09	48.11
Number of ATMs per 100,000 adults	11.43	9.88	7.63	2.29	22.00
Number of ATMs per 1,000 sqkm	35.41	29.24	25.50	5.93	71.86
Number of credit union and credit cooperative branches per 100,000 adults	25.21	24.30	2.84	22.41	31.55
Number of credit union and credit cooperative branches per 1,000 sqkm	73.98	72.74	3.15	71.50	81.90
Number of life insurance offices per thousand adults	1.07	1.15	0.32	0.39	1.41
Number of insurance offices (Life) per 1000 sq km	2.89	3.36	0.93	0.91	3.66
Number of agents per lakh adults	236.29	236.25	82.95	62.35	350.83
Number of agents per 1000 sq km	634.43	640.55	215.99	146.40	906.01
Outstanding deposits with commercial banks (% of GDP)	59.27	61.36	5.30	48.09	64.79
Outstanding deposits with credit unions and credit cooperatives (% of GDP)	5.95	5.89	0.34	5.54	6.92
Outstanding loans from commercial banks (% of GDP)	44.66	46.26	5.52	31.73	50.39
Outstanding loans from credit unions and credit cooperatives (% of GDP)	5.54	5.29	0.67	4.72	7.04
Insurance penetration	4.08	3.93	0.68	3.14	5.20
Insurance density	53.89	54.50	13.17	22.70	74.00

Source: Authors' calculation

$$D_t^u = \frac{\sum_{j,k=1}^{p} \lambda_j^u P_{kt}^u}{\sum_{j=1}^{p} \lambda_j^u} \tag{7}$$

Here each component P_k in the three equations is a linear combination of the indicators in each of the dimensions. λ_j is the variance of kth principal component denoting weights to each component. The weights to each subsequent component keep decreasing which indicates that the first component explains the largest proportion of variance in each dimension and hence the pth component accounts for the least variance. Thus the first component of p orthogonal principal components representing a data-set of correlated variables of p dimensions explains the largest amount of information from the initial data.

After the dimension indices are determined, the second stage PCA employs the same procedure as the first stage in determining the overall financial inclusion index and its estimator:

$$FI_t = \frac{\sum_{j,k=1}^{p} \lambda_j P_{kt}}{\sum_{j=1}^{p} \lambda_j} \tag{8}$$

Each component P_k is again a linear combination of the three-dimension indices and can be represented in terms of eigen vectors as:

$$P_{1t} = \varphi_{11} D_t^{ba} + \varphi_{12} D_t^{fsa} + \varphi_{13} D_t^{u} \tag{9}$$

$$P_{2t} = \varphi_{21} D_t^{ba} + \varphi_{22} D_t^{fsa} + \varphi_{23} D_t^{u} \tag{10}$$

$$P_{3t} = \varphi_{31} D_t^{ba} + \varphi_{32} D_t^{fsa} + \varphi_{33} D_t^{u} \tag{11}$$

Thus (8) can be represented as:

$$FI_t = \frac{\sum_{j=1}^{3} \lambda_j \left(\varphi_{j1} D_t^{ba} + \varphi_{j2} D_t^{fsa} + \varphi_{j3} D_t^{u} \right)}{\sum_{j=1}^{3} \lambda_j} \tag{12}$$

Rearrangement of the terms will give us,

$$FI_t = \frac{\sum_{j=1}^{3} \lambda_j \varphi_{j1}}{\sum_{j=1}^{3} \lambda_j} D_t^{ba} + \frac{\sum_{j=1}^{3} \lambda_j \varphi_{j2}}{\sum_{j=1}^{3} \lambda_j} D_t^{fsa} + \frac{\sum_{j=1}^{3} \lambda_j \varphi_{j3}}{\sum_{j=1}^{3} \lambda_j} D_t^{ba} \tag{13}$$

So the financial inclusion can be represented as a weighted average of the dimensions- bank access, access to other financial services, and usage (Equation 1) where the weights reflect the relative importance of the dimension in measuring the financial inclusion index calculated as:

$$w_t = \frac{\sum_{j=1}^{3} \lambda_j \varphi_{jk}}{\sum_{j=1}^{3} \lambda_j}, \quad k = 1,2,3 \tag{14}$$

The weights are also normalised to 1.

Further, as suggested in the study of Camara and Tuesta (2017), all the components are retained which equals the number of explanatory variables and hence the common practice of replacing the set of causal variables with a few principal components is not followed. The reason for this is to avoid discarding important information that can affect the accurate estimation of financial inclusion.

Results

The first stage PCA enabled the computation of weights for the indicators and estimation of the dimension indices. Tables 1.3, 1.4, and 1.5 exhibit the principal

Table 1.3 PCA estimates for indicators of 'Access to Banking services' dimension

Indicators	PC1	PC2	PC3	PC4	PC5	PC6	Norm weight
Number of deposit accounts with commercial banks per 1,000 adults	0.4113	0.0068	–0.8282	0.2970	0.1683	–0.1680	0.1672
Number of loan accounts with commercial banks per 1,000 adults	0.3909	0.8951	0.2008	0.0082	–0.0609	–0.0436	0.1679
Number of commercial bank branches per 100,000 adults	0.4118	–0.2331	0.0026	–0.5409	–0.5060	–0.4771	0.1659
Number of commercial bank branches per 1,000 sq km	0.4129	–0.1120	–0.0298	–0.5432	0.4043	0.5979	0.1674
Number of ATMs per 100,000 adults	0.4105	–0.2764	0.4929	0.2953	0.5195	–0.3937	0.1655
Number of ATMs per 1,000 sq km	0.4117	–0.2356	0.1726	0.4867	–0.5279	0.4793	0.1661
Eigen values	5.85370	0.13113	0.01373	0.00126	0.00013	0.00006	

Access to banking services

Principal components	Proportion of variance	Cumulative variance
PC1	0.97562	0.97562
PC2	0.02185	0.99747
PC3	0.00229	0.99976
PC4	0.00021	0.99997
PC5	0.00002	0.99999
PC6	0.00001	1

Source: Authors' calculations

component estimates for the indicators of the three dimensions. The weights for each indicator for the dimension of bank access are almost the same which reflects that none of the indicators is dominant in determining bank access. It is also observed that the first component has an even contribution of the six indicators reflecting the same latent structure measured by these indicators. The lower panel of Table 1.3 shows the variance explained by each component which is a measure of ratio of the Eigen value of each component to the sum of the Eigen values. For access to banking services, the first component explains almost 98% of the total information in this dimension.

In case of 'access to other financial services' dimension, we again see a similar weighing structure, although the demographic and geographic penetration of credit

Table 1.4 PCA estimates of 'access to other financial services' dimension

Indicators	PC1	PC2	PC3	PC4	PC5	PC6	Norm weight
Number of credit union and credit cooperative branches per 100,000 adults	−0.3655	−0.6872	−0.2116	−0.5151	0.2836	0.0597	−0.7288
Number of credit union and credit cooperative branches per 1,000 sq km	−0.4136	−0.0321	−0.7103	0.5525	−0.1320	−0.0250	−0.7011
Number of life insurance offices per thousand adults	0.4294	0.0121	−0.4802	−0.4227	−0.4476	−0.4537	0.6389
Number of insurance offices (life) per 1000 sq km	0.4219	0.2563	−0.4635	−0.1275	0.4715	0.5503	0.6791
Number of agents per lakh adults	0.3924	−0.5766	0.0724	0.2663	−0.4549	0.4801	0.5123
Number of agents per 1000 sq km	0.4230	−0.3583	0.0053	0.4044	0.5220	−0.5066	0.5996
Eigen values	5.10356	0.63304	0.22984	0.03332	0.00022	0.00003	

Access to other financial services

Principal components	Proportion of variance	Cumulative variance
PC1	0.85059	0.85059
PC2	0.10551	0.9561
PC3	0.03831	0.99441
PC4	0.00555	0.99996
PC5	0.00004	0.99999
PC6	0.00001	1

Source: Authors' calculations

Table 1.5 PCA estimates of 'usage' dimension

Indicators	PC1	PC2	PC3	PC4	PC5	PC6	Norm weight
Outstanding deposits with commercial banks (% of GDP)	0.4513	–0.1388	0.3617	–0.4933	0.1590	–0.6145	0.7884
Outstanding deposits with credit unions and credit cooperatives (% of GDP)	–0.4373	–0.1415	–0.1763	–0.8199	0.0707	0.2836	–0.9833
Outstanding loans from commercial banks (% of GDP)	0.4522	–0.1739	0.4816	–0.0572	0.0858	0.7230	0.8360
Outstanding loans from credit unions and credit cooperatives (% of GDP)	–0.4566	–0.1187	0.3797	0.2243	0.7604	–0.0684	–0.8153
Insurance penetration	–0.0548	0.9408	0.2801	–0.1711	0.0296	0.0570	0.3649
Insurance density	0.4349	0.1767	–0.6193	–0.0391	0.6191	0.1065	0.8092
Eigen values	4.30504	1.07685	0.35143	0.21308	0.04460	0.00899	

Usage of financial services

Principal components	Proportion of variance	Cumulative variance
PC1	0.71751	0.71751
PC2	0.17948	0.89698
PC3	0.05857	0.95555
PC4	0.03551	0.99107
PC5	0.00743	0.9985
PC6	0.0015	1

Source: Authors' calculations

union and cooperative branches gives us negative weights suggesting that the access to other financial services is hampered due to poor penetration of cooperatives over the years. The geographical penetration of life insurance offices contributes highest to the dimension index of access to other financial services. The first component explains 85% of the information and has an even contribution of the indicators.

A similar pattern is seen in the principal components of usage dimension. The weight of each indicator is almost similar but negative weights have been evident for the indicator of credit union and credit cooperatives reflecting negative contribution of this indicator in the overall index of usage dimension. The contribution of insurance penetration is also less as compared to the other indicators. 'Outstanding loans from commercial banks' are is the most important indicator for determining the usage dimension followed by insurance density. The first two components explain nearly 90% of the total information in this dimension. An important insight in this case is reflected by the insurance penetration indicator adding some extra information through the second principal component and gaining significance in the explanation of the usage dimension.

Table 1.6 shows the dimension indices of the financial inclusion of India from 2005–2018. It is seen that there has been an increasing trend in the dimension index of bank access from 2005–2018. The negative values till 2012 reflects that the achievement in this dimension has not been adequate for financial inclusion. There is a noticeable increase in the access to banks since 2014 which can be attributed to the success of 'Pradhan Mantri Jan Dhan Yojana' launched in 2014 resulting in a notable reduction of unbanked population in the country. This reflects consistency of the results with the theory.

Access to other financial services shows an increasing trend in the index values up to 2012 after which it has declined. However, it has improved from 2017–2018. This might be attributed to the negative or falling trend in the access and usage indicator of credit unions and credit cooperatives. The usage dimension also has an increasing trend over the years; however the trend is not consistent.

Table 1.6 Dimension indices values from 2005–2018

Year	Access to banking services	Access to other financial services	Usage of financial services
2005	−1.23036	−8.61304	−10.6747
2006	−1.14973	−7.18169	−5.61067
2007	−0.9942	−1.96243	−2.53012
2008	−0.84489	0.675019	−1.33153
2009	−0.72111	2.590128	1.062157
2010	−0.50369	2.948349	1.873446
2011	−0.34279	2.413971	2.330247
2012	−0.06796	2.026399	1.942246
2013	0.124053	1.052136	1.368802
2014	0.596659	1.647603	1.727685
2015	0.881147	1.372477	2.0352
2016	1.2298	1.253766	1.749236
2017	1.429038	0.834632	2.467143
2018	1.594033	0.942694	3.590901

Source: Authors' calculations

Table 1.7 depicts the second stage PCA estimates and normalised weights for the three financial inclusion dimensions considered in the study. The weights reflect access to banks as the most important dimension contributing to the overall financial inclusion followed by usage dimension. However, bank access is not a dominant dimension and usage of financial services is assigned nearly the same weight. This reflects that usage of financial services is also important and access is not adequate for determining the financial inclusion.

The structure of the principal components reflects the first component explaining 81% of the total variation and the first two components together explaining 99% of the total information in financial inclusion. Also, the first component explaining 81% of the information has an even contribution of the three dimensions reflecting an identical latent structure of the dimensions. Dimension of access to banking services adding additional information through the second principal component gains significance in the explanation of the overall financial inclusion.

Finally, Table 1.8 shows the values of financial inclusion index for India from 2005–2018.

The table depicts that there has been an increase in the overall level of financial inclusion over the years. The index of overall financial inclusion doesn't reflect a significant change in the level of financial inclusion after 2014 as in the case of access to banks. This reflects that mere access to banking services will not improve the overall level of financial inclusion. To have a sustainable increase in the financial inclusion level, usage of financial services also has to be consistently improved at par with the access dimension.

Conclusion

The proposed financial inclusion index in this paper is likely to help in keeping a track of the progress of the financial inclusion in Indian economy over time. This

Table 1.7 PCA estimates of financial inclusion

Dimensions	PC1	PC2	PC3	Norm weights
Bank access	0.508563	0.828661	0.233848	0.396086232
Other FS access	0.586446	−0.53222	0.610592	0.271580414
Usage	0.630432	−0.17339	−0.75663	0.332333354
Eigen values	2.432423	0.537741	0.029836	

Financial inclusion index

Principal components	Proportion of variance	Cumulative variance
PC1	0.81081	0.81081
PC2	0.17925	0.99005
PC3	0.00995	1

Source: Authors' calculations

Table 1.8 Values of financial inclusion
index of India from 2005–2018

Year (t)	FI_t
2005	–6.37404
2006	–4.27041
2007	–1.76759
2008	–0.59384
2009	0.770795
2010	1.22382
2011	1.294231
2012	1.168884
2013	0.789774
2014	1.257953
2015	1.398113
2016	1.408934
2017	1.612606
2018	2.080768

Source: Authors' calculations

study exhibits an overall improvement in the financial inclusion level over the study period of 14 years. The results show that while there is a notable change in terms of the 'access to banks' after 2014 the usage of financial services does not show consistent improvement over the years. India's financial inclusion has thus improved as far as access to financial services is concerned. However it lags behind in terms of actual usage at par increase in access. This contemplates that the policies of financial inclusion in India focus more on the supply side of the financial inclusion and neglect the demand side which is equally important to reap the benefits of financial inclusion.

For improving the usage of formal financial services, some common challenges involve lack of financial literacy among poor population hindering their knowledge about the financial services available. Transaction cost also prevents the marginalised section from fully utilizing the financial services. To address such challenges is of utmost importance now in order for financial inclusion to expand among the poor in India. The most important area to be addressed now is investment in financial literacy to eliminate ignorance about the benefits of formal financial services. One of the possible ways can be bringing the financial literacy into the mainstream of educational curriculum. Regular surveys in rural areas can prove insightful to comprehend the financial needs of the people which will be helpful in providing tailor-made financial services as per requirements. This will encourage more usage of the services.

This study comes with its limitations. The results of the study depend on the data availability at the national level. Few of the indicators are left due to a lag in data for the time period covered, thus incorporating more dimensions like quality of financial services which may provide a different result. Further, the study incorporates many indicators of financial services to have a comprehensive measure of financial inclusiveness but it has not taken into account the segregation of the indicators based on gender or into rural and urban areas. This can also give us different insights as the access and usage of financial inclusion may be significantly different if taken across gender and different geographical areas. Further research may consider these factors and also construct a state-wise analysis applying this weighting methodology for the indicators and dimensions of financial inclusion. So the index, with further upgrades, can be used to narrow down on locations and communities where financial institutions need to focus their efforts, increasing the efficiency and efficacy of any measures they adopt. This would have a policy implication in shifting focus to those states or geographical areas where financial inclusion is low. The social implication consists in facilitating the policy makers to identify key beneficiaries of financial inclusion schemes and setting up targeted campaigns to increase the coverage thereby allowing for meaningful implementation of any government scheme.

References

Abor, J. Y., Issahaku, H., Amidu, M., and Murinde, V. (2018). Financial Inclusion and Economic Growth: What Do We Know?', Centre for Global Finance, Working Paper Series No 11/2018.

Agyemang-Badu, A. A., Agyei, K., and Duah, E.K. (2018). Financial Inclusion, Poverty and Income Inequality : Evidence from Africa. J. Sprit. Int. J. Pov. Std.2(2).

Allen, F., Carletti, E., Cull, R., Qian, J. Q. J., Senbet, L., and Valenzuela, P. (2014). The African Financial Development and Financial Inclusion Gaps. 23(5):J. Afr. Econ. 614–642.

Ambarkhane, D., Singh, A. S., and Venkataramani, B. (2016). Measuring Financial Inclusion of Indian States. Int. J. Rural Manag. 12(1):72–100.

Amidzic, G., Massara, A., and Mialou, A. (2014). Assessing Countries' Financial Inclusion Standing- A New Composite Index. International Monetary Fund, Working Paper 14/36.

Arora, R. U. (2010). Measuring Financial Access. Economics and Business Statistics Working Paper Series, 1–21.

Barboni, G., Cassar, A., and Demont, T. (2017). Financial Exclusion in Developed Countries: A Field Experiment Among Migrants and Low-Income People in Italy. J. Behav. Econ. Pol.. 1(2):39–49.

Cámara, N. and Tuesta, D. (2017). Measuring Financial Inclusion: A Multidimensional Index. Bank for International Settlements, September.

Chakravarty, S. R. and Pal, R. (2010). Measuring Financial Inclusion : An Axiomatic Approach. Indian J. Sci. Technol. 35(5):813–837.

Demirgüç-Kunt. and A., Klapper, L. (2013). Measuring Financial Inclusion: Explaining Variation in Use of Financial Services across and within Countries. Brookings Papers on Economic Activity, SPRING 2013, 279–321.

Demirguc-kunt, A., Klapper, L., and Singer, D. (2017). Financial Inclusion and Inclusive Growth: A Review of Recent Empirical Evidence. Policy Research Working Paper, April, 1–27.

Demirguc-Kunt, A., Klapper, L., Singer, D. and Oudheusden, P.V. (2015). The Global Findex Database 2014: Measuring Financial Inclusion Around the World. World Bank Group Policy Research Working Paper 7255.

Goel, S. and Sharma, R. (2017). Developing a Financial Inclusion Index for India. Procedia Comput. Sci. 122:949–956.

Gupte, R., Venkataramani, B. and Gupta, D. (2012). Computation of Financial Inclusion Index for India. Procedia Soc. Behav. Sci. 37:133–149.

Honohan, P. (2008). Cross Country Variation in Household Access to Financial Services. J. Bank. Financ. 32:2493–2500.

Kumar, C. and Mishra, S. (2009). Banking Outreach and Household Level Access: Analyzing Financial Inclusion in India. Indira Gandhi Institute of Development Research (IGIDR). www.igidr.ac.in

Kuri, P. K. and Laha, A. (2011). Financial Inclusion and Human Development in India: An Inter-State Analysis. Indian J. Hum. Dev. 5(1):61–77.

Mehrotra, N., Puhazhendi, V., Nair, G. and Sahoo, B.B. (2009). Financial Inclusion- An Overview. National Bank for Agriculture and Rural Development (NABARD), Occasional paper 48.

Mialou, A. andAmidzic, G. (2017). Assessing Countries' Financial Inclusion Standing – A New Composite Index. J. Bank. Finance. Eco. 2(8):105–126.

Ngo, A. L. N. (2019). Index of Financial Inclusion and the Determinants: An investigation in Asia. Asian Econ. Financ. Rev. 9(12):1368–1382.

Park, C. Y. and Mercado, Jr., R. (2018). Financial Inclusion: New Measurement and Cross-Country Impact Assessment. SSRN Electronic Journal. 539.

Park, C.-Y. and Mercado, R. J. (2015). Financial Inclusion, Poverty, and Income Inequality in Developing Asia. SSRN Electronic Journal. 426. https://doi.org/10.2139/ssrn.2558936

Sarma, M. (2008). Index of Financial Inclusion. ICRIER Working Paper No. 215.

Sarma, M. (2010). Index of Financial Inclusion. Discussion Papers in Economics. 1–28. https://www.jnu.ac.in/sites/default/files/DP05_2010.pdf

Sarma, M. (2012). Index of Financial Inclusion- A Measure of Financial Sector Inclusiveness. Working Paper No. 07/2012.

Sarma, M. (2015). Measuring Financial Inclusion. Econ. Bull. 35(1604–611.

Sarma, M. and Pais, J. (2008). Financial Inclusion and Development: A Cross Country Analysis. Annual Conference of the Human Development and Capability Association.

Sethy, S. K. (2015). Developing a Financial Inclusion Index and Inclusive Growth in India. Indian J. Econ. 63(2):283–311.

Sharma, D. (2016). Nexus between Financial Inclusion and Economic Growth: Evidence from the Emerging Indian Economy. J. Financ. Econ. 8(1):1336.

Soedarmono, W. and Prasetyantoko, A. (2017). Financial Literacy and the Demand for Financial Services in Remote Areas: Evidence from Indonesia. SSRN electronic journal. DOI: 10.2139/ssrn.3000339.

Wang, X. and Guan, J. (2017). Financial Inclusion: Measurement, Spatial Effects and Influencing Factors. Appl. Econ. 49(18):1751–1762.

Yorulmaz, R. (2013). Construction of a Regional Financial Inclusion Index in Turkey. J. Bank. Finan. Mark. 7(1):79–101.

2 Gauging the service quality of App Cabs, post COVID-19: Associating sets of underlying constructs

Swapna Datta Khan

Associate Professor, Globsyn Business School, Kolkata, India

Abstract

In March 2020, the entire nation of India was locked down due to the spread COVID-19 pandemic. App Cabs thereafter, resumed services with a slew of measures to prevent the virus from spreading. A query regarding the comfort levels of the consumers with respect to these measures enabled the exploration the attributes of customer service among the App Cabs that impact customer satisfaction, measured by a single Index Score, computed in this research. It is interesting to note that the research revealed that apart from the following of COVID-19 Protocol, the skill of the driver and the helpfulness of the Customer Care Contact Point made significant impact on customer satisfaction.

Keywords: construct validity, exploratory factor analysis, service quality, SERVQUAL

Introduction

March 2020 saw the entire world getting into the grip of the COVID-19 pandemic. Social distancing, nesting and working from home, and other such measures were taken by governments across the world to control the spread of the virus. Nevertheless, business organizations saw a loss in revenue and had to re-engineer their process around the COVID-19 protocol and pandemic-guidelines. The App Cabs, whose innovative business models spelt sustainability a few years back, now had to rethink their service. This paper examines and unearths the attributes of customer service among the App Cabs that impact customer satisfaction, measured by a single Index Score, computed by the researcher.

Objective

To find the attributes of customer service of the App Cabs which impact the satisfaction level of the customer

Methodology

The objective of the research is translated into the need to measure the impact of the underlying construct of each SERVQUAL dimension on an Index Score which spells customer satisfaction levels, created by the researcher, with the help of the underlying construct revealed by using the 22-item multidimensional SERVQUAL on all dimensions taken together. A convenience sample of size 570 was created by survey, during which respondents (demographically homogeneous, as all are adult residents of urban areas in India) submitted measurements of their perceptions of the 35 variables over a 5-point Likert Scale. The data collection was followed by cleaning and some simulation using random numbers. A part of the said respondent-sample has been earlier used in a study by the same researcher. The primary data has been revised for this research. However, the list of 35 variables has been created after a discussion of the SERVQUAL instrument among a Focus Group and is shared by both the research (Datta Khan and Meel, 2021).

The research is divided into four parts: A: Identification of 35 variables relating to customer satisfaction with the help of a Focus Group for use of the 22-item multidimensional SERVQUAL instrument. Collection of adequate primary data using a 5-point Likert Scale (we shall refer to this as the "MasterData").

B: Performance of exploratory factor analysis (EFA) on the Master Data (EFA-Master Data) to unearth an underlying construct and saving of factor scores. Usage of factor scores to create an index score relevant to the reply of each respondent.

C: Performance, within each dimension (Reliability-Responsiveness-Assurance-Empathy-Tangibles) of an EFA, revealing in only three cases, an underlying construct, within the dimension and saving of factor scores.

D: Study the attributes that affect customer satisfaction by checking on the correlation of the factor scores, computed from the EFA within the dimensions and the index score. SPSS 22 Statistical Computational Software is used.

Literature review

Similar studies

Ghosh and Mitra, 2019, in their paper, said that meeting customer expectation impacted the satisfaction levels of the App Cab drivers, who expressed problems with the methodology of the compensation, safety mechanisms, and the assignment of trips to the cars. Datta Khan and Meel, 2021, in their research with the same variables and a separate database, said that pandemic-wary customers put safety and comfort above all else, apart from the driver and customer care service. R and John, 2019 based their research in Ernakulam district and found that factors influencing customer satisfaction of App Cabs are safety, availability, and cashless transactions and laid special emphasis on the App Cab organisation's drivers' knowledge of the routes and road-map. Kumar and Kumar, 2016 found that a sensitivity to pricing and discounts offered seemed to affect customer satisfaction. Customers were also surprised by the innovative nature of the App Cab systems. The brand image of the App Cab organization also played a role in enhancing customer satisfaction. Bappy and Haque, 2018 said that much of customer satisfaction is dependent on the driver's behaviour and driving skills. Promotional discounts, offered through coupons and the safety enabler, for instance the ride-sharing option also appealed to the customers. Paul et al. 2021 found that the educational level of the customer impacted the choice between a pooled cab service and a private cab service. Customers were found to be less sensitive to price, comfort, waiting time, and ease of booking. Pahwa and Goyal, 2019 said that the customers are conscious in the reduction of carbon footprints, as they use App Cabs. Most contemporary customers find an environmentally friendly lifestyle and lifechoices appealing and this translates to cab bookings, as well.

SERVQUAL: The instrument

The SERVQUAL is a 22-item multidimensional instrument to ascertain service quality. Applicable and prominently used, it was developed by Parasuraman *et al*. The 22-item multidimensional scale comprised of dimensions: Reliability, assurance, tangibles, empathy, responsiveness with 4,5,4,5,4 items in the scale, respectively (Buttle, 1996). Ciavolino and Calcagnì, 2005 proposed a method for SERVQUAL Gap Analysis with the generalized cross entropy (GCE) approach allowing to read similtaneously the expectations and perceptions in a unified model representation. They also noted the necessity of weighted SERVQUAL models. Calabrese and Scoglio, 2012 analysed the SERVQUAL (service quality) instrument which is based on a discontinuation pattern checking on the gap between the expectations and perceptions of the customer. They integrated the SERVQUAL gap structure with a Critical Success Factor Analysis.They also recommended the usage of a higher-point (>5 Point) Likert Scale for better results Calabress and Scoglio, 2012. Jiang et al 2002 preliminarily indicated that SERVQUAL had a common structure across diverse populations. However the use of SERVQUAL in rigorous research requires methodological, statistical, and empirical compliance. SERVQUAL has demonstrated stability in marketing literature and the authors, herein, recommended its use as a diagnostic tool in marketing research.

A look into the pandemic related measures taken by the three common Indian App Cabs is given as the Table 2.1 below.

Analysis

In all EFA, coefficients (in the rotated component matrix) below 0.55 have been suppressed; factors have been selected based on Eigen values (>1) and there are no restrictions on the number of iterations required for convergence; Varimax rotation is used to ensure maximum lack of correlation between factors and Bartlett factor scores are saved to enable further computation. In the EFA of dimensions, at the results of the tangibility dimension, 11 variables were reduced to 2. Thus, loadings that were comparatively lower were ignored on the discretion of the researcher. The list of 35 variables defining attributes related to customer satisfaction is shown in the Table 2.2, descriptively

A basic assumption of an EFA is that an underlying construct does exist hidden within 35 variables Hair et al. (2019). However, the 35 variables are further decomposed into 6+4+6+8+11 of the dimensions of the SERVQUAL instrument: reliability, responsiveness, assurance, empathy, tangibles, connoting the acronym, RATER and it is, thus, assumed that there exists an underlying construct in each of the said dimensions separately. Since the interpretation of the factors are given by the loadings directly, the factor analysis model is said to be scale invariant (Härdle and Simar, 2014).

EFA (MasterData): The observed Kaiser-Meyer-Olkin Measure of Sampling Adequacy (KMO-MSA) = 0.897; 6 components (now known as MasterFactors,

Table 2.1 The pandemic related measures taken by the three common Indian App Cabs

Issues/cab aggregators	Uber	Ola	Meru
Wear a mask (driver & customer)	Yes	Yes	Yes
Wear gloves (driver)	Yes	Yes	Yes
Sanitization of car	Yes	Yes	Yes
Air protect barriers	No	No	Yes
Body temperature check of driver	Yes	Yes	Yes
Carrying of hand sanitizers	Yes	Yes	Yes
No use of car air conditioner	Yes	Yes	Not known
Others	Assistance to frontline workers	Assistance to frontline workers	Nil
Source of information	(Uber announces new safety features amid COVID-19, masks now mandatory for both driver and riders, 2020)(Our approach to COVID-19, n.d.)	(Ola launches '10 Steps to a Safer Ride' for driver-partners and customers as services resume in 100+ cities in green and orange zones across the country, n.d.), (Ola Cabs: Ride Safe, n.d.)	(Meru: Ride in Ultra-Hygienic cab, n.d.)

Source: App Cab websites

forming an underlying construct) have shown a cumulative % variance of 69.035. It may be noted in this EFA (and also in the following ones), coefficients below 0.55 have been suppressed in the Rotated Component Matrix. While the rotations converged in 8 iterations. The 6 Factors are shown in the Table 2.3 below, with the factor loadings.

Computation of index scores (Research output): We have performed EFA on the 35 variables of the SERVQUAL instrument and unearthed six factors, that explain 69.035% of the total variance created by the said 35 variables (Note the KMO MSA of 0.897). The variances explained by each of the factors (post Varimax Rotation) could relate to the 'comparative importance' of each factor and is taken as a weight and an Index Score is developed that could substitute as a measure of customer satisfaction. The factors and the weights assigned are shown in Table 2.4. Thus, if the Factor Scores corresponding to 570 cases form the matrix F_{570x6} and the Weights form the vector W_{6x1}, we get the Index Scores I_{570x1} by $F_{570x6} W_{6x1} = I_{570x1}$. It is with these scores that we shall bivariately correlate factor scores unearthed within each dimension, to conclude our research, by finding the extent to which the factors, corresponding to these underlying constructs contribute to the index score and, thus also to customer satisfaction.

Table 2.2 List of variables (research output)

Sno	SERVQUAL Acronym	Question	Sub Question	Variable
1	Reliability (Rel)	Providing services as promised (Promise)	The App Cab reaches me within an appropriate time	Rel_Time
2			The App Cab takes me to my destination as promised	Rel_Promise
3		Dependability in handling customer service problems	The App Cab Customer Care responds whenever I have contacted them	Rel_CustCare
4			The App Cab Customer Care has always solved my problem	Rel_ProbSolv
5		Maintaining Error Free Records	My profile in the App is always correctly updated	Rel_Profile
6			The App has an undertaking that the passenger is not suffering from Covid or Covid-related ailment	Rel_Covid
7	Responsiveness (Res)	Keeping customers informed about when services will be performed	The App informs me about the time when the Cab should be expected	Res_InfoArrival
8			The App informs me about the time when the Cab would reach	Res_InfoDestination
9		Prompt Service to Customers	The App Cab always reaches on time	Res_Prompt
10		Readiness to respond to customer enquiries	Whenever I have asked the driver a question, he has eagerly answered me correctly	Res_Answer
11	Assurance (Ass)	Employees who instill confidence in customers	I always feel confident about the driving skills of the driver	Ass_Driving
12			Whenever I have interacted with the Customer Care of the App Cab, I have felt confident regarding their efforts	Ass_CustCare
13		Making customers feel safe in their transactions	The payment system is transparent	Ass_Paymt
14		Employees who are constantly courteous	The driver of the App Cab is always courteous	Ass_Courtesy
15		Employees have the knowledge to answer customer queries	The driver has knowledge about the App and the Cab system	Ass_DriverKnow
16			The Customer Care executives are knowledgeable enough to answer my queries	Ass_CustCareKnow
17	Empathy (Emp)	Giving customers individual attention	The App communicates with me on an individual basis (remembering my profile settings)	Emp_Attn
18		Employees deal with customers in a caring fashion	I feel well cared for when I interact with the Customer Care staff	Emp_Care
19		Having the customer's best interests at heart	The Customer Care staff keep my interests above all	Emp_CustInt1
20			The behaviour of the driver makes me feel that my interests are above all else	Emp_CustInt2
21		Employees who understand the needs of the customers	The Customer Care Staff understands my needs when I interact with them	Emp_CustNeed1
22			The driver understands my needs very well and helps	Emp_CustNeed2
23		Convenient Business Hours	The App Cabs are active 24x7	Emp_Convenience1
24			The Customer Care is active 24x7	Emp_Convenience2

(continues)

Table 2.2 Continued

Sno	SERVQUAL Acronym	Question	Sub Question	Variable
25		Modern Equipment	The App Cab is equipped with modern amenities	Tan_Equip1
26			The App Cab has wifi which I can access	Tan_Equip2
27			The App Cab has sanitizing equipment on offer	Tan_Equip3
28			The driver has a body-temperature checking equipment	Tan_Equip4
29	Tangibles (Tan)	Visually Appealing Facilities	The App Cab exterior is visually appealing	Tan_VisAppeal1
30			The App is visually appealing to use	Tan_VisAppeal2
31		Employees have a neat professional appearance	The driver is always neatly dressed	Tan_EmpHygiene1
32			The driver always wears a clean mask	Tan_EmpHygiene2
33			The driver wears gloves	Tan_EmpHygiene3
34		Visually appealing materials associated with service	The App Cab interior is comfortable	Tan_CanInterior1
35			The App Cab interior is visually appealing	Tan_CanInterior2
			Total Number of Variables	35

Table 2.3 Factors of EFA (MasterData)

Variable Description	Loadings	Description of the Factor by describing the attributes of the consumer it may relate to	Variable Description	Loadings	Description of the Factor by describing the attributes of the consumer it may relate to	Variable Description	Loadings	Factor by describing the attributes of the consumer it may relate to
The App Cab interior is visually appealing	.550		I feel well cared for when I interact with the Customer Care staff	.583		The App Cab reaches me within an appropriate time	.557	
The App Cab interior is comfortable	.573		The driver understands my needs very well and helps	.605		The App Cab takes me to my destination as promised	.644	This customer is concerned with the punctuality and discipline of the App Cab organization and its frontline staff; Factor3: PunctualityDiscipline
The App Cab is equipped with modern amenities	.578		The Customer Care executives are knowledgeable enough to answer my queries	.612	Such a Customer is satisfied if all contact points demonstrate a Caring Approach, with awareness of the needs of the customer: Factor2: CustomerNeedsAboveAll	The driver has knowledge about the App and the Cab system	.665	
The App Cab has wifi which I can access	.622	The consumer is extremely conscious of the Covid Protol and is also affected positively by modern amenities and comfort: Factor 1: ComfortWithProtocolCompliance				The App informs me about the time when the Cab would reach	.781	
The App has an undertaking that the passenger is not suffering from Covid or Covid-related ailmen	.675		The App Cab interior is visually appealing	.619		The App informs me about the time when the Cab should be expected	.825	
The App Cab has sanitizing equipment on offer	.685		The Customer Care staff keep my interests above all	.685				
The driver is always neatly dressed	.701		The behaviour of the driver makes me feel that my interests are above all else	.689				
The driver has a body-temperature checking equipment	.824							
The driver wears gloves	.836		The Customer Care Staff understands my needs when I interact with them	.747		Variable Description	Loadings	Description of the Factor by describing the attributes of the consumer it may relate to
The driver always wears a clean mask	.861					The App Cabs are active 24x7	.814	Factor 6: 24x7Service
Variable Description	Loadings	Description of the Factor by describing the attributes of the consumer it may relate to				The Customer Care is active 24x7	.871	
The App Cab Customer Care responds whenever I have contacted them	.739	Solution of Issues by CustomerCare: Factor4: CustomerCare	Variable Description	Loadings	Description of the Factor by describing the attributes of the consumer it may relate to			
The App Cab Customer Care has always solved my problem	.751		The payment system is transparent	.701	The customer needs Financial Transparency; Factor 5: FinancialTransparency			

Source: EPA master data

Table 2.4 The master factors and weights assigned to compute the index scores

Factor No	Factor name	% of variance explained by the factor	Weights assigned, W_{6x1}
1	Comfort with protocol compliance	17.128	0.1713
2	Customer needs above all	16.714	0.1671
3	Punctuality discipline	14.779	0.1478
4	Customer care	7.876	0.0788
5	Financial transparency	6.316	0.0632
6	24×7 service	6.222	0.0622

Source: EPA master data

Table 2.5 EFA reliability dimension

Loading		Interpretation of Factors	Factors	
		Description of Variables	1	2
.825		The App Cab reaches me within an appropriate time		
.821		The App Cab takes me to my destination as promised	Reliability of AppCab as a	
.703		The App Cab Customer Care responds whenever I have contacted them	TaxiService; Factor 1:	
.659		The App Cab Customer Care has always solved my problem	ReliableTaxiService	
.691		My profile in the App is always correctly updated		
	.859	The App has an undertaking that the passenger is not suffering from Covid or Covid-related ailment		Factor 2: ReliableProtocolCompliant

Source: EFA Reliability Output

Table 2.6 EFA empathy dimension

Loading		Interpretation of Factors	Factors	
		Description of Variables	1	2
.596		The App communicates with me on an individual basis (remembering my profile settings)		
.719		I feel well cared for when I interact with the Customer Care staff		
.770		The Customer Care staff keep my interests above all	Factor 1:	
.807		The behaviour of the driver makes me feel that my interests are above all else	CustomerMostImportant	
.828		The Customer Care Staff understands my needs when I interact with them		
.820		The driver understands my needs very well and helps		
	.895	The App Cabs are active 24x7		Factor 2: Service24X7
	.906	The Customer Care is active 24x7		

Source: EFA Empathy Output

Table 2.7 EFA tangibles

Loading		Interpretation of Factors	Factors	
		Description of Variables	1	2
.661		The App Cab is equipped with modern amenities		
.638		The App Cab has wifi which I can access		
.583		The App Cab has sanitizing equipment on offer	Loadings which are low	
.816		The driver has a body-temperature checking equipment	(<.7), are ignored as	
.626		The driver is always neatly dressed	outliers; Factor 1:	
.859		The driver always wears a clean mask	CovidProtocolEquipment	
.850		The driver wears gloves		
	.738	The App Cab interior is comfortable		
	.678	The App Cab interior is visually appealing		Factor 2:
	.763	The App Cab exterior is visually appealing		Comfort_Looks
	.830	The App is visually appealing to use		

Source: EFA Tangibles Output

Note: This research ascertains how the underlying construct within each dimension contributes to an index measure created from the underlying construct unearthed after taking 35 variables as a whole.

Bartlett factor scores are refined factor scores, computed procedurally when principal component analysis (PCA) and common factor extraction methods are used within EFA. Most refined factor scores are linear combinations of the variables that throw up the underlying construct. Bartlett factor scores are set to present the unbiased estimates of the true factor scores and Bartlett factors are uncorrelated to other orthogonal factors (Stefano et al., 2009). Though, not pursued in this research, it would be intriguing to ascertain the validity of the Factor Scores as measures of the underlying construct. Regression factor scores are avoided in this research as there may be correlation even after the Varimax Rotation. Bartlett factor scores have a mean of 0 and minimize the sum of squares of the factors over the range of variables (Hahs-Vaughn, 2017).

EFA reliability dimension: Number of variables = 6; EFA results are as follows and are depicted in Table 2.5. KMO-MSA = 0.736; Cumulative % variance of 67.219 explained by two factors, whose details are given in Table 2.5.

EFA responsiveness dimension: Number of variables = 4; EFA results are as follows. KMO-MSA = 0.717; cumulative % variance of 65.596 explained by one factor, whom we shall name 'OrganizationalResponsiveness'.

EFA assurance dimension: Number of variables = 6; EFA results are as follows. KMO-MSA = 0.823; cumulative % variance of 60.174 explained by 1 factor, whom we shall name, after a study of the rotational component matrix: 'SkilledDriver_CustomerCare'.

Note: EFA, so conducted, however failed to throw up more than one factor for dimensions: responsiveness and assurance.

EFA empathy dimension: Number of variables = 8; EFA results are as follows and are depicted in Table 2.6. KMO-MSA = 0.819 cumulative% variance of 69.184 explained by two factors, whose details are given in Table 2.6.

EFA tangibles dimension: Number of variables = 11; EFA results are as follows and are depicted in Table 2.7. KMO-MSA = 0.885; cumulative % variance of 67.414 explained by two factors, whose details are given in Table 2.7:

The Bivariate Pearsonian correlation performed between each of the factors unearthed, within each dimension with the computed index scores are shown in Table 2.8.

Findings: Managerial implications

From the analysis, we read that the opinions regarding comfort and visual appeal while riding an App Cab contributes sparsely to the customer satisfaction level, in general, as also a sense of reliance in the Covid protocol maintained by the App Cabs or a 24×7 service. The reliability of the App Cab as a taxi service, the sense of responsiveness of the organization toward the needs of the customer and paying utmost importance to the individual as also the momentary needs of the customer do play a role in the enhancement of customer satisfaction. However, the factors that contribute largely towards the levels of customer satisfaction are the skills of the driver (gloved and masked, as per Covid protocol), the efficiency of the customer care contact point and the carrying of sanitisation and pandemic-protocol related equipment, such as body-temperature measuring thermometers.

Also, it has been noted by associated readings that in 2016–2019, which is the pre pandemic era, customers and the drivers showed sensitivity to pricing decisions and compensation strategies respectively, apart from the facilities such as efficient customer care and the connect with the customer. However, post-pandemic,

Table 2.8 Correlation between unearthed factors within SERVQUAL dimensions and the index scores computed

SERVQUAL Dimension	Factor	Correlation with Index Score (r)	Rsq, the Coefficient of determination (%)
Reliability	ReliableTaxiService	0.658	43.30
	ReliableProtocolCompliant	0.497	24.70
Responsiveness	Organizational Responsiveness	0.773	59.75
Assurance	SkilledDriver_CustomerCare	0.907	82.26
Empathy	CustomerMostImportant	0.809	65.45
	Service24×7	0.35	12.25
Tangibles	CovidProtocolEquipment	0.88	77.44
	Comfort_Looks	0.248	6.15

Source: Simple Correlation computed on MSExcel

customer desires and needs shifted toward safety from the pandemic, safety during the drive, and environmentally safety, above all else.

Findings: Research implications

It is to be noted that the EFA on the 35 variables of the SERVQUAL instrument taken as a whole and the five EFAs conducted on the variables within each dimension of the SERVQUAL instrument are all done with the same set of data, with a single set of variables, obtained after a common Focus Group discussion. Thus, many degrees of freedom related to the data are lost. The same can be addressed by separating the sets of respondents. The study could be furthered by exploring the option of generating statistically more efficient and sufficient Index Scores and also, considering partial correlation between scores.

The study is entirely cross sectional. Made in the backdrop of the pandemic, the variables and the questionnaire address the particularities related to the pandemic explicitly in exactly three variables. Also, with the changing nature of the environment and the pandemic, the generic format will be relevant and could be extrapolated to get renewed results. Further research could also take into account the demography of the respondents on the Factor Scores, the Index Score and the relationship within.

Conclusions

The hardships faced in the pandemic has forced the urban customer of the App Cab to rethink his priorities. Pre pandemic, the customer appreciated price-related attributes such as the promotional offers and discounts. Post pandemic, the customer is increasingly conscious of his safety related to the pandemic and the skills of the driver and attention paid by customer care.

References

Bappy, T. A. and Haque, S. S. (2018). Examining the Factors Affecting Passengers' Satisfaction with Uber Car Services: Evidences from Dhaka City. Manag. Dev. 32(1): 25, 23.

Buttle, F. (1996). SERVQUAL: Review, critique, research agenda. Eur. J. Mark. 30(1):8–32. Retrieved from: http://140.117.77.118/2009/m954011064/References/20080927Buttle1994

Calabrese, A. and Scoglio, F. (2012). Reframing the past: A new approach in service quality assessment. TQM. 23(11):1329–1343. doi:http://dx.doi.org/10.1080/14783363.2012.733259

Ciavolino, E. and Calcagnì, A. (2005). Generalized cross entropy method for analysing the SERVQUAL model. J. Appl. Stat.42(3):520–534. doi:http://dx.doi.org/10.1080/02664763.2014.963526

Datta Khan, S. and Meel, D. (2021). Factors that Satisfy the Users of App Cabs in a Covid Stricken Nation: An Insight into Urban India. Epra *Int. J.* Econ. Bus. Manag. Stu. 8(4):19–29. doi:https://doi.org/19 10.36713/epra1013

Ghosh, R. and Mitra, D. (2019). An Analytical Study on the Satisfactionlevel of App Cab Drivers in Kolkata. Impact: Mpact: Ijrhal. 7(5):289–298.

Hahs-Vaughn, D. L. (2017). Exploratory Factor Analysis. In D. L. Hahs-Vaughn, *Applied Multivariate Statistical Concepts* (pp. 362–433). New York: Taylor's & Francis.

Hair, J. F., Black, W. C., Babin, B. J., and Anderson, R. E. (2019). Exploratory Factor Analysis. In J. F. Hair, W. C. Black, B. J. Babin, and R. E. Anderson. *Multivariate Data Analysis* (8th ed., pp. 121–189). Cengage Learning EMEA.

Härdle, W. K. and Simar, L. (2014). Factor Analysis. In W. K. Härdle and L. Simar. *Applied Multivariate Statistical Analysis* (4th ed., pp. 359–382). Springer.

Jiang, J. J., Klein, G., and Carr, C. L. (2002). Measuring Information System Service Quality: Servqual from the Other Side1. MIS Quarterly. 26(2):145–166.

Kumar, K. P. and Kumar, R. N. (2016). A Study on Factors Influencing the Consumers in Selection of Cab Services. Int. J. Soc. Sci. Humanit. Res. 4(3):557–561.

Meru: Ride in Ultra-Hygienic cab. (n.d.). Retrieved from: https://www.meru.in/: https://www.meru.in/coronavirus

Ola Cabs: Ride Safe. (n.d.). Retrieved from: https://www.olacabs.com: https://www.olacabs.com/RideSafeIndia

Ola launches '10 Steps to a Safer Ride' for driver-partners and customers as services resume in 100+ cities in green and orange zones across the country. (n.d.). Retrieved from: https://www.olacabs.com: https://www.olacabs.com/media/in/press/ola-launches-10-steps-to-a-safer-ride-for-driver-partners-and-customers-as-services-resume-in-100-cities-in-green-and-orange-zones-across-the-country

Our approach to COVID-19. (n.d.). Retrieved from: https://www.uber.com: https://www.uber.com/in/en/coronavirus/

Pahwa, M. S. and Goyal, M. (2019). Sustainable Business Model for Cab Aggregators: A Confirmatory Factor Analysis. Humanit. Soc. Sci. Rev. 7(1):376–384. doi:https://doi.org/10.18510/hssr.2019.7144

Paul, P., Luke, P. A., Pramanik, S., and Veluchamy, R. (2021). Factors of Consumer's Choice on Online Cab Booking. An Anthology of Multi-functional perspectives in Business and Management Research. 2:229–239.

R, D. and John, A. M. (2019). A Study on Factors Influencing Customersfor Using Uber Cab Booking Apps with Special Reference to Ernakulam District. IJBMI. 8(4, Series V):42–45.

Stefano, C., Zhu, M., and Mîndrilă, D. (2009). Understanding and Using Factor Scores: Considerations for the Applied Researcher. Pract. Assess. Res. Eval. (20):1–11.

Uber announces new safety features amid COVID-19, masks now mandatory for both driver and riders. (2020). Retrieved from: https://www.thehindu.com: https://www.thehindu.com/news/national/uber-announces-new-safety-features-amid-covid-19-masks-now-mandatory-for-both-driver-and-riders/article31612490.ece

3 An analysis of barriers affecting implementation of humanitarian supply chain management approaches in India

Priyanka Saini and Rajat Agrawal

Research Scholar, Department of Management Studies, Indian Institute of Technology Roorkee, Roorkee, Uttrakhand, India

Abstract

Purpose: Developing a humanitarian supply chain (HSC) is full of challenges. HSC is very diverse and dissimilar from ordinary supply chains and as such challenges faced in developing HSC are more stimulating and demanding. The present paper identifies some specific barriers in the implementation of humanitarian supply chain management (HSCM) pertaining to India.

Design/methodology/approach: Expert interviews are used to verify the barriers for HSCM identified through the literature review. The interpretive structural modelling (ISM) and MICMAC analysis are done to get contextual relationships among the barriers.

Findings: The ISM model suggests the two most significant driving barriers are the lack of prediction ability and high uncertainty. The seven-level model suggests the relationship among various barriers which can be used effectively by the policymakers and stakeholders involved in disaster management for improving the performance of HSCM so that the effect and impact of a disaster can be alleviated.

Research limitations/implications: The model is constructed by the subjective opinion of the experts and could be further validated statistically. This study can be further carried out by the use of another technique like Fuzzy-TISM with more number of barriers.

Originality/value: Few published articles have highlighted the barriers/challenges in developing the humanitarian supply chain and logistics in various contexts. This paper contributes to the factors/barriers/challenges in the implementation of HSCM and puts forth the interrelationship of barriers through a model. Suggestive measures are also enumerated.

Keywords: Disaster management, disaster relief, humanitarian relief humanitarian supply chain, natural disaster

Introduction

Vulnerabilities like earthquakes, floods, landslides, tsunamis turn into a disaster when they hit the environment and cause loss of valuable human and animal life along with loss to property. Damages due to the occurrence of natural hazards or disasters attacking various settled areas worldwide are rising every year (Kunz and Reiner 2012). According to Centre for Research on the Epidemiology of the Disasters (CRED) a disaster is "*a situation or event that overwhelms local capacity, necessitating a request at the national or international level for external assistance; an unforeseen and often sudden event that causes great damage, destruction and human suffering*". Increasing population, urbanisation, industrialisation, environmental degradation, climate change and development into high-risk areas aggravate intensity of disasters. Natural disasters cause an inadvertent loss to life and property.

The National Disaster Management Authority (NDMA), Government of India, has placed India into a 'very high risk' country due to its unique geo-climatic conditions- surrounded by mountains and sea. These conditions lead to an array of natural disasters of distinct types and properties (National Disaster Management Plan, 2016). The increasing population of India, approximately 1.39 billion (Census of India, 2021), compels the inhabitants to pervade the sensitive risk-prone areas, which increased vulnerabilities of the disaster. Table 3.1 presents the main disasters which took place in the various regions of India in recent years. It also indicates the increase in occurrence of disaster in India year by year.

Due to the disaster-prone profile of India, a proper disaster planning, management and mitigation are inevitable. The growing frequency of disasters requires an effective and well planned HSCM to deal with the disaster and lessen its impact. The HSCM involves managing the different factors in the system such as goods and materials, information, manpower, political authorities, available infrastructure, etc., to reduce the impact of a disaster (Beamon and Balcik, 2008; Altay, 2008). Thomas and Kopczak, (2005) defined HSCM as "*The process of planning, implementing and controlling the efficient, cost-effective flow and storage of goods and materials, as well as related information, from the point of origin to the point of consumption to alleviate the suffering of vulnerable people*". HSCM can comprise deeds ranging from effectively managing disaster and /or development of assistance for health care operations during disasters and public sector management (Tabaklar et al, 2015).

HSCs are developed to maximize the benefits to disaster hit crowd and to provide relief material and services in time to the affected population. Most of the supply chains are developed with the primary aim of increasing the supply chain access in every aspect. The traditional meaning of supply chain surplus is to maximize the gain and minimize the cost. The primary objective of the HSCs is the welfare of the society. Therefore, a variety of challenges are encountered during making and

Table 3.1 Major disasters in India in recent years

S. No.	Year	Major disasters
1.	2013	Uttrakhand floods (Kedarnath Disaster)
2.	2015	Jammu and Kashmir floods
3.	2016	Assam floods, Uttarakhand forest fire
4.	2017	Assam floods, Gujrat floods, West Bengal floods, Bihar floods, and Mumbai floods
5.	2018	Kerala floods
6.	2019	Gujrat floods, Karnataka floods, Maharashtra floods, Madhya Pradesh floods, Cyclone Fani
7.	2020	Uttarakhand forest fire, Kerala floods, Assam floods, Hyderabad floods, Cyclone Nisarga, Cyclone Nivar, Cyclone Burevi

Source: Prepared by author

execution of HSCs. An effective humanitarian supply chain should be flexible to be able to reduce the impact of disaster. Disaster resilience, and its management, is an essential segment of HSCs (Behl and Dutta, 2018).

This paper outlines some specific and key barriers of HSCM which are noticeable in the Indian scenario. HSCM could be one of the noticeable and effective methods to get situations back to normal (Blecken et al. 2009; Whybark et al. 2010). Hence, we need to identify challenges or barriers and their inter-relationship to improve HSCM.

The hierarchical model is used to represent the inter-relationship between the various factors involved in a problem. It is used to split various inter-related factors into different interconnected levels to understand the entire system. Interpretive structural modeling (ISM) method has been used to build different inter-related elements and is structured into a comprehensive systemic model (Warfield, 1974; Sage, 1977). ISM is often used to provide a fundamental understanding of complex situations, as well as to put together a course of action for solving a problem (Nath et al. 2014, Rathore and Agrawal, 2021). So this study used ISM and MICMAC analysis. This study used experts' practical experience and knowledge with the help of semi-structured interviews for the verification of barriers which were identified through literature review. The main objectives in this paper are:

(i)   To identify the barriers of HSCM with special reference to India
(ii) To establish the interrelationships among the identified barriers and classify them on the basis of driving-dependence power.

The rest of the paper is organised as follows. Section 2 presents a brief review of the literature related to the proposed study. Section 3 deals with the identification and explanation of the barriers from the literature review and experts' discussions. Section 4 outlines and demonstrates the ISM methodology used for identifying the interrelationship between barriers in this study. Section 5 of the study presents the results and discussions of the ISM model followed by research implications in Section 6. Section 7 comprises conclusions and limitations of the present study.

Literature review

For the present study, literature review covered articles on disaster management, published in online databases like Google Scholar, Scopus, and Web of Science. The keywords which were used for searching include 'Disaster', 'Disaster Management', Disaster Risk, 'Barriers in disaster Relief', 'Disaster Preparedness', 'Humanitarian Operations', and 'Barriers in Humanitarian supply chain' connected with Boolean connectors (AND, OR, AND NOT). This metasearch provided 1691 relevant papers, 586 papers after eliminating duplicates. The abstract analysis gave 180 papers, of which 76 papers were selected after analysis of full paper. Barriers were identified and the selected literature also helped in developing questionnaires for semi structured interviews with the experts.

According to Wohlgemuth et al. (2012) disaster prone areas often lack in adequate logistic infrastructure, facilities related to transport and relief supplies to reach the affected level are inappropriate and insufficient. Sheu (2007) has put forth the key challenges in emergency logistics. The humanitarian logistics in distant areas have manual supply chain processes as lack of logistics results in inefficient, ineffective, inadequate collaboration among various actors of HSCM.

Lack of proper coordination makes the relief chain more challenging (Kovács and Spens, 2007). Absence of resources makes communication and coordination between decision makers and humanitarian agencies difficult to attain.

The various key challenges towards execution of efficient humanitarian supply chain as advocated by Ergun et al. (2010) are impact of socioeconomic and conditions related to culture of the affected region, political, high uncertainty in location of the area which will be hit by disaster, timing of disaster, and demand of relief during disaster, collaboration and coordination among the multiple players, limited information and communications infrastructure, and robust dependency of last mile operations.

Other researches concentrated on interpretations of humanitarian activity in a particular calamity. Kovács and Spens (2009) assimilated the output of their research which they carried out in Ghana by proposing a theoretical model which highlighted the key challenges with regard to different phases of disaster, relief focusing on humanitarian organisations. They found challenges like lack of funding causing dearth of supplies and relief dependence, poor coordination, lack of trained staff, absence of clear directives for emergency, lack of in-country warehouses, ineffective and inefficient managing of in-kind donation are identified in this study.

Da Costa et al. (2014), in their research work, have studied the impact of six main natural disasters which took place during 2000 to 2011. The focus of their study was to study and analyse the role of logistics in various situations- in practices followed for relief operations, conditions prevalent during relief operations, logistics process and other critical aspects related to various important post disaster activities.

According to Yadav and Barve (2016), the primary barriers of humanitarian relief operations are insufficient safe shelters which are very less in number and have inadequate shelter capacity while poor strategic planning is another barrier. This study identifies the barriers and challenges based on post disaster phase which includes the response, recovery, and reconstruction phases in cyclone affected regions of Odisha. In another study in the Indian scenario, John and Ramesh (2016), have identified 14 barriers obstructing appropriate management of relief phase. According to Sahebi et al. (2017), barriers such as educational cultural and managerial barriers are the important barriers in the context of a case study of the Tehran Red Crescent Societies.

According to Ozdemir et al. (2020) inter-organizational barriers are the most challenging barrier. While Patil et al. (2020) considered skill set of personnels engaged in disaster management as important barrier. Patil et al. (2020) mentioned lack of effective and decisive funding for information technology (IT) infrastructure, chaotic operative environment and conflicting objectives of HO also as important barriers.

Negi and Negi (2020) propose a framework that has been developed to manage humanitarian logistics in the disaster relief operation, which would improve the humanitarian supply chain in India and help to effectively manage natural disasters in the preparedness and response stage at the state and district levels.

It can be understood from the review of available literature that only limited research has been done towards the improvement in understanding of the dissimilar barriers of the humanitarian supply chain (HSC). The review articles address the potential challenges of humanitarian logistics and supply chains and conclude that most of the articles are concentrated on either the preparedness or immediate response oriented.

Verification and identification of the HSCM barriers through experts

The output of literature review was verified with expert reviews of different experts including policymakers, bureaucrats, academicians, and NGOs. The interaction of researchers with beneficiaries of HSCM was already available to make a meaningful contribution of the experts' interviews. 14 experts were used for interview. Out of 14 experts 5 were from academia; academic experts were carefully selected for knowledge related to disaster and supply chain management. A total of five experts were from humanitarian organisations or NGOs who have practical experience to deal with real conditions of disaster. The detailed profile of experts is given in Table 3.2. These experts were aware of all the hitches of the disaster management in their respective fields related to disaster. Hence, the diversified group of experienced experts gave their valuable insights to select the barriers of HSCM.

The review of selected literature provided 12 barriers. These identified barriers were agreed upon by the experts. The detailed discussion with the experts added three more different barriers like poor crowd management, no perception of direct economic advantages, and lack of agility in humanitarian supply chain. With the expert discussions, these barriers found more significant for the proper planning and implementation of HSCM and pose major challenges in the performance of HSCM. So finally, with the help of literature review and expert interviews, a total of 15 most influencing barriers were identified which cause hindrance in the successful planning and implementation of HSCM.

Table 3.2 Detailed profile of the experts

Organisation	No. of Respondent	Designation	Experience
State Disaster Management Authority (SDMA), Uttrakhand, India	2	Government Executive	12 years
National Disaster Response Force (NDRF), India	1	Commandant	12 years
State Disaster Response Force (SDRF), Uttrakhand, India	1	SAR Team Commander (Inspector)	10 years
National & International Non-Government Organisation (NGOs)	5	Secretary, Members	15 years
Academicians	5	Professor	15 years

Source: Prepared by author

Limited prediction ability

The inadequate availability of past data and statistics of disaster related facts (Richey et al., 2009) is the reason for the inability to predict the assessment of the relief needs for the response phase. The assessment of the loss of lives, properties and livelihoods caused by any disaster is used to estimate the needs of victims like food, medicines, shelter and other basic needs.

Reactive funding

All the relief activities take place only when funds are allocated. Funding in case of disaster-related matters is done in the form of charity and is mostly done post-disaster. Most relief organisations depend mainly on funding received from donors. Hence relief teams cannot begin response action to disaster till funds are made available to them (Seaman, 1999).

Non-availability of permanent government officials

Indian Disaster Management Act, 2005, makes provision for a centralised author-ity National Disaster Management Authority (NDMA) and a State Disaster Management Authority (SDMA) in every state followed by District Disaster Management Authority (DDMA) in all districts. District Magistrate (DM) of the district is generally chairperson of DDMA. DM is already occupied with a large number of other routine activities and developing the supply chain for disaster management during pre-disaster phase is not a priority work. Government aid does not reach at the right time to face this situation in a better way because of non-availability of permanent government officials (Kala, 2014).

Non-availability of proper tools and equipment

Uncertain occurrence of disaster events leads to non-uniform demand levels and left very slight time to supply the relief aids. The time constraints do not allow using proper tools and equipment even if they are available (Richey et al., 2009). After the disaster takes place, the very first step is rescue and relief. For this, proper tools and equipment like boats, life jackets in case of floods, crane and stature in case of an earthquake, and various other tools and machinery which are used in the rescue and relief operation are needed for easy and timely evacuation of the affected peo-ple to safer places.

Lack of skilled workforce

Lack of skilled workforce is another challenge for successful HSCM operations. It is emphasised by various authors in their studies (Allen et al., 2013; Thomas & Mizushima, 2005; Pettit and Beresford, 2009).

Lack of involvement of local people

During the disaster, local people are the first responders to help themselves and oth-ers (Bremer, 2003; Hilhorst and Schmiemann, 2002). They are also the only channel for providing information on an initial and original situation to the authority to deliver the rescue and relief aid to the much-needed people. But sometimes they are not aware of the process. "Whom to and how to disseminate the information" is not clear to local people.

Lack of co-ordination between inter and intra supply chains

The coordination between inter and intra supply chains is also a very important challenge because misinterpretation or obscurity in the actions of any inter and intra agency would cause challenges in the implementation of HSCM (Rietjens et al., 2014; Kabra and Ramesh, 2013; Balcik et al., 2010). It can lead to various problems in relief aid operation like an excess of relief items reaches one place and nothing or small amount reaches another place.

Poor capacity development of people

Capacity development of people is a very important challenge in execution of HSCM. Local people on the catastrophe site are very much affected physically, psychologically, and economically by the impact of a disaster (Sandwell, 2011). Capacity development of people can provide training, rehearse and mock drills to make the people aware about the disaster, its consequences, do's and don'ts etc. They can prepare themselves to face the disaster in a better way with proper planning.

Poor inventory management

Poor inventory management is another important barrier for HSCM. Relief operations depend upon the inventory management in humanitarian supply chain (Baemon and Kotleba, 2006; Balcik et al., 2010; Bagchi et al., 2011). The management of inventory becomes tedious in the pre-disaster as well as in the other stages including the post-disaster stage for reconciling the demand and supply (Lee and Zbinden 2003, Ozdamar et al., 2004).

High uncertainty

The occurrence of disaster has high uncertainty in nature; the time, the place of occurrence, and the strength of disaster is highly uncertain (Richey et al., 2009; Altay et al., 2009; Rawls and Turnquist, 2010). The demographic profile of the affected areas is not available beforehand for the assessment of affected people and to predict the rescue and relief supplies.

Lack of IT and communication infrastructure in a distant area

IT & Communication infrastructure is another important barrier for HSCM. Without efficient communication devices, it is very hard to get exact information about the situation. Information system and utilissation of technology needs to be upgraded for efficiency in proving helpful in organizing the relief activities, minimizing the effect of disasters like earthquake, floods, hurricanes, wildfires, etc. (Altay and Labonte 2014; Kabra and Ramesh, 2015).

Lack of physical infrastructure

Inadequate proper physical infrastructure is also a significant barrier to perform response and relief aid. The proper infrastructure like alternate route, evacuation, shelter, helipads is not available in many disaster-prone distant areas. The rescue and relief operation becomes difficult in the absence of proper physical infrastructure (Balcik and Baemon, 2008; Richey et al., 2009).

Poor crowd management

Poor crowd management is also an essential barrier to HSCM. A massive gathering is also a cause of calamities. There is a need for effective planning to deal with such events. Sometimes during the disaster , we do not know the exact statistics of the people in the affected site supplies. A well-defined crowd management system can improve the performance of HSCM.

No perception of direct economic advantages

In disaster management, the stakeholders have no insight of direct economic advantages which is also a very important barrier for HSCM. Agencies do not show interest in investing in return for profit to provide funding aid for HSCM because there is no direct economic benefit associated.

Lack of agility in humanitarian supply chain

The HSCM should be agile because of the presence of uncertain circumstances. Agility is used where demand is less predictable and the responsive requirement of high variety (Oloruntoba and Gray, 2006). Generally, inventory in a humanitarian supply chain is static, and replenishments are not very frequent. This reduces agility of the supply chains and creates an obstacle to the effective management of the humanitarian supply chain.

ISM methods

According to Warfield (1974) and Sage (1977) ISM is knowledge process which uses a set of directly related but different elements arranged in a comprehensive systemic model to build the relationship between more than one different variable to handle the complexity of that system. ISM alters poorly-structured mental models about the system under study into a clear consistent well-structured set of system elements (Warfield and Cárdenas 1994).

Structural Self-Interaction Matrix (SSIM)

According to ISM methodology, various techniques which are highly dependent on experts' advice like brainstorming, nominal group technique, etc. along with questionnaire surveys should be used for obtaining the SSIM., but the questionnaire surveys can also be used to identify the relationship between the variables. A group of 14 experts was used for identifying the appropriate variable and contextual relationship between the barriers. On the basis of the expert opinion, we came to an agreement on the SSIM which is shown in Table 3.3. As part of ISM methodology

Table 3.3 Structural self-interaction matrix (SSIM)

Barrier	15	14	13	12	11	10	9	8	7	6	5	4	3	2	1
Limited prediction ability (B1)	V	V	V	V	X	V	V	V	V	V	V	V	V	V	
Lack of skilled work force (B2)	V	X	A	V	A	V	V	V	V	V	A	V	V		
Non-availability of government officials (B3)	V	A	A	X	A	A	V	A	X	A	A	V			
Reactive funding (B4)	V	A	A	A	A	A	X	A	A	A	A				
Non-availability of proper tools, equipment (B5)	V	O	X	V	A	V	V	V	V	V					
Lack of involvement of local people (B6)	V	A	A	V	A	X	V	X	V						
Lack of Co-ordination between inter & intra supply chain (B7)	V	A	A	X	A	A	V	A							
Poor capacity development of people (B8)	V	A	A	V	A	X	V								
Lack of inventory management system (B9)	V	A	A	A	A	A									
Poor crowd management (B10)	V	A	A	V	A										
High uncertainty (B11)	V	V	V	V											
Lack of IT & communication infrastructure in distant areas (B12)	V	A	A												
Lack of physical infrastructure like roads (B13)	V	O													
No perception of direct economic advantages (B14)	V														
Lack of agility in humanitarian supply chain (B15)															

Source: Prepared by author (It is a part of ISM methodology)

four symbols V, A, X, O having different denotations in different situations were used to identify the path between the two variables (i and j):

- V=barrier "i" influences barrier "j".
- A=barrier "j" influences barrier "i".
- X=barriers "i" and "j" influence each other.
- O=barriers "i" and "j" are unrelated.

Level Partitions

The reachability set is a set of the barrier which easily gets influenced by the effect of other barriers, including it. The antecedent set of barriers is those barriers which influence others including it. The intersection of the reachability set and the antecedent set is the intersection set. Highest priority is given and is placed at the top of the ISM model to the variable for which both the reachability set and the intersection set are the same.

Results and discussion

The final partition levels are presented in Table 3.6. This level partition results in a hierarchical structure model which is shown in Figure 3.1. Table 3.6 illustrates that 'Lack of agility in humanitarian supply chain' is at Level I of the ISM model. 'Low prediction ability' and 'High Uncertainty' are at the bottom level-VII. The detailed ISM model for all barriers is shown in Figure 3.2. High uncertainty and low prediction abilities are two such barriers that are having the highest driving power of 15 and the lowest dependence of 2. The reviewed literature and experts also support that the high uncertainty about the event, where it will occur, at what time, of what magnitude and intensity, and how much area will be affected by it, are the key barriers of HSCM. Response operations should be agile in nature so that their implementation can provide prompt relief after the catastrophe. An agile strategy

Table 3.4 Calculation of driving power and dependence for final reachability matrix

Barrier	1	2	3	4	5	6	7	8	9	10	11	12	13	14	15	D.P
B1	1	1	1	1	1	1	1	1	1	1	1	1	1	1	1	15
B2	0	1	1	1	0	1	1	1	1	1	0	1	0	1	1	11
B3	0	0	1	1	0	0	1	0	1	0	0	1	0	0	1	6
B4	0	0	0	1	0	0	0	0	1	0	0	0	0	0	1	3
B5	0	1	1	1	1	1	1	1	1	1	0	1	1	1*	1	13
B6	0	0	1	1	0	1	1	1	1	1	0	1	0	0	1	9
B7	0	0	1	1	0	0	1	0	1	0	0	1	0	0	1	6
B8	0	0	1	1	0	1	1	1	1	1	0	1	0	0	1	9
B9	0	0	0	1	0	0	0	0	1	0	0	0	0	0	1	3
B10	0	0	1	1	0	1	1	1	1	1	0	1	0	0	1	9
B11	1	1	1	1	1	1	1	1	1	1	1	1	1	1	1	15
B12	0	0	1	1	0	0	1	0	1	0	0	1	0	0	1	6
B13	0	1	1	1	1	1	1	1	1	1	0	1	1	1*	1	13
B14	0	1	1	1	0	1	1	1	1	1	0	1	0	1	1	11
B15	0	0	0	0	0	0	0	0	0	0	0	0	0	0	1	1
Dependence Power	2	6	12	14	4	9	12	9	14	9	2	12	4	6	15	130

Source: Prepared by author (It is a part of ISM methodology)

in supply chain is aimed at being flexible in adapting quick and effective services to overcome rapidly changing needs of the victims in the relief operation. The agility in humanitarian supply chain is the final outcome which improves the effectiveness and efficiency of disaster management as a whole.

Damaged physical infrastructure (driving power = 13) directly affects the relief activity and as such another plan has to be implemented. It becomes a very challenging task for HSCM.

Unavailability and almost no exposure of tools and equipment leads to a lack of skilled workforce (driving power = 11). In the initial findings, no perception of direct economic advantage (driving power = 11) was rated as the least important factor but the outcome of ISM model suggested that it is of moderate importance and can't be ignored. Involvement of local people and commercial organisations (driving power = 9) in awareness training programs and post-disaster management is negligible. Lack of trained workforce is unable to offer a capacity development program on regular and continuous mode. Information sharing is also not possible because of deprived IT& communication infrastructure in the distant area (driving

Table 3.5 ISM analysis (iteration results)

Barrier	R S	A S	I S	Level
B1	1,2,3,4,5,6,7,8,9,10,11,12,13, 14,15	1,11	1,11	VII
B2	2,3,4,6,7,8,9,10,12,14,15	1,2,5,11,13,14	2,14	V
B3	3,4,7,9,12,15	1,2,3,5,6,7,8,10,11,12, 13,14	3,7,12	III
B4	4,9,15	1,2,3,4,5,6,7,8,9,10,11,12, 13,14	4,9	II
B5	2,3,4,5,6,7,8,9,10,12,13,14,15	1,5,11,13	5,13	VI
B6	3,4,6,7,8,9,10,12,15	1,2,5,6,8,10,11,13,14	6,8,10	IV
B7	3,4,7,9,12,15	1,2,3,5,6,7,8,10,11,12, 13,14	3,7,12	III
B8	3,4,6,7,8,9,10,12,15	1,2,5,6,8,10,11,13,14	6,8,10	IV
B9	4,9,15	1,2,3,4,5,6,7,8,9,10,11,12, 13,14	4,9	II
B10	3,4,6,7,8,9,10,12,15	1,2,5,6,8,10,11,13,14	6,8,10	IV
B11	1,2,3,4,5,6,7,8,9,10,11,12,13 ,14,15	1,11	1,11	VII
B12	3,4,7,9,12,15	1,2,3,5,6,7,8,10,11,12, 13,14	3,7,12	III
B13	2,3,4,5,6,7,8,9,10,12,13,14,15	1,5,11,13	5,13	VI
B14	2,3,4,6,7,8,9,10,12,14,15	1,2,5,11,13,14	2,14	V
B15	15	1,2,3,4,5,6,7,8,9,10,11, 12,13,14,15	15	I

Source: Prepared by author (It is a part of ISM methodology)

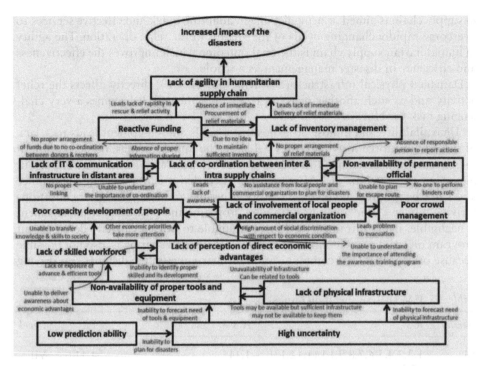

Figure 3.1 Multilevel hierarchy structure through ISM model of barriers for HSCM in India
Source: Prepared by author (It is a part of ISM methodology)

power = 6) which leads to poor coordination between supply chain actors, inter and intra supply chains (driving power = 6). Lack of regional permanent officials (driving power = 6) is also responsible for information dissemination to the central authority to make a decision in dealing with the unfortunate circumstances.

The MICMAC analysis is done to bring forth the driving and dependence power of the identified barriers. The variables are categorised into four distinct clusters as illustrated in Figure 3.2. Autonomous variables, dependent variables, linkage variables, and independent variables are the four categories of variables. Those variables which have both weak driving power and weak dependence power are termed as autonomous variables. These variables do not influence the overall system.

Research Implication and conclusion

An ISM model explaining major barriers of HSCM and their interrelationship (Figure 3.3) has been developed. The barriers need to be overcome in the most effective manner for the successful implementation of HSCM. From the ISM model (Figure 3.3), the stakeholders can classify that the low prediction ability and high uncertainty are the primary barriers which are placed at the lowest level of the ISM model and hence contribute for a chaotic situation during the disasters. The policymakers and the managers should use the resources in the most optimal manner

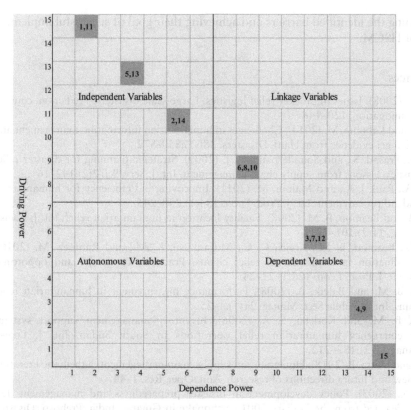

Figure 3.2 MICMAC analysis
Source: Prepared by author (It is a part of ISM methodology)

to improve the level of predictability simultaneously reducing the uncertainty in the occurrence of the disasters. Early warning systems need to be focused and their accuracy should be worked upon. Capacity development programs for local people is an important factor which various agencies like govt. organisations, NGOs and other community based learning centres should emphasise upon. The local people should be apprised about the economic benefits of HSCM in long run. They should be trained towards adoption of various standing operating procedures during disasters. New mechanisms should be developed to improve present level of coordination amongst the various actors of HSCM along with optimizing the available scarce resources to provide new avenues for coordinating them by minimizing the sufferings caused to beneficiaries of HSCM. The constraints in prepositioning of ware houses, training of professional, relationship between various actors including long term relationship with suppliers and other allied areas should be worked upon in a holistic manner to improve the accuracy of HSCM and reducing the loss of valuable human lives and properties.

The valuable insights related to characteristics of barriers provided by MICMAC analysis (Figure 4) can assist the mangers to plan and act in a proactive manner for overcoming the identified barriers and achieving their goal of successful implementation of HSCM.

References

Altay, N. (2008). Issues in disaster relief logistics. Large-scale disasters: Prediction, control, and mitigation, 120–146.

Altay, N. and Labonte, M. (2014). Challenges in humanitarian information management and exchange: evidence from Haiti. Disasters. 38(s1):S50–S72.

Altay, N., Prasad, S., and Sounderpandian, J. (2009). Strategic planning for disaster relief logistics: lessons from supply chain management. Int. J. Serv. Sci. 2(2):142–161.

Bagchi, A., Paul, J. A., and Maloni, M. (2011). Improving bid efficiency for humanitarian food aid procurement. Int. J. Prod. Econ. 134(1):238–245.

Balcik, B. and Beamon, B. M. (2008). Facility location in humanitarian relief. Int. J. Logist. Manag. 11(2):101–121.

Balcik, B., Beamon, B. M., Krejci, C. C., Muramatsu, K. M., and Ramirez, M. (2010). Coordination in humanitarian relief chains: Practices, challenges and opportunities. Int. J. Prod. Econ. 126(1):22–34.

Beamon, B. M. and Balcik, B. (2008). Performance measurement in humanitarian relief chains. Int. J. Public Sect. Manag. 21(1):4–25.

Beamon, B. M. and Kotleba, S. A. (2006). Inventory management support systems for emergency humanitarian relief operations in South Sudan. Int. J. Logist. Manag.17(2):187–212.

Behl, A. and Dutta, P. (2018). Humanitarian supply chain management: a thematic literature review and future directions of research. Ann. Oper. Res. 1–44.

Bremer, R. (2003). Policy development in disaster preparedness and management: lessons learned from the January 2001 earthquake in Gujarat, India. Prehosp. Disaster. Med. 18(4):372–384.

Centre for Research on the Epidemiology of Disasters – CRED, (2018). Cred Crunch 52 - Economic Losses, Poverty and Disasters: 1998–2017.

da Costa, S. R. A., Bandeira, R. A. M., Mello, L. C. B. B. and Campos, V. B. G. (2014). Humanitarian supply chain: an analysis of response operations to natural disasters. Eur. J. Transp. Infrastruct. Res. 14(3).

Ergun, O., Karakus, G., Keskinocak, P., Swann, J., & Villarreal, M. (2011). Operations Research to Improve Disaster Supply Chain Management. Operations Research and Management Science. https://doi.org/10.1002/9780470400531.EORMS0604

Hilhorst, D. and Schmiemann, N., (2002). Humanitarian principles and organizational culture: everyday practice in Meédecins Sans Frontiéres-Holland. Dev. Pract. 12 (3-4):490–500.

John, L. and Ramesh, A. (2016). Modeling the barriers of humanitarian supply chain management in India. In *Managing humanitarian logistics*, ed. B. S. Sahay, S. Gupta, and V. C. Menon, 61–82 India: Springer.

Kabra, G. and Ramesh, A. (2015). Analyzing drivers and barriers of coordination in humanitarian supply chain management under fuzzy environment. 22(4), 559–587.

Kabra, G. and Ramesh, A., (2013). Coordination in humanitarian supply chain management in India: modeling the barriers, In Proceedings of the Thirteenth Global Conference on Flexible systems Management, Indian Institute of Technology Delhi.

Kala, C. P., (2014), Deluge, disaster and development in Uttarakhand Himalayan region of India: challenges and lessons for disaster management. Int. J. Disaster Risk Reduct. 8:143–152.

Kovács, G. and Spens, K. (2009). Identifying challenges in humanitarian logistics. Int. J. Phys. Distrib. Logist. Manag. 39(6):506–528.

Kunz, N. and Reiner, G. (2012). A meta-analysis of humanitarian logistics research. J. Humanit. Logist. Supply Chain Manag. 2(2):116–147.

National Disaster Management Plan, 2016. A publication of the National Disaster Management Authority, Government of India. May 2016, New Delhi.

Nath, V., Kumar, R., Agrawal, R., Gautam, A., and Sharma, V. (2014). Impediments to adoption of green products: An ISM analysis. *Journal of Promotion Management*, 20(5), 501–520.

Negi, S. and Negi, G. (2020). "Framework to manage humanitarian logistics in disaster relief supply chain management in India". Int. J. Emerg. Serv. 10(1):40-76.

Oloruntoba, R. and Gray, R., (2006), Humanitarian aid: an agile supply chain? Int. J. Supply Chain Manag. 11(2):115–120.

Ozdamar, L., Ekinci, E., and Küçükyazici, B., (2004), Emergency logistics planning in natural disasters. Ann. Oper. Res. 129(1-4):217–245.

Ozdemir, A. I., Erol, I., Ar, I. M., Peker, I., Asgary, A., Medeni, T. D., and Medeni, I. T. (2020). The role of blockchain in reducing the impact of barriers to humanitarian supply chain management. Int. J. Logist. Manag. 32(2):454-478.

Patil, A., Shardeo, V., and Madaan, J. (2020). Modelling performance measurement barriers of humanitarian supply chain. Int. J. Product. Perform. Manag. 70(8):972–2000.

Pettit, S. and Beresford, A. (2009). Critical success factors in the context of humanitarian aid supply chains. . Int. J. Phys. Distrib. Logist. Manag. 39(6):450–468.

Rathore, R. S. and Agrawal, R. (2021). Performance indicators for technology business incubators in Indian higher educational institutes. Manag. Res. Rev. DOI 10.1108/MRR-12-2019-0515

Rawls, C. G. and Turnquist, M. A. (2010). Pre-positioning of emergency supplies for disaster response. Transp. Res. B: Methodol. 44(4):521–534.

Richey G., Kovács, G., and Spens, K. (2009). Identifying challenges in humanitarian logistics. Int. J. Phys. Distrib. Logist. Manag. 39(6):506–528.

Rietjens, S., Goedee, J., Van Sommeren, S. and Soeters, J. (2014). Meeting needs: value chain collaboration in stabilisation and reconstruction operations. J. Humanit. Logist. Supply Chain Manag. 4(1):43–59.

Sage, A. P. (1977). Methodology for large-scale systems.

Sahebi, I. G., Arab, A., and Moghadam, M. R. S. (2017). Analyzing the barriers to humanitarian supply chain management: a case study of the Tehran Red Crescent Societies. Int. J. Disaster Risk Reduct.24:232–241.

Sandwell, C. (2011). A qualitative study exploring the challenges of humanitarian organisations. J. Humanit. Logist. Supply Chain Manag., 1(2):132–150.

Seaman, J. (1999). Malnutrition in emergencies: How can we do better and where do the responsibilities lie? Disasters. 23(4):306–315.

Sheu, J. B. (2007). Challenges of emergency logistics management. Transp. Res. E. 43(6):655–659

Tabaklar, T., Halldórsson, Á., Kovács, G., and Spens, K. (2015). Borrowing theories in humanitarian supply chain management. J. Humanit. Logist. Supply Chain Manag. 5(3):281–299.

Warfield, J. N. (1974). Developing interconnection matrices in structural modeling. IEEE Trans. Syst. Man Cybern. 1:81–87.

Whybark, D. C. (2007). Issues in managing disaster relief inventories. Int. J. Prod. Econ. 108(1-2):228–235.

Whybark, D. C., Melnyk, S. A., Day, J. and Davis, E. D. (2010). Disaster relief supply chain management: new realities, management challenges, emerging opportunities. Decision Line. 41(3):4–7.

Wohlgemuth, S., Oloruntoba, R. and Clausen, U. (2012). Dynamic vehicle routing with anticipation in disaster relief. Socio-Econ. Plan. Sci. 46(4):261–271.

Yadav, D. K. and Barve, A. (2016). Modeling post-disaster challenges of humanitarian supply chains: A TISM approach. Glob. J. Flex. Syst. Manag. 17(3):321–340.

4 Role of AI on HRM functions: An empirical study on private IT and educational sectors in India

Sourabh Jain[1] and Smita Barik[2]

[1]Assistant Professor, Global Nature Care Sanghtan's Group of Institutions, Jabalpur, India

[2]Assistant Professor, Institute of Technology & Science, Mohan Nagar, Ghaziabad, India

Abstract

Artificial intelligence (AI) is a well-known technology now a day. We cannot think of a life where AI is not there in this technological era. As it has been implemented almost in all sectors and all business processes, our study will focus on its impact on different human resource management (HRM) functions like, recruitment and selection, training and development, compensation, performance management, emotional intelligence & employee retention. Also, we will study whether AI is being accepted by the employees working in different organisations or not.

Purpose: The basic objective of the study is to identify the acceptance of AI between employees of an organisation. The main objective is to identify the role of AI in different HRM functions.

Methodology: A structured questionnaire was designed to collect the data on the dimensions related to different HRM functions. The sample size of the study is 390. The convenient sample technique was used for data collection. Correlation, regression and ANOVA technique is used for hypothesis testing.

Findings: It is found that there exists a positive relationship between various dimensions of HRM functions with AI and there is a positive acceptance of employees towards AI.

Keyword: Artificial intelligence, human resource management, HRM functions, private IT sectors, educational institution.

Introduction

Covid-19 has given high time to companies to redefine their business process through new innovation technologies and giving it a different direction to earn competition. Innovative technologies are being tested and implemented in the organisation (The Financial Express, 2020). Technology is now considered as an integral part of every business plan. Most of the businessmen consider technology to start and scale their companies. But the correlation between business and innovative technology started few years back and traditional processes like quality management, employee and customer retention, process control has been replaced by improved technologies like business process reengineering, total quality control, customer relationship building etc. (Saxena, 2020). In the field of human resource too, it has brought a radical change in almost all the sectors. As it has a number of advantages, AI is being integrated with the business process globally in a more rapid way. It has been implemented in compensation management, performance management, career planning, emotional intelligence and many more. Artificial intelligence can be understood as a recreation of human intellect in modern day technology that plans to impersonate human like actions. The advent of artificial intelligence (AI), chatbots, and advancements have transformed efficiency, improved employee-employer relationships and employee assessments, accelerated internal processes, and heightened accuracy in results (Peoplematters, 2021), so HR professionals have to adopt AI in order to keep themselves in the race of increasing productivity and efficiency of organisation. In this research, the researcher has tried to find out the role of AI in modern day workforce management and also how far AI is being accepted by employees of organisation, Also this study will try to find out the challenges of AI in different HR functions.

Objective of study

Keeping the above aspects in mind, this study provides a sound rationale for researchers, so the objectives of the research are summarised below:

1. To identify role of AI on HRM functions.
2. To measure the acceptance of AI on HRM functions and the impact of AI on HRM functions.

Literature review

AI and HR: The concept AI was first coined by McCarthy (1956), and it is now used in solving various complex cognitive problems, performs task like an intelligent system and it has now been incorporated in various business processes (George, 2019). It was based on the concept that human thoughts can be mechanised and also can be used intelligently. AI has its unique role in HR and various researchers have also shared their views on use of AI on HR (Kapoor, 2010), in his research has studied on use of business intelligence in human resource management. He has suggested business intelligence vendors to incorporate data analytics into human resource management modules (Jain, 2018) in his research, has also studied the role of AI on HRM and found out that modern technology is being adopted by most of the companies, even into their HR related functions (Dirican, 2015). In his research paper has studied the impact of robotics on modern day business, almost into all HR related functions. He also suggested that AI and robotics may have negative impact on overall function of the organisation (Buzko et al., 2016). The researchers studied challenges faced by AI technologies in human resource are and he found out that AI was not that much effective in finding out training cost (R and D, 2018). The researchers have explained the role of AI as an effective and integral tool to recruitment process. Artificial intelligence helps in almost all end-to-end process of recruitment.

*   *Impact of AI on recruitment and selection*: AI for recruiting means applying AI to conduct the recruitment function. AI helps conducting the same by Application Tracking System to scan multiple resumes at a time and finding out

required applications by identifying keywords and phrases. This way recruiters can conduct the process quickly and efficiently (Digitalhrtech, 2021). More specialised softwares are also used to check candidates' credibility to demonstrate their skills. Filtered is such kind of a software used by Tech Talent Recruiting (Talent Lyft , 2021).

- *Impact of AI on training and development*: In the training process, AI technology helps to record training data automatically. Then the data can be analysed to show the degree and effect of employee training. It can lead managers to save training time and also to get quick training results. In addition, voice technology, learning content database, and core algorithm can also be used-to achieve a fast and efficient learning experience (Jia et al., 2018).
- *Impact of AI on performance management*: AI provides a data-driven performance management system where information is collected in a single place, managers can easily extract insights from real time analysis, and psychological bias is eliminated (People Hum, 2021).
- *Impact of AI on compensation*: Compensation system is a very integral part of organisation. A fair compensation system is what is expected from a successful organisation. AI can assist to facilitate a fair compensation system. BP neural network is an advanced AI technology which can imitate the human nervous system (Richard and Lippmann, 1991) and can be used as a strong decision support system to provide fair salary (Jia et al., 2018).
- *Impact of AI on emotional intelligence*: When AI can read the facial expression, gesture, voice tone of keystrokes of a human being, it is called artificial emotional intelligence. In other words, AI can read the emotions of human beings by analysing employee data. Affective, Real eyes, Companion Mx, Bio Essenceet care some companies that use advanced AI system where multiple tools are used to analyse emotions of human beings (Bernard Marr, 2021).
- *Impact of AI on employee retention*: As AI eases out the work of employees, and saves processing time of work, it provides a great support for work-life balance. It also plays a great role in increasing productivity and also its self-scheduling mode saves human efforts of doing a job. This way it eases out the major processes for employees and employees are unlikely to get overburdened. This way AI helps achieving low employee turnover in organisations (Hrci, 2021).

Rationale of study

AI is a growing concept in modern technologies. AI has now been incorporated into business processes. It has also been implemented into various HR functions. There are very few researches done to find employees acceptance towards AI, which gives strength to explore more on this dimension. Further research can be done in different industries apart from IT Industry. Our study focuses on private IT and education sector of India. It will also show employees' acceptance level for AI and will also find out the challenges of AI on HR functions. Further this study can be a base for further research on the employees' acceptance towards AI implementation. Keeping the above aspects in mind, this study provides a sound rationale for researchers.

Hypothesis_1

H_0 There is no significant relationship between AI and HRM functions.

H_{01} There is significant relationship between AI and recruitment and selection.

H_{02} There is significant relationship between AI and training and development

H_{03} There is significant relationship between AI and performance management.

H_{04} There is significant relationship between AI and compensation.

H_{05} There is significant relationship between AI and emotional intelligence.

H_{06} There is significant relationship between AI and employee retention.

Hypothesis_2

H_1 There is no significant impact of AI on HRM functions

H_{11} There is significant impact of AI on HRM functions

Research methodology

Data analysis

Table 4.1 represents the demographic analysis of the respondents.

Table 4.2 represents the descriptive analysis of the HRM functions.

Table 4.3 represents the reliability analysis of dimensions of hrm. The value of Cronbach's Alpha for all the items used in our research are more than 0.700 which clearly indicates that the data is reliable for study.

Table 4.1 Demographical variables

Industry	IT	Educational		
	139 (36.77%)	239 (63.23%)		
Gender	Male	Female		
	207 (54.76%)	171 (45.24%)		
Age	25–35	36–45	46–55	55 & above
	81 (21.42%)	117 (30.95%)	139 (36.77%)	41 (10.84%)
Salary	20000–30000	31000–45000	46000–60000	60000 & above
	79 (20.89%)	111 (29.37%)	149 (39.41%)	39 (10.31%)

These tables are based on Authors Primary Source of Data Collection and Analysis is done through SPSS 20

Table 4.2 Descriptive analysis

Items	Mean	Std. dev.
Recruitment and selection	2.28	1.284
Training and development	2.27	1.289
Performance management	2.25	1.295
Compensation	2.25	1.293
Employee intelligence	2.24	1.299
Employee retention	2.23	1.290

These tables are based on Authors Primary Source of Data
Collection and Analysis is done through SPSS 20

Table 4.3 Reliability analysis

Items	No. of items	Cronbach's Alpha
Recruitment and selection	03	.889
Training and development	03	.893
Performance management	03	.895
Compensation	03	.891
Employee intelligence	03	.892
Employee retention	03	.897

These tables are based on Authors Primary Source of Data Collection and Analysis is done through SPSS 20

Testing of Hypotheses

Hypothesis-1

H_0 There is no significant relationship between AI and HRM functions.
H_1 There is significant relationship between AI and recruitment and selection.
H_{11} There is significant relationship between AI and training and development
H_{12} There is significant relationship between AI and performance management.
H_{13} There is significant relationship between AI and compensation.
H_{14} There is significant relationship between AI and emotional intelligence.
H_{15} There is significant relationship between AI and employee retention.

Area of study	Respondents are taken from private IT and educational sectors of India.
Research design	Causal research design is preferred
Sample size	390 (385 is standard sample size according to Cochran at 95% confidence level). Total responses received from respondents are 378.
Sampling technique	Convenient sampling
Data collection	Primary data is collected through structured questionnaire. Researcher has used Likert Scale to conduct the survey. Secondary data is collected through various sources like journals, white papers, web references and articles.
Tools Used for Analysis	Correlation, regression & ANOVA analysis

Table 4.5 represents the correlation analysis and how the AI and HRM functions are related to each other. The relationships of the AI & HRM functions are generally accepted. Pearson correlation was applied on the data to check the relationship between AI and HRM functions with recruitment and selection (r=.792), training and development (r=.782), performance management (.789), compensation (r=.779), emotional intelligence (r=.760), employee retention (r=.774). The results indicates that all the functions of HRM are statistically significant and accepted at ($p<0.05$).

Table 4.4 Correlation analysis

		Correlation analysis						
		AI	RS	TD	PM	Comp	EI	ER
AI	Pearson correlation	1	.792**	.782**	.789**	.779**	.760**	.774**
	Sig. (2-tailed)		0	0	0	0	0	0
RS	Pearson correlation	.792**	1	.995**	.989**	.992**	.988**	.987**
	Sig. (2-tailed)	0		0	0	0	0	0
TD	Pearson correlation	.782**	.995**	1	.994**	.995**	.987**	.990**
	Sig. (2-tailed)	0	0		0	0	0	0
PM	Pearson correlation	.789**	.989**	.994**	1	.998**	.991**	.995**
	Sig. (2-tailed)	0	0	0		0	0	0
Comp	Pearson correlation	.779**	.992**	.995**	.998**	1	.993**	.995**
	Sig. (2-tailed)	0	0	0	0		0	0
EI	Pearson correlation	.760**	.988**	.987**	.991**	.993**	1	.993**
	Sig. (2-tailed)	0	0	0	0	0		0
ER	Pearson correlation	.774**	.987**	.990**	.995**	.995**	.993**	1
	Sig. (2-tailed)	0	0	0	0	0	0	

**Correlation is significant at the 0.01 level (2-tailed)
**Correlation is significant at the 0.05 level (2-tailed)
These tables are based on Authors Primary Source of Data Collection and Analysis is done through SPSS 20

Table 4.5 Summary of hypothesis result correlation analysis

	Hypothesis	Correlation	Result
H1	There is significant relationship between AI and recruitment and selection.	.792	Accepted
H11	There is significant relationship between AI and training and development	.782	Accepted
H12	There is significant relationship between AI and performance management	.789	Accepted
H13	There is significant relationship between AI and compensation	.779	Accepted
H14	There is significant relationship between AI and emotional intelligence	.760	Accepted
H15	There is significant relationship between AI and employee retention	.774	Accepted

*Correlation is significant at 0.05 level (2- tailed)
**Correlation is significant at 0.01 level (2- tailed)
These tables are based on Authors Primary Source of Data Collection and Analysis is done through SPSS 20

Hypothesis-2

H_1 There is no significant impact of AI on HRM functions
H_{11} There is significant impact of AI on HRM functions

Regression and ANOVA analysis

Table 4.6 shows the multiple regression analysis and Table 4.7 shows the ANOVA model. In this study the level of significance is 0.000. The value of r^2=.860 (almost 86%). The results are justified (i.e., the null hypothesis is rejected and alternate hypothesis accepted), that means there is positive significance of AI on Human resource functions.

Findings and Conclusion

From the above research, it is clearly shown that there is a strong correlation between AI and different HR functions. All the dimensions of HR functions under study have more than 0.700 correlation value with AI which signifies that AI and HRM functions are strongly correlated. ANOVA shows the P value to be 0.00 that means null hypothesis is rejected and our test is statistically significant. In other words, there is significant impact of AI on different HRM functions. This may happen because our dimensions under study (recruitment & selection, training & development, performance management, compensation, emotional intelligence, employee retention) are being strongly affected by AI systems used or adopted in an organisation. AI has entered and is being adapted successfully into almost all discussed HRM functions. It eases out employees work burden in a much better way so that they can sustain in an organisation culture and also apply their skills in a more productive way. Similarly, an organisation where AI is implemented successfully attracts and retains talent by facilitating them an advanced technological environment where employees can work more comfortably and with fewer burdens in long run.

- After taking response from employees, it was also found by the researchers that they have accepted AI in their work life in a broader way. Although some initial

Table 4.6 Regression Analysis

Model	R	R^2	Adjusted R^2	Std. Error of the Estimate	Sig. F Change
1	.921[a]	0.860	0.857	0.64556	0.00

a. Predictors: (Constant), AI
b. Dependent Variable: HRM functions
These tables are based on Authors Primary Source of Data Collection and Analysis is done through SPSS 20

Table 4.7 ANOVA

Model		SS	df	MS	F	Sig.
1	Regression	69.402	6	34.701	380.985	.000[b]
	Residual	39.348	371	0.091		
	Total	108.75	377			

a. Predictors: (Constant), AI
b. Dependent Variable: HRM functions
These tables are based on Authors Primary Source of Data Collection and Analysis is done through SPSS 20

challenges are faced like taking proper training to learn AI and implement it in their work correctly, but later on after taking proper training, it has been proved to ease out tasks in day-to-day life in the organisation.

- It can also be suggested to the organisations implementing AI to give proper and timely training so that the employees can be benefitted out of it in a much-advanced way.

References

AI For Recruiting: A Definitive Guide for HR Professionals | Ideal, accessed on 8th Aug 2021.

AI in performance management people Hum, accessed on 8th Aug 2020.

Article: Changing trends in HR Technology — People Matters, accessed on 8th Aug, 2021.

Buzko, I., Dyachenko, Y., Petrova, M., Nenkov, N., Tuleninova, D., and Koeva, K. (2016). Artificial Intelligence technologies in human resource development. Comput. Model. New Tech, 26–29.

Dirican, C. (2015). The Impacts of Robotics, Artificial Intelligence on Business and Economics. Procedia Soc. Bheav.Sci, 564–573.

George, G., and Thomas, M. R. (2019). Integration of artificial intelligence in human resource. Int. J. Innov. Technol. Explor. Eng, 9(2), 5069–5073.

How AI Is Helping Improve Employee Retention (hrci.org), accessed on 8th Aug,2021.

Jain, S. (2017). Is Artificial Intelligence–The Next Big Thing in HR? International Conference on *Innovation Research in Science, Technology and Management* (220–224). Rajasthan: Modi Intitute of Management & Technology.

Jia, Q., Guo, Y., Li, R., Li, Y., and Chen, Y. (2018) A conceptual artificial intelligence application framework in human resource management. In Proceedings of the International Conference on *Electronic Business* (106–114).

Kapoor, B. (2010). Business Intelligence and Its Use for Human Resource Management. *J Hum Resour. Adul. Leae.* 6(2), 21–30.

R, G., and D, B. S. (2018). Recruitment Through Artificial Intelligence: a Conceptual Study Int. J. Mech. Eng. Technol 9(7): 63–70. Retrieved from: http://www.iaeme.com/ijmet/issues.asp?JType=IJMET&VType=9&IType=7

Richard, M. D., and Lippmann, R. P. (1991). Neural network classifiers estimate Bayesian a posteriori probability. Neur. Compu., 3(4): 461–483.

Saxena, A. (2020). The growing role of artificial intelligence in human resource. EPRA *Int. J. Multidiscip. Res.* 152–158. 10.36713/epra4924.

The future of artificial intelligence adoption in India - The Financial Express, accessed on 9th Nov., 2020.

The impact of AI on recruitment | AIHR Digital (digitalhrtech.com), accessed on 8th Aug 2021.

The Role of Artificial Intelligence (AI) in Recruitment | Talent Lyft, accessed on 8th Aug 2021.

What Is Artificial Emotional Intelligence? | Bernard Mar, accessed on 8th Aug 2021.

5 Revolutionising supply chains with Industry 4.0 concepts to attain sustainability

Swayam Sampurna Panigrahi[1] and Rajesh Kumar Singh[2]

[1]Assistant Professor, International Management Institute, Bhubaneswar, India

[2]Professor, Management Development Institute, Gurgaon, India

Abstract

Supply chains (SC) are progressing towards a smart, automated, and digitised age with the advent of Industry 4.0 revolution. The core functions of the of the SCs need to align with the Industry 4.0 concepts which requires focused attention from the researchers. This article aims to integrate the sustainability goals with the concepts of Industry 4.0 which will lead to a Smarter SC or SC 4.0 which has been described as well as presented in a framework. This framework will act a roadmap for practitioners and decision makers to adopt Industry 4.0 concepts in their organisations while attaining sustainability.

Keywords: Industry 4.0, Supply chains, sustainability triple bottom line

Introduction

Manufacturing firms today not only aspire to become lean, flexible, or world class but all the three and more that is sustainable. Firms have started to believe that aligning their long-term strategies with sustainable development goals can bring them the competitive advantage they long for. 'Sustainable development' is the buzz word of the decade which rose to prominence in the 1980s in the World Conservation Strategy published by World Conservation Union. Since then, it has become a rage and has now turned as a mandate in many countries. The basic idea behind sustainability is to meet the requirements of the present while preserving the requirements of the future. With rapid industrialisation, our natural resources are fast depleting, the carbon emissions are harming the ozone layer and polluting the environment. Growth of industries is crucial for the economy, and we need to keep evolving and in order to do that, we must not hamper technological or industrial advancements. It is crucial to focus on developing strategies, policies, and technologies that aid the economy but at the same time conserve the environment and society.

The world has witnessed four industrial revolutions till date. The key elements in the first three industrial revolutions included steam engines, moving assembly lines, use of electronics and information technology, respectively. With each revolution the manufacturers realised the importance of developing machines with relatively superior abilities to increase productivity. The fourth industrial revolution also known as Industry 4.0 is the most recent revolution that the manufacturers are aiming to adopt. It comprises of several components such as, Internet of Things (IoT) cyber physical system, cloud computing, Big data, augmented reality, additive manufacturing, digital twin etc. These components aim to integrate men and machines, create storage systems, and production facilities that can autonomously communicate for useful decision making without human intervention. Industry 4.0 involves the collection of huge amounts of data which can be processed to predict fault/defects in the assembly line/work-in-progress inventory much before its occurrence. This enables the decision makers in a factory to not conduct periodic maintenance regimes, rather conduct a maintenance routine as and when the system prompts. With the population expansion leading to the dynamic patterns of production and consumption, it is crucial to establish and implement efficient quality control mechanisms. Industry 4.0 enabled manufacturing ensures effective quality management. Industry 4.0 also aims to bring in flexible robotic systems which can collaborate with humans and new manufacturing techniques such as 3D-printing which support the zero waste criteria of lean manufacturing (Peng et al., 2018).

Industry 4.0 has the ability to aid industrial growth and simultaneously foster sustainability along the supply chain (SC). The SC core functions when linked with the Industry 4.0 principles will revolutionise the same by enhancing operational efficiency and thereby ensuring profitability. The paper is an attempt to develop a conceptual framework which justifies the investment done by industries in adopting the Industry 4.0 concepts. This investment is going to be fruitful when the industry is planning for sustainability of their SCs. Before linking sustainability with Industry 4.0, we must understand the basics of both the concepts. The following sections will throw light on the matter discussed above.

Theoretical background

Before conceptualising the framework to revolutionise the SCs using the Industry 4.0 concepts to attain sustainability, it is imperative to explore the three concepts from the existing literature. The various perspectives from the literature have also been tabulated in Table 5.1 at the end of Section 2.

Sustainability goals

Sustainability is a term that can bridge the gap between the all-round development and the environment. It is about how we can still keep developing while taking care of the environment. It deals with questions like, how many trees can we cut yet have forest growth? How much of ground water can we use yet not exhaust the aquifer? However, if we think deeply, even when these maximum levels are monitored, we cannot ensure the sustainability of the eco-system as these are just a few components. The major discussion on sustainable development was found in the World Commission of Environment and Development, a body founded under UN general assembly in 1983. Gro Brundtland was the leader of this commission who was also the then Prime Minister of Norway. Hence, a report by this body in the year 1987 is often referred as the Brundtland Commission Report that defined sustainable development as the development that 'meets the needs of the present without compromising the ability of future generations to meet their own needs (WCED, 1987).' There have been numerous definitions of sustainability by different authors, but the bottom line remains the same. Sustainability can be achieved if the triple bottom line aspect of sustainability is addressed uniformly which are, the economic, ecological, and socio-cultural aspects. The term sustainability is associated with stability, balance, and conservation of nature. Attaining sustainability is about carrying day-to-day activities in a way to preserve the environment yet gain profits, without disrupting the society. It should be done in an integrated manner (Dubey et al., 2017). Today, globalisation is under a pressure to meet the day to day needs of the world population of goods and services and concurrently assure a sustainable evolvement of the human race in the social, ecological, and economic aspects (Stock and Seliger, 2016). This issue can be addressed by aligning the industries toward sustainable development.

The environment is under a huge threat of devastation in the near future. There are several environmental and social issues that require immediate attention. The atmospheric and oceanic pollution, rampant use of fossil fuels leading to climate change, soil erosion, and subsequent salinisation and degradation are some of the key fallouts of large-scale industrialisation (Reid, 2013). Hence, it is our duty and responsibility to move towards an enlightened and a more responsible form of manufacturing and industrialisation. After a period of 20 years, industrialisation and manufacturing have been marked as significant enablers for research, productivity, and employment generation in the Western economic agenda (Rezk et al., 2015; Prause, 2015). A truly promising approach that is the fusion of the real world with the virtual one called Industry 4.0 is gaining worldwide acclaim because of its guaranteed long-term benefits and linkage with sustainable development goals. In the next section, Industry 4.0 has been elaborately explained.

Industry 4.0

A new revolution termed as Industry 4.0 has begun which is being recognised as the fourth industrial revolution. The vision of the revolution is to build smart factories where the shop floor would have intelligent equipment. The intelligent equipment referred would comprise of numerous sensing devices and actuators called the cyber-physical systems (CPS). The CPS which are embedded with mechatronic components will aid in carrying out the manufacturing activities on the shop floor (Ramsauer, 2013). The mechatronic components comprise of applied sensor systems to collect data and actuator systems to control physical processes (Gausemeier et al, 2015). The CPSs are intelligently interlinked with one another which continually exchange information virtually like in a cloud space in real time. They constitute of human-machine interfaces to interact with users (Stock and Seliger, 2016).

The concept of Industry 4.0 aims at a creation of a highly flexible and digitised production mode. The objectives of Industry 4.0 also go beyond the development of CPS and dynamic production networks that is, it aims for energy and resource efficiency, higher productivity, digital integration of engineering (Kagermann et al., 2013). Internet aided manufacturing facilities, interlinked manufacturing systems through networks enable machine to machine communication called M2M, which provides the basis to identify, name, and trace every single product in the production line (Bauer et al., 2014; Brettel et al., 2014; Prause, 2015). This kind of information is going to be helpful in various SC operations like product development and design, logistics, management etc.

The advent of Industry 4.0 has a significant effect on the manufacturing processes. It promotes the adoption of smart factories, smart products, and smart services which are embedded in the IoT or the industrial internet (Stock and Seliger, 2016).

Industry 4.0 has five design principles as follows; the first is termed as 'interoperability' which refers to the ability of the CPS, machines, and humans to get connected and communicate with each other through the internet. This will lead to the creation of a highly integrated ecosystem. The second is 'virtualisation' which aims at the creation of virtual models and simulations for the physical factory. The virtual models are counterparts of the physical processes created through the sensory data. The third principle is known as the 'real-time capability', which focuses on the collection of real time data from a machine during a process. This will enable developing online monitoring and control of the system. The plant head would have a real time insight of the shop floor and immediate control of the processes would be possible. In addition to this, the continuous gathered data can be used to extract information regarding the health of the equipment. The fourth principle is the 'decentralisation' which aims at making the equipment autonomous, that is the machines will be able to self-configure themselves, self-monitor, and self-heal. This will be possible with the dressing of the equipment with various machine learning algorithms. The fifth and last principle is known as 'modularity' which refers to the ability of the machine to adopt and sustain with varying circumstances.

These five principles would serve the purpose of smart production and will lead to the creation of a smart factory. The principles of the concept aim at increasing the productivity achieving unpredictable efficiency through the integrated use of automation and artificial intelligence. The real time data will be used to improve the product quality and reduce the wastage of raw materials and downtime of the machines. Also, the uninterrupted data flows from the machines will speed-up the traceability.

Integrating Sustainable Development Goals to Industry 4.0

In simple terms, Industry 4.0 is about the complete integration of equipment with electronics to get real time sensory data. The Industry 4.0 is like an umbrella that encompasses the Information and Communication Technology (ICT) techniques like embedded systems, IoT, CPS etc. and directs us toward the way in which the industrial production is heading. It mostly focuses upon CPS and hence, there is a requirement for newer and compatible techniques to manage and store information which could leverage a diligent business administration. The ultimate objective is to enhance the business competitiveness by increasing the efficiency and flexibility of the production process via the integration of ICT techniques (Gabriel and Pessl, 2016). The revolution will not only have an impact on the inter-organisational matters like production technologies, employees, profitability etc. but also on the external factors like the social and ecological aspects which are the core of sustainable development. The triple bottom lines perspectives of sustainable development i.e., environment, economy, and society deserve equal attention. There is a myth associated with environmentally responsible operational practices that they are not going to be cost effective. Sustainable supply chains promote the adoption of

Table 5.1 Perspectives from the literature

S. no.	Perspectives	Reference
1.	Sustainability – • Stability, balance, and conservation of nature. • Attaining sustainability is about carrying day-to-day activities in a way to preserve the environment yet gain profits, without disrupting the society.	(Dubey et al., 2017)
2.	Growing environmental threats • Population expansion leading to peculiar production and consumption trends. • Assuring a sustainable evolvement of the human race in the social, ecological, and economic aspects.	(Stock and Seliger, 2016)
3.	Rapid industrialisation and its aftermath, • Atmospheric and oceanic pollution, • rampant use of fossil fuels leading to climate change, • soil erosion and subsequent salinization, and • ecosystem imbalance degradation.	(Reid, 2013)
4.	Sustainable operational and manufacturing practices • Industrialisation and manufacturing have been marked as significant enablers for research, productivity, and employment generation. • Cleaner technologies, lean principles, sustainable supply chains	(Rezk et al., 2015; Prause, 2015) (Dubey et al., 2017)
5.	Industry 4.0 • Big data, CPS, IoT, IIOT, cloud computing, AI • Mechatronic components assistance in shop floor • Advanced sensory systems to collect data and • Actuator systems to control physical processes • Smart production- smart factories, smart products and smart services	(Ramsauer, 2013); (Gausemeier et al., 2015) (Stock and Seliger, 2016)
6.	Future of Industry 4.0- • Looking beyond smart and dynamic production networks, • aiming for energy and resource efficiency, • higher productivity, • digital integration of engineering, • Internet aided manufacturing facilities, and • interlinked manufacturing systems through networks enable machine to machine communication.	(Kagermann et al., 2013) (Bauer et al., 2014; Brettel et al., 2014; Prause, 2015).
7.	Five principles of Industry 4.0- • Interoperability, virtualisation, real-time operability, decentralisation, modularity	(Mishra et al., 2021)

environment-friendly operational activities that are not only profitable in the long run but also foster societal harmony. Therefore, it is imperative to consider all the three perspectives of sustainable development. The following sections shall provide clarity about how the revolution integrates the sustainable development with Industry 4.0 which energises the supply chains.

Social perspective

Expert opinion suggests that even if there is a higher level of automation involved people will still hold a crucial position in the industry. In one of the papers, the authors conducted an empirical study on 661 number of companies and 21 Industry 4.0 experts and concluded that 60.2% of respondents stated that human work is going to play an important role in future manufacturing (Gabriel and Pessl, 2016). Industry 4.0 will restore some of the classical manually running processes that have to be accomplished by workers' skill, expertise, intelligence and creativity; however, the positioning of the workers within the manufacturing units and the tasks that they have been performing will change (Gabriel and Pessl, 2016). Authors have stated that workers will play the role of coordinating, conducting, and monitoring the production processes where major muscular work along with a part of mental work will be assigned to the machines (Spath et al., 2013). Industry 4.0 would ensure workers' health by protecting them from adverse working conditions where now the machines would operate. New professions for workers would emerge as a result of the revolution. The employees will require adequate training to grow closely with the machines while operating them. This strong network between man and machine is expected to promote job satisfaction and job content among the employees.

Skilled knowledge and expertise in the field of information and communications technologies will be the call of the day to sustain in the Industry 4.0 environment. Skilled employees will be responsible for planning, executing, and decision making along with controlling, programming, and correcting the errors in the coding involved in these intelligent sensors embedded machines in an integrated manner (Nyhuis, 2010; Kurz, 2012; Kagermann et al., 2013). There will also be a demand for employees who have interdisciplinary knowledge in corresponding disciplines of the production unit (Kurz, 2012; Gabriel and Pessl, 2016). As a result of large-scale automation of production processes, the physical strain on laborers will decrease which will be particularly advantageous for the older workers (Gabriel and Pessl, 2016). In fact, there will be an opportunity for hiring the older workers who could no longer do the hard muscular work but have a lifetime of experience of the process. Not only can their experience be used to train the machines for decision making under critical conditions but also, they can be involved in the actual process with adequate training. It is a matter of fact that women are not as physically strong as men. And since the Industry 4.0 reduces the muscular work involved in production, it would increase the opportunity to hire female employees at the shop floor. This would also enhance the decision-making skills of the female employees who aim to become leaders in future. In developing countries like India, having a female in the board of directors is a mandate according to The Companies Act, 2013, thus, it would be advantageous for organisations across nations to hire more female employees. This would address the gender inequality in the organisation and would lead to women empowerment. This in turn would further boost the productivity in an organisation along with ensuring the SD. With the boon comes the bane; although the physical stress would drop, but the mental stress might rise (Kagermann et al., 2013). when there would be a lack of communication and cooperation between man and the machine or the work allocation being done by a machine could cause mental strain on the employee. Thus, it is important to consider the risk and identify measures to address the same.

Apart from the larger corporations, the Micro, Small and Medium Enterprises (MSMEs) could also benefit from adopting Industry 4.0 into their SCs. There is a challenge to find skilled workforce for the MSMEs which could be addressed by adopting Industry 4.0 which in turn will also help them attain sustainability. Hence, the discussion above justifies that the social aspect of sustainable development will be aptly addressed by Industry 4.0.

Environmental perspective

The aftermath of large-scale industrialisation is seen in form of climate change, global warming, water scarcity, ozone depletion, air contamination, soil contamination, imbalance in ecosystem and extinction of animal species. It is high time we realised the need to adopt environmentally sustainable production and consumption. Stricter regulations are already coming up in most of the nations and the industries are the first where these laws shall be imposed. Industrial adherence to environmental standards is highly essential in the present day. Industries today deal with huge amounts of wastage. A part of the waste is the result of non-conformance to product quality standards. The lean manufacturing concept that highlights the zero-waste principle is one of the ways to handle industrial waste before it is even created (De la Vega-Rodriguez et al., 2018). National governments and industry associations have felt the need to adopt environmentally conscious manufacturing since a long time (Richards, 1994). However, environment today is still under the threat of devastation. Industry 4.0 has the potential to incorporate the concepts of lean and environmentally conscious manufacturing concepts and lead the organisation to sustainable development. It can provide support by continuous energy and resource management. The sensor embedded machines have the ability to produce real time information at each stage of production and the subsequent energy and resource use. Further, the systems can be optimised during the process of production with minimum energy and resource utilisation and keep emission levels in check at all times (Gabriel and Pressl, 2016). Industry 4.0 also allows effective production planning to optimise resource and energy consumption by planning the design of rooms, spaces, pathways, lines to create close energy and resource cycles (Kagermann et al., 2013). Industry 4.0 promotes the optimisation of industrial production processes that reduce the carbon emissions to minimum. With this, it is possible to get environmental clearance from governments to operate plants even at urban areas which would enable a social (work life balance of employees) and environmental sustainability. Industry 4.0 will promote advanced manufacturing processes like additive manufacturing. For instance, 3D printing is a technology that has been gaining momentum with time. It produces products using layer by layer printing using raw materials like ceramics, polymers, metals etc. It generates zero waste and is called a sustainable manufacturing process (Huang et al., 2013). Hence, such environmental measures in organisations would help in ecological conservation as well as motivate the employees to perform better in such clean and healthy surroundings.

Economic perspective

Digital transformation in the engineering sector will yield profits in the long run. Authors have stated that Industry 4.0 in conjunction with SCs will reduce the operational costs by 30% and decrease inventories by 75% (Alicke et al., 2017). Most countries have already put themselves on the path of digitisation. In developing countries like India and China, the respective national governments have introduced several programs and campaigns to proliferate digital transformation. For example, the 'Make in India' and 'Digital India' campaigns have reaped an economic growth rate of 7.5% in the year 2015 which is greater than China (Bilimoria, 2016). This is proof of how profitable Industry 4.0 is. When the machines, tools, components, assemblies, sub-assemblies, and modes of transport in a production unit are connected to the internet, sensors, radio frequency identification (RFID), etc., it enables the exchange of valuable real time information and a platform for the above to communicate with each other. It is quite advantageous to attain the overall goal of optimised manufacturing. Customised manufacturing will also be possible by the implementation of Industry 4.0 into manufacturing reality that would yield high customer satisfaction (Wang et al., 2016) which has a direct link to profitability. This platform of data collection, information sharing, decision making, coordination and transparency between organisational disciplines and SC stakeholders results in a reduction of waste, shortened lead times, and decreased operational costs which is, in fact, a direct consequence of integration of Industry 4.0 and economic aspect of sustainability. Greigarn, 2016 stated that the revolution can also be called the New Economic Revolution that would not only conserve the people and planet but also ensure profit.

The contributions of various Industry 4.0 components to the attainment of the triple bottom line perspectives of sustainability have been presented in Table 5.2.

Revolutionising the supply chains

Over the three decades, SCs have undergone a significant paradigm shift. From ones which had simple tasks in the SCs such as, manufacturing, logistics, and delivery to customers have been revolutionised to lean, customised manufacturing, optimised transportation and logistics, customer feedback, and planning product end of life. They have seen a sea change in processes, techniques, technologies, and decision making. In the era of digitisation, organisations are forced to re-design their SCs accordingly. Although SCs in the present have the ability to support the ICT to share information along the chain through a number of interfaces, they lack the ability for a global overview of product manufacturing in real time (Brettel et al., 2014; Prause, 2015). Several authors have marked that the Industry 4.0 principles that incorporate internet aided production and networked production lines that can monitor the product life cycle serves as a crucial contributor in organisational decision making and progress towards sustainable development (Bauer et al., 2014; Dubey et al., 2017; De Sousa Jabbour et al., 2018).

There are projects that have adopted the Industry 4.0 concepts and are making profits out of the same. The AMATRAK project at ISL, Bremen makes use of self-guided container transportation systems which have various sensors and artificial

Table 5.2 Contribution of Industry 4.0 components for attaining sustainability

S. No.	Industry 4.0 components	Scope	Sustainability perspective it addresses
1)	Internet of things	This contributes to connecting the machines to the internet and ultimately to one another wherein useful information is shared in the shopfloor in real time.	Economic
2)	CPS	These systems connect the computations, networks and physical processes which are required for automation of the production systems.	Economic
3)	Big data	This facilitates the analysis of the large and complex data sets (which are collected from previous instances) to predict and control a manufacturing process in the future. It can predict the pollution levels in a factory which can be checked before it occurs.	Economic, environmental
4)	Cloud computing	Complete automation of production systems is only possible when large data sets are collected which require to be stored before further analysis.	Economic
5)	Intelligent robot/cobots	In addition to reducing the manual load/muscular strain on workers in an assembly line, the intelligent robots/cobots can collaborate with humans to aid intelligent manufacturing.	Economic, social
6)	Augmented reality/virtual reality	This technology aids the workers to not work in hazardous conditions but still are able to be actively involved in the production process by creating a computer simulated reality.	Social, environmental
7)	Additive manufacturing	This supports the *lean* concept of zero waste manufacturing which is the call of the hour.	Economic, environmental, social
8)	Digital twin	The digital counterpart of a physical object or process aims to revolutionise the present-day manufacturing. This not only aids in health monitoring of the machines, ensuring safety of workers but also in determining the most economical way of production.	Economic, environmental, social

intelligence technologies integrated to them that allows them to choose optimal means of transportation systems based on their own requirements (ISL, 2015). Industry 4.0 has the capacity of revolutionising the SCs by reforming the roles of the SC members like designers, suppliers, consumers, and logistics providers. And this integration of Industry 4.0 into the SC can be called 'Supply Chain 4.0.' When the supply chain management will adopt Industry 4.0 innovations like IoT, higher order robotics, Big data, etc. to enhance the business performance with the purpose of satisfying the customers, this will pave a way for Supply Chain 4.0 (Alicke et al., 2017). This SC 4.0 will borrow the Industry 4.0 networked manufacturing, adaptive logistics systems, customer integrated manufacturing, etc. SC 4.0 will aim to horizontally integrate networks by digitisation of processes across the chain, end to end engineering over the product life cycle while vertically integrating the manufacturing systems. The horizontal integration implies the cross-organisational interlinking and digitisation of a product's value chain and the interlinked value chains that are involved in the production. The end-to-end engineering implies the cross-connecting and digitising of the phases in the product life cycle that is acquiring raw materials to manufacturing and finishing, delivering, and product use and product end of life. Vertical integration of manufacturing systems means the intelligent cross-connecting and digitising the hierarchical levels of a SC from manufacturing stations through cells, lines, units, factories and also linking the other SC functions like marketing and technological innovation (Stock and Seliger, 2016). SC 4.0 will have smart factories that include flow of smart data via the cloud which would manufacture smart products. These factories will receive the electricity required from smart grids.

There are some guaranteed benefits to the SC core functions that accompany the adoption of Industry 4.0. SC planning will benefit from big data and predictive analytics to evaluate and forecast demand by using machine learning algorithms to derive a befitting demand plan. Logistics and transportation is going to hugely benefit from the components of Industry 4.0. Wearable, human-friendly interfaces can be used on the shop floor to allow location-based directions to workers for guiding and picking up processes. High end robotics and exoskeletons can dramatically improve human productivity in manufacturing (Alicke et al., 2017). Collaborative relationship among stakeholders is likely to improve because of the available cloud platforms where there is information transparency among the customers, suppliers, and manufacturers. They can jointly make decisions and find solutions to several issues. Figure 5.1 shows how the principles of Industry 4.0 can be integrated into the supply chain functions.

Conclusion

Operational effectiveness will increase with eliminations of digital waste and adoption of new technologies. This hybrid strategy of integrating Industry 4.0 with SCs for the overall motive to attain sustainability is expected to minimise the operational costs and inventories of an industry. SCs will become more agile and flexible that can cater to needs of the present. SC sustainability is a topic that has been researched over the years and is still under consideration as experts believe that if we make the SCs sustainable, then we can achieve overall sustainable

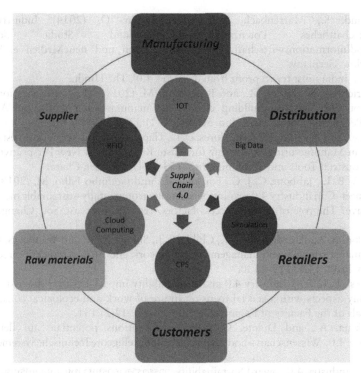

Figure 5.1 Supply chain 4.0 integration with Industry 4.0
Source: Created by authors

development. It is seen that principles and practices of Industry 4.0 will unleash the ability of organisations to attain sustainable development A nation's progress towards sustainability is directly linked to its ability of adopting innovative technologies that conserve the environment as well as generate profits. Sustainable development and Industry 4.0 are major trends in the current production scenario and their synergy can create an industrial wave that has the capacity to revolutionise today's manufacturing system. Organisational sustainability has developed over the years in concurrence to Industry 4.0. Hence, it is important to understand the nature of the interaction and synergy of both the concepts. This article is dedicated to integrating the idea of sustainability with the concepts of Industry 4.0. Through this research, we urge the researchers worldwide to dive further into the literature to develop ways and suggest means that can provide clarity to this concept and further derive models, action plans, and road maps to transform this into reality.

References

[WCED] World Commission on Environment and Development, B. C. (1987). Our common future. *Report of the world commission on environment and development.*
Alicke, K., Rexhausen, D., & Seyfert, A. (2017). Supply Chain 4.0 in consumer goods. Mckinsey & Company, 1(11).

Bauer, W., Schlund, S., Marrenbach, D., and Ganschar, O. (2014). Industrie 4.0-Volkswirtschaftliches Potenzialfür Deutschland, Studie des BundesverbandInformationswirtschaft, Telekommunikation und neueMedien e. V. (Bitkom). Berlin, Germany.

Bilimoria, K. (2016). India must try to profit from 'Industry 4.0'. The Hindu.

Brettel, M., Friederichsen, N., Keller, M., and Rosenberg, M. (2014). How virtualization, decentralization and network building change the manufacturing landscape: An Industry 4.0 Perspective. Int. J. Mech. Ind. Sci. Eng. 8(1):37–44.

De la Vega-Rodríguez, M., Baez-Lopez, Y. A., Flores, D. L., Tlapa, D. A., and Alvarado-Iniesta, A. (2018). Lean Manufacturing: A Strategy for Waste Reduction. In New Perspectives on Applied Industrial Tools and Techniques (pp. 153–174). Springer, Cham.

de Sousa Jabbour, A. B. L., Jabbour, C. J. C., Foropon, C., and Godinho Filho, M. (2018). When titans meet–Can industry 4.0 revolutionise the environmentally-sustainable manufacturing wave? The role of critical success factors. Technol. Forecast. Soc. Change. 132:18–25.

Dubey, R., Gunasekaran, A., Papadopoulos, T., Childe, S. J., Shibin, K. T., and Wamba, S. F. (2017). Sustainable supply chain management: framework and further research directions. J. Clean. Prod. 142:1119–1130.

Gabriel, M. and Pessl, E. (2016). Industry 4.0 and sustainability impacts: critical discussion of sustainability aspects with a special focus on future of work and ecological consequences. Annals of the Faculty of Engineering Hunedoara. 14(2):131.

Gausemeier, J., Czaja, A., and Dülme, C. (2015). Innovations potentiale auf dem WegzuIndustrie 4.0. Wissenschafts-und IndustrieforumIntelligenteTechnischeSysteme. 10.

Greigarn, K. (2016). Industry 4.0 toward Sustainability. วารสารวิชาการมหาวิทยาลัยอีสเทิร์นเอเซียฉบับวิทยาศาสตร์และเทคโนโลยี EAU Heritage Journal: Science and Technology. 10(2): 15.

Huang, S. H., Liu, P., Mokasdar, A., and Hou, L. (2013). Additive manufacturing and its societal impact: a literature review. Int. J. Adv. Manuf. Techn.. 67(58):1191–1203.

ISL. 2015. AMATRAK Project, www.isl.org, Bremen

Kagermann, H., Helbig, J., Hellinger, A., and Wahlster, W. (2013). *Recommendations for implementing the strategic initiative INDUSTRIE 4.0: Securing the future of German manufacturing industry; final report of the Industrie 4.0 Working Group.* Forschungsunion.

Kurz, C. and METALL, I. (2012). Arbeit in der Industrie 4.0. Information Management and Consulting. 3:56–59.

Mishra, D., Pal, S. K., and Chakravarty, D. (2021). Industry 4.0 in Welding. Weld. Technol. 253–298.

Nyhuis, P. (2010). WandlungsfähigeProduktionssysteme, Schriftenreihe der HochschulgruppefürArbeits-und Betriebsorganisation e. V. (HAB), GITO-Verlag, Berlin,, Germany.

Peng, T., Kellens, K., Tang, R., Chen, C., and Chen, G. (2018). Sustainability of additive manufacturing: An overview on its energy demand and environmental impact. Addit. Manuf.. 21:694–704.

Prause, G. (2015). Industry 4.0: New Perspectives for Smart Production and Logistics in the Baltic Sea Region. Baltic Rim Economies. 4, 41.

Ramsauer, C. (2013). Industrie 4.0–Die Produktion der Zukunft. WINGbusiness. 3:6–12.

Reid, D. (2013). Sustainable development: an introductory guide. Routledge, London, United Kingdom

Rezk, M. R., Ibrahim, H., TvaronaviÄienÄ, M., Sakr, M., Piccinetti, L., and Piccinetti, L. (2015). Measuring innovations in Egypt: case of industry. Entrep. Sustain. Issues 3(1):47–55.

Richards, D. J. (1994). Environmentally conscious manufacturing. World Class Design to Manufacture. 1(3):15–22.

Spath, D., Ganschar, O., Gerlach, S., Hämmerle, M., Krause, T., and Schlund, S. (2013). Produktionsarbeit der Zukunft–Industry 4.0, fraunhofer, Stuttgart, 155p.

Stock, T. and Seliger, G. (2016). Opportunities of sustainable manufacturing in industry 4.0. Procedia Cirp. 40:536–541.

Wang, G., Gunasekaran, A., Ngai, E. W., and Papadopoulos, T. (2016). Big data analytics in logistics and supply chain management: Certain investigations for research and applications. International Journal of Production Economics. 176:98–110.

6 Spiritual leadership – A systematic review and call for future research

Jerin Jose and Arun Antony Chully

Assistant Professor, School of Business and Management, CHRIST (Deemed to be University), India

Correspondence: jerin.jose@christuniversity.in

Abstract

Spiritual leadership is considered to be a human-centred and value-oriented leadership theory, where the leaders intrinsically motivate their followers and themselves. It emerged in the late 1990s and early 2000s as a response to lack of job security and multiple other factors. Anchored on Intrinsic motivation, spiritual leadership is comprised of vision, hope/faith, and altruistic love. Spiritual leadership is considered to be the synthesis of value-based leadership constructs like servant leadership, principle-centred leadership, charismatic leadership, and transformational leadership.

A systematic review, also known as the research synthesis, focuses on providing a comprehensive and unbiased body of knowledge of multiple studies in a single form. Attending to the existing and emerging importance of spiritual leadership, we focus on the cause-effect framework i.e. the causes of spiritual leadership - vision, hope/faith, and altruistic love and effects of spiritual leadership – calling and membership. Based on the review of literature on spiritual leadership across 44 articles in 20 journals spanning over 20 years, we sorted and summarised the literature around the cause-effect framework of spiritual leadership. The significant possibility of future research is also pointed out.

Keywords: Spiritual leadership, Leadership, Individual outcome, Organizational outcome

Introduction

The emergence of the human spirit is one of the major driving forces of organizations in the 21st century, thus the importance of spirituality is gaining importance (Pio et al., 2020). Spiritual leadership is considered to be a spirit-centred and value-oriented leadership theory, where the leaders intrinsically motivate their followers and themselves and are comprised of vision, hope/faith, and altruistic love (Fry, 2003). By helping followers to find value and meaning in their work, these leaders will satisfy the natural need for spiritual life and also enhance spiritual well-being. Intrinsic motivation is the anchoring principle of spiritual leadership. The concept of spiritual leadership in the workplace emerged in the late 1990s and early 2000s as a response to lack of job security and multiple other factors (Darling and Chalofsky, 2004). Fry (2003) in his attempt to connect leadership with spirituality argued that spiritual leadership is a collection of values, attitudes, and behaviour required to motivate a person and others intrinsically (Wahyono et al., 2021) in order to develop a sense of spiritual well-being through calling and membership (Fry, 2008, p. 109).

Spiritual leadership, which comprises vision, hope/faith, and altruistic love, is the synthesis of value-based leadership constructs like servant leadership (Greenleaf, 1977), principle-centered leadership (Covey, 1992), charismatic leadership (House and Shamir, 1993), and transformational leadership. We believe there is a need for an extensive and systematic literature review of research on spiritual leadership. Since the early work of Fry (2003) that led to the foundation of the development of spiritual leadership theory, a large volume of empirical and conceptual studies have demonstrated the relationship between spiritual leadership and outcomes; we propose the time is right for a systematic review of the nomological network of spiritual leadership.

Research of spiritual leadership can be classified into three stages. The first stage can be considered as an early stage of conceptual development where spirituality and spiritual leadership was entangled, interwoven with religious dimensions, and had an edge of faith (Fairholm, 1996; Stowell, 1997). The second stage can be considered as the phase of the call for workplace spirituality and differentiation of religion and spirituality (Fry, 2003), developing measures (scale) of spiritual leadership (Fry et al., 2005), and examining the relationship between spiritual leadership and the consequences. The current stage can be considered as the third stage of development where more complex research designs are utilized to further understand the consequences, mediations, and the circumference of spiritual leadership. Our review of spiritual leadership literature is an attempt to analyse the spiritual leadership literature for the past 20 years and understand where it was and give it a future direction.

With the changing business and economic scenario, the call for a more holistic approach to leadership is at an accelerating pace. The up-rise of the holistic approach to leadership is the result of this realization which integrates the body (physical), mind (logical/rational thought), heart (emotions, feelings), and spirit (Fry, 2003; Moxley, 2000). From the traditional, uniform, centralized organizational structure that is driven by fear and authority, a radical paradigm shift to an intrinsically motivated learning organization is the response to the call (Ancona et al., 1999; Moxley, 2000; Fry 2003). Spiritual leadership, which proposes an intrinsic motivation of self and others, is a casual organizational theory designed to have a sense of spiritual survival through calling and membership (Fry, 2003; Fry et al., 2005). It is a paradigm in the leadership school of thought.

We approached the literature analysis with three questions

1. How is spiritual leadership defined and understood among leadership literature?
2. What is our depth of understanding about spiritual leadership through existing research?
3. What is the future of spiritual leadership research?

Review methodology

To answer the above questions, we conducted a systematic review of the literature to identify the literature relevant to spiritual leadership. The primary criterion for the selection of articles was the focus on spiritual leadership. Research articles whose primary focus is on spiritual leadership are considered for the review. We searched on databases (Google scholar, Jstor, emerald, Proquest central, and APApsycNET) with keyword search and included the combinations of words - spiritual leadership, spirituality, workplace spirituality, leadership, leader. Following keyword search, articles were sorted by reading the abstract and selected the articles that broadly address spiritual leadership. After reading the full article, the selection was done on the basis of relevance to the topic. We also explored and examined the reference list of articles with the purpose of identifying additional literature excluded in the database.

We considered the articles published over 20 years (2001–2021) from the first casual model of spiritual leadership proposed by Fry (2003). Altogether we reviewed 44 published articles across 20 ABDC listed journals (Table 6.1).

Based on our research questions, we have organized our review mainly into three segments. First, we examine how spiritual leadership is understood in the school of leadership literature; second, we discuss our depth of understanding and map the network by reviewing the literatures on spiritual leadership; and third recommend an agenda for future research.

Table 6.1 List of articles reviewed

Sl. No	Journal Name	No. of Papers
1	Educational Management Administration & Leadership	1
2	Human Resource Management	1
3	Human Resource Management International Digest	1
4	International Journal of Business and Information	1
5	International Journal of Culture, Tourism and Hospitality Research	1
6	International Journal of Law and Management	1
7	International Journal of Public Administration	1
8	Journal of Applied Social Psychology	1
9	Journal of Business Ethics	7
10	Journal of Economic and Administrative Science	1
11	Journal of Educational Administration	1
12	Journal of Environmental Planning and Management	1
13	Journal of Hospitality and Tourism Management	1
14	Journal of Managerial Psychology	1
15	Leadership	1
16	Leadership & Organization Development Journal	5
17	Organization Dynamics	1
18	Personnel Review	1
19	The leadership quarterly	10
20	Journal of Economic and Administrative Sciences	1

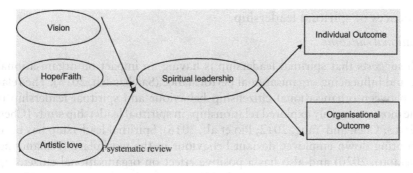

Figure 6.1 Framework of systematic review
Source: Adapted from Fry (2003)

Antecedents of servant leadership

Generally, organisational work culture, personality, demographics, team culture, and policies are considered the antecedents of leader behaviour (Eva et al., 2019). Theories of spiritual leadership developed within the framework of motivation theory include elements of workplace spirituality and spiritual survival (Fry, 2003). Spiritual leadership theory, therefore, comprises vision, hope/faith, and altruistic love (Fry, 2003; Fry et al., 2005).

Vision

Vision is the anticipated future and the substantiation of why we should endeavour for the same. "Vision refers to a picture of the future with some implicit or explicit commentary on why people should strive to create that future" (Kotter, 1996). Vision depicts the organizational purpose and the reason employees and leaders follow the same (Fry, 2003). The leader has to envision the future and should, then, act as a mediator between the present and the future (Polat, 2011). Vision influences the organisational objectives and goals, derives meaning for work, and exhibits ambitions (Draft and Lengel, 1998).

Altruistic love

Altruistic love is defined as a 'sense of wholeness, harmony, and well-being produced through care, concern, and appreciation for both self and others' (Fry, 2003). It is based on integrity, lack of envy, recognition of self and others, and the ability to control oneself (Fry, 2003; Reave, 2005; Salehzadeh et al., 2015).

Hope/faith

Hope/faith in an organisation's vision motivates employees to look forward to achieving the organisational vision and propel the employees through intrinsic motivation to work towards achieving the same (Fry, 2003). Faith is the optimistic outlook established on attitudes, values, and behaviour (Fry, 2003; Fry et al., 2008; Salehzadeh et al., 2015).

Consequences of spiritual leadership

Organisational outcome

Research suggests that spiritual leadership is having an impact on organisational outcome and influencing organisational performance (Salehzadeh, 2015). The relationship between organisational citizenship behaviour and spiritual leadership is one of the most commonly explored relationships in spiritual leadership study (Chen and Li, 2013; Chen and Yang, 2012; Pio et al., 2018). Spiritual leadership has been found to bring down employee deviant behaviour in the workplace (Prihandono and Wijayanto, 2020) and also has a positive effect on organisational citizenship behaviour for environment (Anser et al., 2021), organizational commitment (Tabor et al., 2020), and meaningfulness climate (Yang et al., 2019).

Individual outcome

Spiritual leadership, a value-oriented spirit-centred leadership approach (Jeon and Choi, 2020) based on intrinsic motivation, is associated with a wide range of individual outcomes. The three dimensions of spiritual leadership i.e., vision, hope/faith, and altruistic love, (Fry, 2003) improve the creativity of the employees (Jeon and Choi, 2020). Creativity at work is the task, result, and product of efforts to invent and introduce new products and services to ease the ways of doing work (Hughes et al., 2018). Spiritual leadership is also positively associated with affective commitment (Jeon and Choi, 2020), environmental justice orientation (Anser et al., 2021), productivity and career self-management (Chen et al., 2012), self-esteem, and self-efficacy (Chen et al.,2012; Chen and Li, 2013), performance (Chen and Li, 2013), relational energy, and job performance (Yang et al., 2019) (Table 6.2).

Network analysis of spiritual leadership research

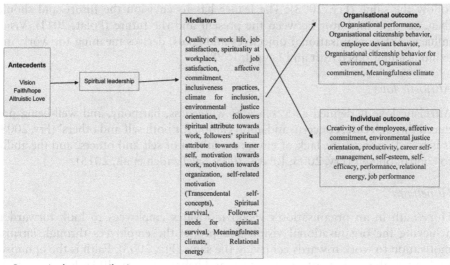

Source: Authors contribution

Table 6.2 Outcomes of spiritual leadership

Mediator	Outcome	Author
	Performance	Salehzadeh, R., Pool, J. K., Lashaki, J. K., Dolati, H., & Jamkhaneh, H. B. (2015).
Quality of work-life, job satisfaction	OCB	Pio, R. J., & Tampi, J. R. E. (2018).
Spirituality at the workplace, job satisfaction	Reduced deviant behaviour in deviant behaviour in workplace	Prihandono, D., & Wijayanto, A. (2020).
Affective commitment	Employee's creativity	Jeon, K. S., & Choi, B. K. (2020).
Inclusiveness practices, climate for inclusion	Follower outcomes, common good outcomes	Gotsis, G., & Grimani, K. (2017)
Environmental justice orientation	OCEB	Anser, M. K., Shafique, S., Usman, M., Akhtar, N., & Ali, M. (2020).
Followers' spiritual attribute towards work, Followers' spiritual attribute towards inner self	Career self-management, productivity	Chen, C. Y., Yang, C. Y., & Li, C. I. (2012)
Motivation towards work, motivation towards organisation, self-related motivation (transcendental self-concepts)	Performance, OCB	Chen, C. Y., and Li, C. I. (2013)
Spiritual survival	OCB	Chen, C. Y., and Yang, C. F. (2012).
Followers' needs for spiritual survival	Organisational commitment productivity employee, well-being	Fry, L. W., Vitucci, S., and Cedillo, M. (2005)
Meaningfulness climate	Team effectiveness	Yang, F., Huang, X., and Wu, L. (2019)
Relational energy	Job performance	Yang, F., Liu, J., Wang, Z., and Zhang, Y. (2019)

Future research directions

Our review on spiritual leadership successfully identified the individual and organisational outcome, but as recognised, there still exist considerable gaps. We categorise the agenda for future research into two parts- theoretical approaches and methodological paths. Theoretical advancement focuses on re-looking at the theoretical dimension of spiritual leadership and to re-establish the way spiritual leadership is analysed and understood. We suggest researchers should take into account upper echelon theory and resource-based view. Secondly, the methodological path is to show the roadmap for spiritual leadership research. The spiritual leadership research was done using longitudinal data but was over-relied on a newly formed Apache Longbow helicopter attack squadron of the US. As the unit of analysis was a recent creation, we have mentioned alternative units of analysis and corresponding research questions to help us authenticate the knowledge on spiritual leadership.

However, the outcomes of spiritual leadership should be able to substantiate practices that add value to the leadership practices instead of adding more variables to the existing network.

Theoretical approach

The theoretical advancement of spiritual leadership is in the developmental stage and has to expand beyond the leadership theories. Spiritual leadership theories helped researchers to understand the impact of organisations and employees. The spectrum of spiritual leadership extends beyond the organizational and follower outcome; additional theoretical advancement is necessary. In an effort to widen the scope of spiritual leadership research and to propose a new roadmap for this research, we propose two theories that will help for enlarging the spiritual leadership framework.

Upper echelon theory

Upper echelon theory (Hambrick and Mason, 1984) can be used to understand, in depth, the individual and organizational outcome of the employees under a spiritual leadership. The upper echelon theory argues that managerial characteristics influence performance, strategic decisions, and organizational results (Hiebl, 2017). Upper echelon theory is a multidimensional approach that includes bounded rationality, observable measures, and top management accountability acting as the drives of decision making (Lee et al., 2018), where top management has a notable role in organisational decision making (Hattke and Blaschke, 2015).

Top executive decisions are driven by personal exposition which is derived from the values, past experience, and characteristics (Hambrick, 2007). The organisational outcome is determined by demographic and non-demographic characteristics of the leaders (Harrison and Klein, 2007), including age, socio-economic roots, educational background, etc. (Hambrick and Mason, 1984; Hattke and Blaschke, 2015). Spiritual leadership is a value-based leadership theory (Fry, 2003) that consists of vision, hope/faith, and altruistic love (Fry et al., 2015) that will result in a positive organizational output (Sapta et al., 2021). Drawing on this model, spiritual leadership majorly focuses on the positive organisational and individual outcomes whereas upper echelon theory affects the top management traits that influence the outcome. We recommend researchers to examine and analyse the traits of the upper echelon and the impact of spiritual leadership in the organizational context.

Resource-based view

Resource-based view, evolved as an alternative for Porter (1980), is an umbrella term (Bromiley and Rau, 2016; Nagano, 2020) and primarily focuses on the possession and disposition of a firm's resources which creates value for the organization (Popli et al., 2017). Organisational resources are the central concept of the resource-based view (Greve, 2021). Amit and Schoemaker (1993: 35) define resources as 'stocks of available factors that are owned and controlled by the firm.' The firm's rare and exclusive resources will give a competitive advantage (Bromiley and Rau, 2016; Kull et al., 2016) and will provide practical alternatives (Nagano, 2020) because resource-based views will show light into the resources on which organisations can rely (Gibson et al., 2021). The resources of the organisation are not only its tangible assets (Wernerfelt, 1984) but they also extend to intangible assets (Greve, 2021) that include leadership (Gibson et al., 2021; Wright et al., 2001). Spiritual leadership, which is based on intrinsic motivation principles (Fry et al., 2005) will increase the competitive advantage of the firm because it has a significant impact on organizational and individual output. We recommend the researcher to analyse the resource-based view in a spiritual leadership framework to understand the impact on competitive advantage.

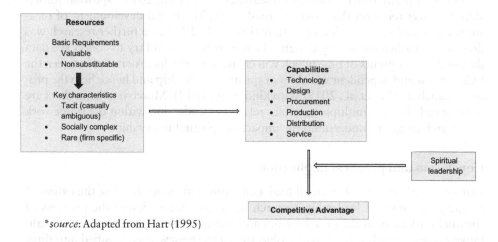

source: Adapted from Hart (1995)

Research design and roadmap

Spiritual leadership school is still dependent on Fry et al., (2005), to measure the spiritual leadership dimension using the Likert scale which was initially developed in a military setting. While the use of rating scale is a subject of debate in many earlier works on leadership (Eva et al., 2019), spiritual leadership is still following the initial set boundaries. Taking into account the progress made in the statistical analysis of leadership studies, the measurement of spiritual leadership should also advance and develop.

The initial scale was developed in a military leadership setting but further research lacked field experiments which are commonly observed in leadership studies. The lack of field study is giving an opportunity for the spiritual leadership scholars to make a breakthrough intervention. Spiritual leadership studies have emerged into mainstream leadership schools of thought only in the past two decades. No major studies have been done to measure how spiritual leadership is developed in the organisational context, so researchers can organise training, workshops, and other programs to understand how spiritual leadership training increases spiritual leadership among the participants. The researchers can adopt an intervention study where one group can be given training on spiritual leadership during various time periods whereas the other group remains a non-intervention group. During the time period, researchers can measure the spiritual leadership traits displayed by the trainees and also associated possible behaviours to illustrate whether servant leadership can be taught and implemented for the benefit of the organization. The researcher can further analyse how leaders who consider practicing spiritual leadership are intrinsically motivating their followers (Fry, 2003).

Our review on spiritual leadership identified a significant focus given to the top management but is not addressing the middle and lower-level managers and leaders. However, middle and lower-level managers and leaders could be potential actors in the disposition of spiritual leadership. Middle and lower-level managers of the organisation take part in different activities and hold recognisable positions which make them key actors in the leadership role. Therefore, we propose to focus on middle and lower-level management on theorizing the impact of spiritual leadership

Similar to many other leadership researches (Eva et al., 2019), spiritual leadership also over-relies on the cross-sectional study. The initial development of measures was based on a longitudinal study (Fry et al., 2005), no further research was done to strengthen the survey design. The researchers should try to collect the data during different points of time which will create a timely disassociation between the independent and dependent variables of spiritual leadership and hence help the process of analysis (Eve et al., 2019; Wittekind et al., 2013). Moreover, researchers are recommended to use multiple variables related to leadership within the framework of research design to understand the impact of spiritual leadership.

Conclusion and practical implication

Our systematic review of spiritual leadership aimed at understanding the extent of progress the spiritual leadership research has made. We reviewed the progress of spiritual leadership in the past 20 years and included both quantitative and qualitative research articles. The broader objective of the review was classified into three parts. First, how spiritual leadership is defined and understood in the leadership school of thought; second, analysing the depth of our understanding about spiritual leadership using the existing research; analysing the current literature we mapped the consequences of spiritual leadership as 'individual outcome' and 'organizational outcome'. Last, we proposed a future research agenda for the researchers with an aim to improve the studies on spiritual leadership.

With the current momentum for spiritual leadership, the practitioners can employ the suggestions we mentioned. The persistent positive relationship of spiritual leadership with individual and organizational outcomes favours spiritual leadership as a leading school of thought to be practiced by organizations and leaders. Instead of focusing only on top management alone, a holistic effort including middle and lower levels could be more effective.

Limitations of the review

While we restricted our review only to the research that follows Fry et al. (2005) spiritual leadership framework, there are few limitations in our approach. We focus only on articles that explicitly followed the Fry et al., (2005) framework, we could not include articles that address spiritual leadership out of this framework as well as those address spiritual leaderships connected with spirituality and religion. While we omitted them to fix our review in a framework, we acknowledge that including them would have resulted in a comprehensive review.

References

Amit, R. and Schoemaker, P. J. (1993). Strategic assets and organizational rent. Strateg. Manag. J. 14(1):33–46.

Ancona, D., Kochan, T., Scully, M., Van Maanen, J., Westney, D. E., Kolb, D. M., ... and Ashford, S. J. (1999). Organizational behavior and processes. *Boston: South-Western College Publishing*.

Anser, M. K., Shafique, S., Usman, M., Akhtar, N., and Ali, M. (2021). Spiritual leadership and organizational citizenship behavior for the environment: An intervening and interactional analysis. J. Environ. Plan. Manag. 64(8):1496–1514.

Chen, C. Y. and Li, C. I. (2013). Assessing the spiritual leadership effectiveness: The contribution of follower's self-concept and preliminary tests for moderation of culture and managerial position. Leadersh Q. 24(1):240–255.

Chen, C. Y. and Yang, C. F. (2012). The impact of spiritual leadership on organizational citizenship behavior: A multi-sample analysis. J. Bus. Ethics. (1):107–114.

Chen, C. Y., Yang, C. Y., and Li, C. I. (2012). Spiritual Leadership, Follower Mediators, and Organizational Outcomes: Evidence From Three Industries Across Two Major Chinese Societies 1. J. Appl. Soc. Psychol. 42(4):890–938.

Covey, S. R. (1992). *Principle centered leadership*. Simon and Schuster.

Daft, R. L. and Lengel, R. H. (1998). *Fusion leadership: Unlocking the subtle forces that change people and organizations*. Berrett-Koehler Publishers.

Darling, J. and Chalofsky, N. (2004). *Spirituality in the workplace*. EOLSS, Oxford.

Eva, N., Robin, M., Sendjaya, S., van Dierendonck, D., and Liden, R. C. (2019). Servant leadership: A systematic review and call for future research Leadersh Q. 30(1):111–132.

Eva, N., Robin, M., Sendjaya, S., van Dierendonck, D., and Liden, R. C. (2019). Servant leadership: A systematic review and call for future research. Leadersh Q. 30(1):111–132.

Fairholm, G. W. (1996). Spiritual leadership: Fulfilling whole-self needs at work. Leadersh. Organ. Dev. J. *17*(5), 11–17.

Fry, L. W. (2003). Toward a theory of spiritual leadership. Leadersh Q. 14(6):693–727.

Fry, L. W. (2008). Spiritual leadership: State-of-the-art and future directions for theory, research, and practice. In *Spirituality in business* (pp. 106–124). Palgrave Macmillan, New York.

Fry, L. W., Vitucci, S., and Cedillo, M. (2005). Spiritual leadership and army transformation: Theory, measurement, and establishing a baseline. Leadersh Q. 16(5):835–862.

Gibson, C. B., Gibson, S. C., and Webster, Q. (2021). Expanding our resources: Including community in the resource-based view of the firm. J. Manag. Res. 0149206320987289.

Greenleaf, R. K. (1977). Servant Leadership: A Journey into the Nature of Legitimate Power and Greatness. New York: Paulist Press.

Greve, H. R. (2021). The resource-based view and learning theory: Overlaps, differences, and a shared future. J. Manag. Res. 0149206320967732.

Hambrick, D. C. (2007). Upper echelons theory: An update. Acad Manage Rev. 32(2):334–343.

Hambrick, D. C. and Mason, P. A. (1984). Upper echelons: The organization as a reflection of its top managers. Acad Manage Rev. 9(2):193–206.

Harrison, D. A. and Klein, K. J. (2007). What's the difference? Diversity constructs as separation, variety, or disparity in organizations. Acad Manage Rev. 32(4):1199–1228.

Hattke, F. and Blaschke, S. (2015). Striving for excellence: The role of top management team diversity in universities. Team Perform. Manag: An International Journal. 21(3/4):121–138.

Hiebl, M. R. (2017). Finance managers in family firms: an upper-echelons view. J Fam. Bus. Manag. 7(2):207–220

House, R. J. and Shamir, B. (1993). Toward the integration of transformational, charismatic, and visionary theories.

Hughes, D. J., Lee, A., Tian, A. W., Newman, A., and Legood, A. (2018). Leadership, creativity, and innovation: A critical review and practical recommendations. Leadersh Q. 29(5):549–569.

Jeon, K. S. and Choi, B. K. (2020). A multidimensional analysis of spiritual leadership, affective commitment and employees' creativity in South Korea. Leadersh. Organ. Dev. J. 41(8): 1035–1052

Kotter, J. P. (1996). Leading change. Boston: Harvard Business School Press

Kull, A. J., Mena, J. A., and Korschun, D. (2016). A resource-based view of stakeholder marketing. J. Bus Res. 69(12):5553–5560.

Lee, W. S., Choi, C., and Moon, J. (2018). The upper echelon effect on restaurant franchising: the moderating role of internationalization. Int. J. Cult. Tour. Hosp. R. 12(1): 15–28

Moxley, R. S. (2000). *Leadership and spirit*. San Francisco, CA: Jossey-Bass.

Nagano, H. (2020). The growth of knowledge through the resource-based view. *Management Decision*.

Pio, R. J. and Lengkong, F. D. (2020). The relationship between spiritual leadership to quality of work life and ethical behavior and its implication to increasing the organizational citizenship behavior. J. Manag. Dev. 39(3):293–305.

Pio, R. J. and Tampi, J. R. E. (2018). The influence of spiritual leadership on quality of work life, job satisfaction and organizational citizenship behavior. Int. J. Law Manag. 60(2):757–767.

Polat, S. (2011). The level of faculty members' spiritual leadership (SL) qualities display according to students in faculty of education.Procedia Soc. Behav. Sci. 15:2033–2041.

Popli, M., Ladkani, R. M., and Gaur, A. S. (2017). Business group affiliation and post-acquisition performance: An extended resource-based view. J. Bus. Res. 81:21–30.

Prihandono, D. and Wijayanto, A. (2020). The influence of spiritual leadership on spirituality, conscientiousness and job satisfaction and its impacts on the reduction of workplace deviant behavior.J. Econ. Finance Adm. Sci. 37(1):90–13.

Reave, L. (2005). Spiritual values and practices related to leadership effectiveness. Leadersh Q. 16(5):655–687.

Salehzadeh, R., Pool, J. K., Lashaki, J. K., Dolati, H., and Jamkhaneh, H. B. (2015). Studying the effect of spiritual leadership on organizational performance: an empirical study in hotel industry. Int. J. Cult. Tour. Hosp. R. 9(3):346–359

Sapta, I. K. S., Rustiarini, N. W., Kusuma, I. G. A. E. T., and Astakoni, I. M. P. (2021). Spiritual leadership and organizational commitment: The mediation role of workplace spirituality. Cogent Bus. Manag. 8(1):1966865.

Stowell, J. M. (1997). *Shepherding the church: Effective spiritual leadership in a changing culture*. Moody Publishers.

Tabor, W., Madison, K., Marler, L. E., and Kellermanns, F. W. (2020). The effects of spiritual leadership in family firms: A conservation of resources perspective. J. Bus. Ethics. 163(4):729–743.

Wahyono, Prihandono, D., and Wijayanto, A. (2020). The influence of spiritual leadership on spirituality, conscientiousness and job satisfaction and its impacts on the reduction of workplace deviant behavior. J. Econ. Finance Adm. Sci. 37(1):90–113.

Wittekind, A., Raeder, S., and Grote, G. (2010). A longitudinal study of determinants of perceived employability. J. Organ. Behav. 31(4):566–586.

Wright, P. M., Dunford, B. B., and Snell, S. A. (2001). Human resources and the resource based view of the firm. J. Manag. Stud. 27(6):701–721.

Yang, F., Huang, X., and Wu, L. (2019). Experiencing meaningfulness climate in teams: How spiritual leadership enhances team effectiveness when facing uncertain tasks. Human Resource Management, 58(2):155–168.

Yang, F., Liu, J., Wang, Z., and Zhang, Y. (2019). Feeling energized: a multilevel model of spiritual leadership, leader integrity, relational energy, and job performance. J. Bus. Ethics. 158(4):983–997.

7 Ownership concentration, institutional ownership and stock return: The case of India

Brahmadev Panda

Assistant Professor, SIBM Nagpur, Symbiosis International University, India

Abstract

The main focus of this paper is to find out the effect of ownership concentration and institutional ownership on the stock return during the pre and post-crisis period. To carry this study, two study periods are used- the pre-crisis and the post-crisis period- and the global financial crisis 2008 considered as a base. The pre-crisis period is covered from FY2000–01 to FY 2007–08, whereas post-crisis period is covered from the FY 2008–09 to FY 2016–17. Further, NSE-500 listed companies are used as the sample size for this study. Dynamic panel data methodology, for instance system GMM, is employed to test the research hypotheses. Firm-specific factors such as firm size, age, risk, profitability, leverage, liquidity, and dividend pay-out are considered as control variables. The model findings indicate that ownership concentration has a negative effect, while institutional ownership has no effect on the stock returns during the pre-crisis phase. Firm-specific factors such as firm age and profitability improves the stock return in the pre-crisis period. In the post-crisis phase, it is observed that institutional ownership has an adverse effect, while concentrated ownership has no effect on the stock return. In the context of firm-specific factors, it is found that firm age and higher leverage led to a decline in the stock returns.

Keywords: Financial Crisis; Ownership Structure; Stock return; Panel data

Introduction

Ownership structure is considered as one of the key governance mechanisms for the enhancement of the corporate efficiency and performance (Shleifer and Vishny, 1986). Hence, early literature has studied the effect of the ownership structure on the financial performance, where it witnessed a mixed effect of ownership holdings. However, there is a dearth of studies on the effect ownership structure on the stock return as most of the studies in this line have investigated the ownership effect on the accounting and financial measures. Stock return is different from these measures as it reflects the earning and management efficiency information of the firms, which depends upon the ownership control and engagement in the management decision making. Early studies opined that ownership control and engagement may affect positively or negatively, hence the emphasis of this paper is on the concrete role of ownership structure on stock return.

The existence, and the role, of differential ownership structure and types of equity ownership fuel the debate of determining the stock return. It is observed that developed countries like USA, UK, and Canada mostly witness dispersed ownership structure, while emerging countries like India have concentrated ownership (Laporta, Lopez-de-Silanes and Shleifer, 1999). Further, it found institutional investors as one of the key owners in the corporate ownership structure, where they influence the management through their holdings and monitoring (McNulty and Nordberg, 2016). Due to the existence of differential ownership, the debate on the effect of ownership holdings on stock return becomes very intense. Here, this paper is mostly based on the effect of differential ownership holdings.

This paper investigates the effect of ownership concentration and institutional ownership on the stock return during the pre- and post-crisis phases and analyses the difference in the effect due to distinctive economic conditions. For this the S&P NSE 500 companies are selected as a sample and system-GMM estimation is applied to control the endogeneity issue. This study tries to define the monitoring and expropriation effect of the large owners and institutional ownership by contributing the existing literature through the following ways. First, this study considers two sets of study periods by taking the global financial crisis 2008 as a base, such as the pre-crisis and the post-crisis period. Second, this studies two major parts of the ownership structures such as concentrated ownership and institutional ownership. Third, the system-GMM is considered for this study to control the endogeneity problems in the ownership-performance models. Fourth, the considerations of an emerging market like India add a new field of study.

Rest of the paper is structured as follows. Section-2 reviews the extant literature. Section-3 describes the sample and variables. Section-4 explains the research methodology. Secttion-5 discusses the empirical findings. Section-6 summarises the paper.

Literature Review

Ownership concentration and stock return

Early evidence on the relationship between the ownership concentration and firm performance can be traced back to the work of Demsetz and Lehn (1985); their study showed a non-significant association. Further, the study of Clark and Wojcik (2005) on the German corporates revealed that concentrated ownership negatively affect the stock return. Another study by Othman et al. (2010) in the Malaysian context found that large ownership holding is detrimental to the stock return. Another school of thought inferred that large ownership has a positive monitoring effect of stock return. Zou and Adams (2008) examined the different ownership holdings effect on stock return, where they inferred that block holdings have a positive effect on the stock return. Some other studies have found a positive effect of ownership concentration on stock return through their effective monitoring. Zou and Adams (2008) tested various forms of ownership holdings on stock returns in Chinese firms, where they found that large block holdings significantly improved the stock returns in China. From these studies, it is reasonably apparent that large ownership holdings have a mixed effect on stock performance, which diverges from country to country.

H1: Ownership concentration has a significant effect on the stock returns

Institutional ownership and stock return

The empirical evidence of Han and Suk (1998) indicated that institutional investors in US market have efficient monitoring abilities that result in a higher stock return. Similarly, Ovtcharova (2003) reported that institutional ownership reflected a positive stock return in stocks with high institutional ownership than stocks with low institutional ownership, which is in line with the findings of the Gompers and Metrick (2001). Another research by Brockman et al. (2014) in the US market provided the evidence on the positive role of institutional monitoring in improving the stock return of the real estate investment trusts (REITs).

H2: Institutional Ownership leads to higher firm-level stock return.

Cella (2009) made a study on European firms to examine the effect of ownership structure on stock returns, where it was concluded that institutional holdings deleteriously affect the stock returns. Additionally, in an emerging market like China, it is found from the analysis of Ying, Kong and Luo (2015) that institutional owners enhance the price efficiency. Similarly, Dyakov and Wipplinger (2020) indicated a weak positive association between the equity holdings of the institutional investors and stock returns in sixteen emerging and developed economies. The study of Chuang (2020) demonstrated that institutional trading has a short term positive effect as well as a negative long term effect on stock returns of Taiwanese firms, which is consistent with the works of Dasgupta et al. (2011).

H3: Institutional Ownership has an adverse effect on the firm-level stock return.

Data and Variables

Study period and sample

The study period spans over 16 years from FY 2000–01 to FY 2016–17, which is categorised into two study periods such as pre-crisis and post-crisis by taking FY 2008–09 as the crisis year. Pre-crisis phase includes 08 years from FY 2000–01 to FY 2007–08, while post-crisis phase covers 08 years from FY 2009–10 to FY 2016–17. The US financial crisis 2008–09 is considered to be one of the worst financial epidemics in the last century, which halted the growth of the world economy (Sikorski, 2011). Emerging markets like India could not be decoupled from the crisis and got affected through the financial and trade channels (Singh & Singh, 2016). Due to the surfacing of the US financial crisis, India witnessed the decline of foreign investment, collapse of stock market and export dip, which deteriorated its corporate financial health. Prior to the crisis, Indian market and economy have shown a growth and a positive trend. The economic and market performance of pre-crisis is better than the post-crisis phase in India, which specifies that pre-crisis period was a growth phase and post-crisis was a sluggish phase. Hence, consideration of these two periods would furnish the fluctuations that occurred in investors' sentiment, equity investments and stock performances during these phases.

To construct the sample for this study, NIFTY-500 indexed companies are selected from the National Stock exchange (NSE), India. The selected sample size for the both the pre-crisis and post-crisis period is decided according to the data availability of the variables (ownership holdings, stock return, and company-specific). Balanced panel dataset of 316 listed companies is selected for the pre-crisis period while the post-crisis period comprises 404 balanced panel datasets of listed companies. The dataset related to the ownership holdings, stock return, company-specific data are extracted from the CMIE (Centre for Monitoring Indian Economy) database.

Dependent variable

Stock return: It is a widely used measure to quantify the profitability of the stock that affects the investors' sentiment profusely.

Independent variable

This study considers two major ownership structure measures such as ownership concentration and institutional ownership as independent variables. Emerging markets witness concentrated ownership, where they exert their influence on the management and governance of the firm hugely. Two measures such as holdings of the single largest shareholder and total holdings of the five largest shareholders are used to represent the ownership concentration. Fractions of shareholdings of the institutional investors are utilized as a measure for institutional ownership.

Control variables

Certain firm-specific factors based on previous studies are considered to control their effect on the stock return. This study includes firm size, firm age, firm risk, profitability, leverage, current ratio, and dividend pay-out to gauge the effect.

Methodology and model specifications

This study used dynamic panel models to curb endogeneity issue due to the unobserved heterogeneity and simultaneity (Wooldridge, 2013). Under dynamic panel models, two-step system-generalized method of moments (GMM) is considered. This econometric tool eliminates the endogeneity problem through internally generated instrumental variables. Subsequently, certain model specification tests like Arellano–Bond test, Sargan test and Wald Chi-square (χ^2) test are applied to check the serial correlation and over-identification issues. The insignificant autoregressive terms (AR) of Arellano–Bond test indicates the absence of serial correlations. The insignificant p-values of Sargan test indicate no over-identifications issues. Wald test with significant p-value implies the overall robustness of the model results.

Model specifications

Here, it is hypothesised that ownership concentration and institutional ownership affects the stock return of listed companies. Based on this hypothesis, the following empirical research models are developed.

$$SR_{it} = \alpha + \beta_1 OC_{it} + \beta_2 FS_{it} + \beta_3 FA_{it} + \beta_4 FR_{it} + \beta_5 FP_{it} + \beta_6 LEV_{it} \\ + \beta_7 LIQ_{it} + \beta_8 DP_{it} + \varepsilon_{it} \tag{1}$$

$$SR_{it} = \alpha + \beta_1 IO_{it} + \beta_2 FS_{it} + \beta_3 FA_{it} + \beta_4 FR_{it} + \beta_5 FP_{it} + \beta_6 LEV_{it} \\ + \beta_7 LIQ_{it} + \beta_8 DP_{it} + \varepsilon_{it} \tag{2}$$

Where, *SR, OC, IO, FS, FA, FR, FP, LEV, LIQ* and *DP* denote stock return, ownership concentration, institutional ownership, firm size, firm age, firm risk, firm performance, leverage, liquidity, and dividend payout. Ownership concentration includes two proxies such as holdings single largest shareholder (OC1) and five largest shareholders (OC5). The measurements of all these variables are depicted in the Table 7.1.

Table 7.1 Summary of dependent, independent and control variables

Variables	Acronyms	Measurement	Type	Source
Stock return	SR	(Current stock price-Previous stock price)/previous stock price	Dependent	PROWESS
Ownership concentration	OC1; OC5	Percentage of holdings of top largest shareholder; Percentage of holdings of top five largest shareholders	Independent	PROWESS
Institutional ownership	IO	Percentage of shareholdings of institutional investors	Independent	PROWESS
Firm size	FS	Natural logarithm of market capitalization	Control	PROWESS
Firm age	FA	Number of years since the incorporation of the company	Control	PROWESS
Firm risk	FR	Covariance of firm's stock return and market return variance of market return	Control	PROWESS
Firm performance	FP	Net income/average shareholders' equity	Control	PROWESS
Leverage	LEV	Total debt/total assets	Control	PROWESS
Liquidity	LIQ	Current asset/current liability	Control	PROWESS
Dividend payout	DP	Dividend paid/net income	Control	PROWESS

Source: Author's compilation

Empirical results

Pre-crisis estimations

Summary statistics
The summary statistics of dependent, independent and control variables for pre-crisis period are presented in the Table 7.2.

SR varies within –4.203 and 50.044 with a mean value of 0.389. The average values of OC1 and OC5 are 0.334 and 0.577, respectively. Institutional ownership is having an average value of 0.213. In India, the concentration level is very high, which means most of the ownership holdings lies in the hand of few large shareholders.

Correlation analysis
The correlation matrix for the pre-crisis period is depicted in the Table 7.3. It is detected that the co-efficient values between the variables are below the permissible limit of 0.8 (Kennedy, 1985), except between the OC1 and OC5, which validates the empirical models with no collinearity issues.

It is observed that ownership concentration and institutional ownership has no significant correlation with stock return. In the context of control variables, firm performance has a positive correlation with stock return.

Dynamic panel estimations
The two-step GMM estimations (Models: 13) are reported in the Table 7.4.

The model findings indicate that ownership concentration (OC1) has an adverse effect on the stock return during the pre-crisis period, which is similar to the early findings of (Clark and Wojcik, 2005). This shows that investors do not consider

Table 7.2 Pre-crisis summary statistics

Variables	Minimum	Maximum	Mean	Median	Standard deviation	Total observation
SR	-4.203	50.044	0.389	0.27	1.811	2528
OC1	0.05	0.761	0.334	0.27	0.209	2528
OC5	0.25	0.99	0.577	0.58	0.174	2528
IH	0.02	0.909	0.213	0.187	0.127	2528
FS	1.01	15.008	8.864	8.86	1.971	2528
FA	3.349	4.98	0.01	3.301	0.791	2528
FP	-201.09	189.24	16.571	16.96	24.126	2528
FR	-0.77	2.28	0.842	0.83	0.328	2528
LEV	0.01	1.687	0.446	0.458	0.238	2528
LIQ	0.01	139.42	1.687	1.2	3.228	2528
DP	0.01	97.09	26.533	24.075	17.529	2528

Source: Author's compilation

Table 7.3 Pre-crisis correlation matrix

Variables	SR	OC1	OC5	IO	FS	FA	FR	FP	LEV	LIQ	DP
SR	1										
OC1	-0.004	1									
OC5	-0.015	0.802	1								
IO	-0.038	-0.194	-0.231	1							
FS	0.069	0.231	0.138	0.349	1						
FA	-0.021	0.126	0.042	0.094	0.321	1					
FR	0.012	-0.007	-0.063	-0.019	0.157	-0.123	1				
FP	0.086	0.021	-0.016	0.032	0.286	-0.406	-0.039	1			
LEV	0.008	-0.166	-0.076	0.051	-0.308	-0.126	-0.098	-0.231	1		
LIQ	0.014	0.014	0.018	-0.047	0.024	0.052	0.017	0.011	-0.248	1	
DP	-0.016	0.057	-0.004	-0.007	0.074	0.021	-0.149	0.214	-0.123	1	

Source: Author's compilation
Note: Bold values are with p value < 0.05

Table 7.4 Pre-crisis GMM estimations

Models DV IV/methodology	Model-1 SR GMM	Model-2 SR GMM	Model-3 SR GMM
Intercept	−0.319	−0.462	0.616
	(−0.37)	(−0.53)	(0.38)
OC1	−1.325		
	(−2.32)***		
OC5		−0.226	
		(−0.48)	
IO			−0.004
			(−0.01)
FS	−0.201	−0.149	−0.051
	(−2.55)**	(−2.17)**	(−0.33)
FA	0.873	0.712	0.061
	(3.24)***	(3.03)***	(0.15)
FR	−0.298	−0.221	1.201
	(−1.80)*	(−1.36)	(2.02)**
FP	0.033	0.025	0.129
	(3.52)***	(2.77)***	(4.52)***
LEV	0.194	−0.176	−4.171
	(0.37)	(−0.36)	(−4.32)***
LIQ	−0.101	−0.066	−0.02
	(−2.62)***	(−1.83)*	(−0.98)
DP	0.006	0.005	0.011
	(1.95)*	(1.76)*	(1.60)
Wald χ2 test	154.60***	158.64***	88.64***
AR(1)-p value	0.000	0.001	0.002
AR(2)-p value	0.128	0.136	0.082
Sargan test (χ2 value)	22.364	21.251	29.374
P value	0.142	0.156	0.116

Source: Author's compilation
Note: DV and IV represent the dependent and independent variables respectively

high concentration of ownership as a motivating factor because it is believed that higher concentration leads to expropriation of wealth. Further, the institutional ownership is found to be having no significant effect on the stock return. In the meantime, firm age and profitability have a positive effect on the stock return, which reflects that older firms with high profit infer better stock return.

Post-crisis estimations

Summary statistics

The summary statistics of dependent, independent and control variables for post-crisis period are presented in the Table 7.5.

SR varies within –0.094 and 8.525 with a mean value of 0.332. The average values of OC1 and OC5 are 0.374 and 0.618, respectively. Institutional ownership is having an average value of 0.233. Here it is noticed that there is an increase in institutional investment over the pre-crisis period.

Correlation analysis

The correlation matrix for the post-crisis period is depicted in Table 7.6. It is detected that the co-efficient values between the variables are below the permissible limit of 0.8 (Kennedy, 1985), except between the OC1 and OC5, which validates the empirical models with no collinearity issues.

Ownership concentration and institutional ownership have significant negative correlation with stock return while firm performance has a positive correlation with stock return. Other firm-specific variables do not have a significant correlation with stock return.

Dynamic panel estimations

The two-step GMM estimations (models: 13) are reported in the Table 7.7.

Findings for post-crisis indicate that ownership concentration has no effect on the firm-level stock return. In case of institutional ownership, it is found that it has an adverse effect, which means institutional investors acted as negative feedback traders during the post-crisis period. The negative effect of institutional investment is similar to the earlier findings of Cella (2009). Firm age (FA) and leverage (LEV)

Table 7.5 Post-crisis summary statistics

Variables	Minimum	Maximum	Mean	Median	Standard deviation	Total observation
SR	–0.094	8.525	0.332	0.105	0.833	3232
OC1	0.052	0.752	0.374	0.326	0.209	3232
OC5	0.251	0.995	0.618	0.619	0.161	3232
IO	0.02	0.92	0.233	0.209	0.145	3232
FS	5.206	15.425	10.731	10.595	1.528	3232
FA	0.01	5.04	3.469	3.401	0.667	3232
FP	–99.68	129.3	16.237	14.775	19.001	3232
FR	0.08	2.9	1.068	1.03	0.433	3232
LEV	0.01	3.303	0.473	0.435	0.311	3232
LIQ	0.08	148.23	1.811	1.27	4.075	3232
DP	0.01	98.87	25.077	21.03	19.402	3232

Source: Author's compilation

Table 7.6 Post-crisis correlation matrix

Variables	SR	OC1	OC5	IO	FS	FA	FR	FP	LEV	LIQ	DP
SR	1										
OC1	−0.065	1									
OC5	−0.064	0.837	1								
IO	−0.057	−0.242	−0.384	1							
FS	−0.159	0.243	0.116	0.318	1						
FA	−0.045	0.121	0.051	0.071	0.204	1					
FR	−0.003	0.034	−0.101	0.005	0.215	−0.069	1				
FP	0.122	−0.042	0.022	0.051	−0.118	0.035	−0.336	1			
LEV	−0.015	−0.182	−0.146	−0.057	−0.018	−0.125	−0.201	0.241	1		
LIQ	0.009	0.052	0.038	−0.027	0.006	0.041	0.005	−0.053	−0.259	1	
DP	−0.041	0.058	0.032	0.054	−0.071	0.078	0.249	−0.164	−0.185	−0.003	1

Source: Author's compilation
Note: Bold values are with p value <0.05

Table 7.7 Post-crisis GMM estimations

Models DV IV/methodology	Model-1 SR GMM	Model-2 SR GMM	Model-3 SR GMM
Intercept	5909.927	5814.435	5122.33
	(4.76)***	(5.44)***	(3.11)***
OC1	−1350.87		
	(−1.00)		
OC5		−503.13	
		(−0.59)	
IO			−864.821
			(−1.69)*
FS	−10.854	−9.643	−7.936
	(−1.04)	(−0.93)	(−0.95)
FA	−1379.08	−1423.45	−1281.962
	(−3.04)***	(−4.22)***	(−2.94)***
FR	−124.81	−103.89	−84.705
	(−0.76)	(−0.68)	(−0.70)
FP	−5.964	−5.574	−5.994
	(−1.49)	(−1.56)	(−1.89)*
LEV	−438.84	−452.11	−456.53
	(−1.70)*	(−1.84)*	(−1.64)*
CR	2.543	3.043	3.392
	(0.93)	(1.16)	(0.95)
DP	−0.142	−0.025	0.071
	(−0.23)	(−0.04)	(0.13)
Wald $\chi 2$ test	42.86***	43.20***	43.86***
AR(1)-p value	0.000	0.001	0.005
AR(2)-p value	0.328	0.335	0.324
Sargan test ($\chi 2$value)	22.651	23.149	26.327
P value	0.141	0.138	0.121

Source: Author's compilation
Note: DV and IV represent the dependent and independent variables respectively

are found to have a declining effect, which implies that older firms with high leverage provided a negative return.

Conclusion

This study has tested the effect of ownership concentration and institutional ownership on the firm-level stock return for the pre-crisis and post-crisis period. Here it is evidenced that ownership concentration has a negative effect in pre-crisis and no effect during post-crisis period, which signifies that ownership concentration has a time-dependent effect. During the growth phase of the economy, it can be said that concentrated ownership proves to be detrimental. There is no institutional effect during pre-crisis but it has a negative effect during post-crisis, which denotes that it also has a time-dependent effect. Here, it can be inferred that institutional ownership diminishes the stock return during the slowing economy. Further, the effect of firm age also has a time-dependent effect. Overall, this study suggests that firm profitability improves the stock return and high leverage leads to lowering of the stock return. This study can be an exemplary to other emerging market researchers and policy makers.

References

Brockman, P., French, D. and Tamm, C. (2014). REIT organizational structure, institutional ownership, and stock performance. *J. Real Estate Portf. Manag.* 20(1): 21–36.

Cella, C. (2009). Institutional investors and corporate investment. United Sates: Indiana University, Kelley School of Business.

Chuang, H. (2020). The impacts of institutional ownership on stock returns. *Empir. Econ.* 58(2):507–533.

Clark, G. L. and Wójcik, D. (2005). Financial valuation of the German model: the negative relationship between ownership concentration and stock market returns, 1997–2001. *Econ. Geogr.* 81(1):11–29.

Dasgupta, A., Prat, A. and Verardo, M. (2011). Institutional trade persistence and long-term equity returns. *J. Finance.* 66(2):635–653.

Demsetz, H. and Lehn, K. (1985). The structure of corporate ownership: causes and consequences. *J. Polit. Econ.* 93(6):1155–1177.

Dyakov, T. and Wipplinger, E. (2020). Institutional ownership and future stock returns: an international perspective. Int. Rev. Finance. 20(1):235–245.

Gompers, P. A. and Metrick, A. (2001). Institutional investors and equity prices. *Q. J. Econ.* 116(1):229–259.

Han, K.C. and Suk, D.Y. (1998). The effect of ownership structure on firm performance: Additional evidence. *Rev. Financ. Econ.* 7(2):143–155.

Kennedy, P. (1985). *A Guide to Econometrics*, MIT Press, Cambridge.

La Porta, R., Lopez-de-Silanes, F., and Shleifer, A. (1999). Corporate ownership around the world. *J. Finance.* 54(2):471–517.

Manawaduge, A. S., Zoysa, A., and Rudkin, K. M. (2009). Performance implication of ownership structure and ownership concentration: Evidence from Sri Lankan firms. Paper presented at the Performance Management Association Conference. Dunedin, New Zealand.

McNulty, T. and Nordberg, D. (2016). Ownership, activism and engagement: institutional investors as active owners. *Corp. Gov.: Int. Rev.* 24(3):346–358.

Othman, R., Arshad, R., Ahmad, C. S. and Hamzah, N. A. A. (2010).December. The impact of ownership structure on stock returns, In 2010 International Conference on Science and Social Research (CSSR 2010) (pp. 217–221). IEEE.

Ovtcharova, G. (2003). Institutional Ownership and Long-Term Stock Returns. Working Papers Series. Available at SSRN: https://ssrn.com/abstract=410560.

Shleifer, A. and Vishny, R.W. (1986). Large shareholders and corporate control. *J. Polit. Econ.* 94(3):461–488.

Sikorski, D. (2011). The global financial crisis, in Jonathan Batten, A. and PeterSzilagyi, G. (Eds). The Impact of the Global Financial Crisis on Emerging Financial Markets. *Contemporary Studies in Economic and Financial Analysis. Emerald Group Publishing.* 93:17–90.

Singh, A. and Singh, M. (2016). Cross country co-movement in equity markets after the US financial crisis: India and major economic giants. *J. Indian Bus. Res.* 8(2):98–121.

Wooldridge, J. M. (2013). *Econometric Analysis of Cross Section and Panel Data*, The MIT Press, Cambridge: MA.

Ying, Q., Kong, D. and Luo, D. (2015). Investor attention, institutional ownership, and stock return: Empirical evidence from China. *Emerg. Mark. Finance Trade.* 51(3):672–685.

Zou, H. and Adams, M. B. (2008). Corporate ownership, equity risk and returns in the People's Republic of China. *J. Int. Bus. Stud.* 39(7):1149–1168.

8 Environmental perspective of workforce across industries

Soma Sinha Sarkar[1] and Jhumoor Biswas[2]

[1]PhD Research Scholar, Indian Institute of Social Welfare and Business Management (IISWBM), Kolkata, India

[2]Professor, Indian Institute of Social Welfare and Business Management (IISWBM), Kolkata, India

Abstract

Environmental sustainability is the concept and idea of the measures and actions to be taken to conserve the natural resources of the earth and protect the global ecosystems for the current and future generation. We, as human beings, are responsible for respecting and preserving the natural world from the anthropogenic afflictions. Making every stratum of the society environmentally aware is beneficial in developing environmental consciousness. Environmental attitudes are crucial in environmental psychology and many environment scientists have done their part to contribute to this idea. Encouraging environment friendly behaviour in the organisation results in reduction in the problem because employees adopting 'green' behaviour are expected to replicate it in all walks of life. When pro-environmental behaviour (PEB) is undertaken by employees in respect to their jobs, it becomes pro-environmental behaviour at the workplaces. All parts of the management from strategic to operational are required to be involved to implement environment friendly policies in the organization.

This paper attempts to assess the Environmental Awareness, Environmental Attitude, and PEB of the workforce across industries and also check whether Environmental Awareness and Environmental Attitude collectively translate into PEB using multiple regression technique. Random sampling technique has been used to collect data and Likert scale used to note the responses. Primary data has been gathered with the help of adapted versions of the questionnaires.

With environmental sustainability being the buzzword in today's corporate/industrial world and the need of the hour, by behaving in an environmentally positive manner, the companies can place themselves well.

Keywords: environmental attitude, environmental awareness, environmental sustainability, pro-environmental organizational behaviour (PEB), workforce

Introduction

Pro-environmental behaviour or green behaviour or environmentally friendly behaviour has been defined as a helping behaviour towards the environment (Unsworth et al., 2013). Stern (2000) more specifically defines pro-environmental behaviour as a 'behaviour that intentionally pursues reductions of the negative impact of people's actions on the natural world'. When pro-environmental behaviour is demonstrated with respect to individuals' jobs, they become pro-environmental behaviour at workplaces (Ones and Dilchert, 2012).

The adoption of organisational sustainability principles becomes visible through technical solutions, the publication of organisational sustainability reports, the integration of sustainability measures in employee performance evaluation, or employee training (Linnenluecke and Griffiths, 2010). This provides the context for the adoption of sustainability practices (Dunphy et al., 2003).

On a value level, the adoption of organisational sustainability principles takes place through changes in employees' values and beliefs towards more ethical and more responsible values (Crane, 2000). On an underlying level, the adoption of organisational sustainability principles requires a change in core assumptions regarding the interdependence of human and ecological systems (Purser, 1994). The different levels of organisational sustainability suggest a parallel to the different dimensions of organisational culture (Schein, 2004): the observable culture (the visible organisational structure, processes, and behaviours), espoused values (strategies, goals, and philosophies), and underlying assumptions (unconscious beliefs and perceptions which form the ultimate source of values and action). Further, Fairfield et al. (2011) argued that future research should provide "pointed, practical advice" for business to improve their practices. They argued that because of the increasing importance of sustainability issues and their direct link to global welfare, business insights are not only warranted but critical.

The importance of our study lies in the assessment of the environmental awareness and attitude (EAA) and subsequent pro-organisational behaviour (PEB) of the workforce across a range of industries in India. This will help in providing a holistic perspective for organisations regarding environmental awareness, behavioural practices that will aid in implementation of working environment management systems within the organisations.

Literature review

Environmental awareness

Putra et al. (2020) used a qualitative approach to study the activities of Gemilang Garbage Bank raise environmental awareness in the form of 3R behaviour (reduce, reuse, and recycle). The authors found that the management and customers of Gemilang Garbage Bank had respective roles in managing the environment, especially waste management.

Bacsi (2020) compared the environmental awareness in distinct country groups by trying to identify the components of national culture the different approaches of which to the environmental sustainability are most influential. The researcher used Hofstede's cultural dimensions to define the national culture and collected the environmental awareness data through the Eurobarometer surveys of the EU. This study was conducted over a period of seven years from 2012 to 2018. The author found that the environmental awareness of the EU citizens showed an increasing trend with time.

Do Prado and de Moraes (2020) proposed and tested a theoretical model to assess how some aspects of environmental awareness the intention of consuming organic products. They used gender as a control variable in this study. They concluded that environment awareness positively influences the intention on buying organic products and that it is also influenced by the consumer's gender.

Škatarić et al. (2021) tried to gauge the level of consumer awareness with respect to green marketing in Republic of Serbia. The researchers found that consumers do not easily identify with the term 'green marketing' and though they know what a 'green product' is they cannot easily identify it and shall not buy it enough to preserve the environment.

Workforce environmental awareness

Sun and Sun(2021) used attention-based view (ABV) to investigate the relationship between environmental awareness (EA) and eco innovation (EI). They also tried to find whether resource flexibility (RF) plays a mediating role between EA and EI and also whether unabsorbed slack resources (USRs) act as a mediator between them. They found that executives' EA and EI are positively related, RF acts as a mediator between EA and EI and USRs negatively moderate the relationship between EA and EI.

Sanyal and Pal (2017) examined how organisational culture facilitates more sustainable organisation behaviour. It also attempts to capture the relationship between organisational culture in environmental awareness and pro-environmental organisational behaviour. The authors used a random sampling technique and conducted the study across different organisations in the state of West Bengal in India.

Pro-environmental behaviour

Blok et al. (2015) worked on finding factors which could predict pro-environmental behaviour in the workplace. They did a comprehensive literature review and formed two groups of factors: internal and external. They then tested the model among employees of a green university in Netherlands. Based on the results of the study they concluded that Theory of Planned Behavior could explain pro-environmental behaviour in the workplace and also found that these are substantially different from those encouraging pro-environmental behaviour in the households.

Yusliza et al. (2021) in his study focussed on finding elements influencing pro-environmental behaviour in the workplace. The authors conducted a survey among 84 employees of an organisation and inferred that green-efficacy, environmental commitment, environmental consciousness, green lifestyle and green human resource management positively influenced pro-environmental behaviour.

Research objectives and hypothesis

Research objectives

- To assess the environmental awareness, environmental attitude and pro-organisational behaviour of the workforce in organisations across industries.
- To see whether environmental awareness and attitude impact the pro-environmental organisation behaviour of the workforce across industries.
- To see the extent of the influence of environmental awareness and attitude on pro-environmental organisation behaviour of the workforce across industries.

Hypothesis

One hypothesis has been formulated to understand whether 'environmental awareness' and 'environmental attitude' collectively have an impact over the pro-organisational behaviour of the workforce.

- H_O – There is not a statistically significant relationship between 'PEB and 'EAA' taken together.
- H_A – There is a statistically significant relationship between 'PEB' and 'EAA' taken together.

Materials and methods

Data collection

For the purpose of this study, primary data has been collected from professionals of the working group between 25 to 60 years of age. A thorough literature review has been conducted and adapted versions of the questionnaires of the following used:

- Environmental awareness
- Environmental attitude
- PEB

The questionnaire has been distributed amongst the participants by the internet survey method. The survey has been administered online through Google forms. The link to the questionnaire has been sent by email, Whatsapp and Facebook messenger (social media), Linkedin services to all the participants. The link also has been posted in Whatsapp groups with potential respondents. Random sampling method has been used to collect data and the respondents have also been requested to circulate the questionnaire amongst their colleagues, friends, and family resulting in snowball sampling method.

The data has been collected on a 5- point Likert scale of 0 to 5 as follows:

0 – Strongly disagree
1 – Disagree
2 – Neither agree nor disagree
3 – Agree
4 – Strongly agree

There were very few missing data in very few records which was filled up using strong theoretical bases.

Research methods

Reliability test has been conducted for EAA and PEB and results validated using Cronbach's Alpha. Scores of the respondents for EAA and PEB have been assessed and represented in charts. K means cluster analysis has been conducted on environmental awareness and attitude and also on PEB to group the data. One Sample

Kolmogorov-Smirnov Normal test has been conducted on the scores of environmental awareness and attitude and also PEB and results shown in the form of summary table and histogram. The assumption of homoscedasticity has been tested using simple scatter plots. Multicollinearity amongst the independent variables has been checked for using correlation and Collinearity diagnostics and coefficients table. With the data been found suitable for multiple regression, this technique has been used to find whether 'EAA' collectively impact PEB and in the absence of a robust model, PEB has been further divided into 'habit' and 'intention' and multiple regression analyses conducted. The extent of influence of exogeneous variables on endogenous variables has also been found through this method. A basic demographic representation of the respondents has been presented. The scores chart has been created in MS Excel and the analysis has been conducted with the help of SPSS software, version 26.

Data analysis

Reliability tests of the questionnaire

Tables 8.1 and 8.2 represent basic demography of respondents. To measure the internal consistency of the questionnaire, reliability test has been conducted on the two scales of 'EAA' and 'Pro-PEB'.

Environmental awareness and attitude (EAA) scale
Reliability statistics table: In figure 8.1 we observe that Cronbach's Alpha value based on standardised items is 0.717 which is acceptable according to the rule of George and Mallery (2003). Thus, our questionnaire is reliable.

Pro-environmental organisation behaviour (PEB) scale
Reliability statistics table: In figure 8.2 we observe that Cronbach's Alpha value based on standardised items is 0.837 which is acceptable according to the rule of George and Mallery (2003). Thus, our questionnaire is reliable.

Scores
The above bar chart in figure 8.3 gives us the scores of environmental awareness and it can be seen that technology industry has scored the highest with 890 followed by services industry at 625.

While going through the above figure 8.4, it can be inferred that Technology industry has scored the highest followed by financial services and then Education.

The PEB scores in figure 8.5 tell us that the technology industry is well placed followed by financial services and education while mining and media scored the least.

Normality testing

EAA scale
In figures 8.6 and 8.7 we observe that:
　　Null hypothesis – The population is normally distributed
　　Alternate hypothesis – The population is not normally distributed

Table 8.1 Basic demography of respondents

Variables	Categories	Respondents	Total percentage
Age	25–30	5	4
	31–36	16	14
	37–42	63	55
	43–48	18	16
	49–54	8	7
	55–60	5	4
Location	Aurangabad	1	1
	Bangalore	7	6
	Bhilai	1	1
	Bhopal	7	6
	Bhubaneshwar	1	1
	Delhi	4	3
	Howrah	1	1
	Hyderabad	3	3
	Indore	1	1
	Jaipur	4	3
	Jamshedpur	2	2
	Jodhpur	2	2
	Kolkata	41	35
	Mumbai	3	3
	Nagpur	15	13
	Navi Mumbai	1	1
	New Delhi	1	1
	Pune	15	13
	Ranchi	4	3
	Vadodara	1	1
Subject of study at graduate or post-graduate level	Humanities	13	11
	Commerce	38	33
	Science	29	25
	Engineering	27	24
	Medicine	8	7
Study EVS as a subject?	Yes	46	40
	No	69	60

Source: Derived after the data analysis conducted on the statistical software SPSS 26 and MS-Excel for the 'demography' table

Table 8.2 Basic demography of respondents continued

Variables	Categories	Respondents	Total Percentage
Industry Type	E-Commerce	3	3
	Education	21	18
	Financial services	21	18
	Government	6	5
	Manufacturing	9	8
	Media	1	1
	Mining	1	1
	Power and utility	0	0
	Retail	6	5
	Services	8	7
	SME	3	3
	Technology	35	30
	Telecom	1	1
Organisational level	Entry level	5	4
	Leadership	6	5
	Middle Management	59	51
	Senior management	35	31
	Top management	10	9
Turnover of the organisation	<= 5 crore	28	24
	<= 50 crore	10	9
	<= 250 crore	13	11
	> 250 crore	64	56
Employee strength of the organisation	<= 10	10	9
	<= 50	18	15
	<= 250	10	9
	>250	77	67
Annual family income	<= 2 lakhs	3	3
	2 lakhs to 5 lakhs	9	8
	5 lakhs – 10 lakhs	23	20
	10 lakhs – 40 lakhs	65	56
	> 40 lakhs	15	13
Total professional experience	<= 10 years	24	21
	<= 15 years	40	35
	<= 20 years	34	29
	> 20 years	17	15

Source: Derived after the data analysis conducted on the statistical software SPSS 26 and MS-Excel for the 'demography' table

Reliability Statistics

Cronbach's Alpha	Cronbach's Alpha Based on Standardized Items	N of Items
.628	.717	39

Figure 8.1 Reliability statistics – EAA scale
Source: Derived after the data analysis conducted on the statistical software SPSS 26 and MS-Excel for the 'demography' table

Reliability Statistics

Cronbach's Alpha	Cronbach's Alpha Based on Standardized Items	N of Items
.803	.837	21

Figure 8.2 Reliability statistics – PEB scale
Source: Derived after the data analysis conducted on the statistical software SPSS 26 and MS-Excel for the 'demography' table

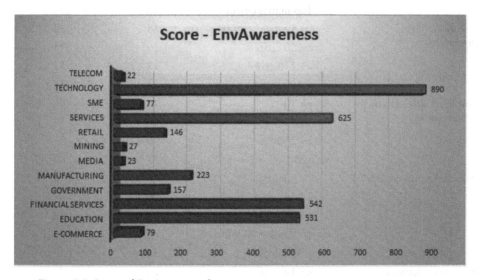

Figure 8.3 Score of Environmental awareness
Source: Derived after the data analysis conducted on the statistical software SPSS 26 and MS-Excel for the 'demography' table

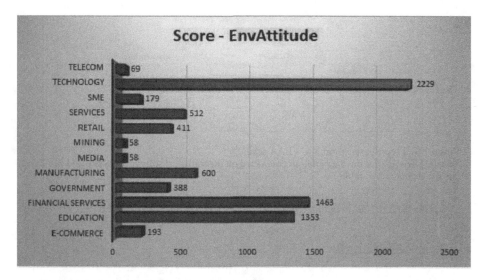

Figure 8.4 Score of environmental attitude
Source: Derived after the data analysis conducted on the statistical software SPSS 26 and MS-Excel for the 'demography' table

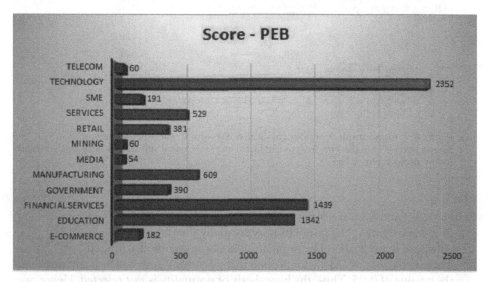

Figure 8.5 Score of PEB
Source: Derived after the data analysis conducted on the statistical software SPSS 26 and MS-Excel for the 'demography' table

The significance is 0.077 for Kolmogorov-Smirnov test which is greater than the p value of 0.05. Thus, the hypothesis of normality is *not rejected*. Hence, we conclude that the scores of EAA are normally distributed.

Figure 8.8 displays that the histogram has a normal distribution with a mean of 90.7 and standard deviation of 9.33

Hypothesis Test Summary

	Null Hypothesis	Test	Sig.	Decision
1	The distribution of ScoreEAAScale is normal with mean 91 and standard deviation 9.329.	One-Sample Kolmogorov-Smirnov Test	.077ᵃ	Retain the null hypothesis.

Asymptotic significances are displayed. The significance level is .050.

a. Lilliefors Corrected

Figure 8.6 Hypothesis summary – EAA scale
Source: Derived after the data analysis conducted on the statistical software SPSS 26 and MS-Excel for the 'demography' table

One-Sample Kolmogorov-Smirnov Normal Test

ScoreEAAScale

One-Sample Kolmogorov-Smirnov Normal Test Summary

Total N		115
Most Extreme Differences	Absolute	.079
	Positive	.079
	Negative	-.044
Test Statistic		.079
Asymptotic Sig.(2-sided test)		.077ᵃ

a. Lilliefors Corrected

Figure 8.7 One-sample Kolmogorov-Smirnov Normal test – EAA scale
Source: Derived after the data analysis conducted on the statistical software SPSS 26 and MS-Excel for the 'demography' table

PEB scale
In figures 8.9 and 8.10 we observe that:
    Null hypothesis – The population is normally distributed
    Alternate hypothesis – The population is not normally distributed
    The significance is 0.187 for Kolmogorov-Smirnov test which is greater than the p value of 0.05. Thus, the hypothesis of normality is *not rejected*. Hence, we conclude that the scores of PEB are normally distributed.

In figure 8.11, the histogram shows that the mean score is 63.48 and standard deviation is 7.607

K Means cluster analysis – EAA
In figures 8.12 and 8.13 it has been noted that three clusters have been formed and the highest scoring cluster is number 3 which has 16 cases. The lowest scoring cluster is number 2 with 45 cases.

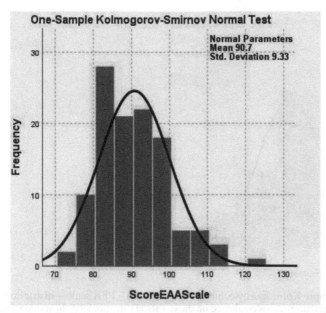

Figure 8.8 One-Sample Kolmogorov-Smirnov Normal Test– EAA scale.- histogram
Source: Derived after the data analysis conducted on the statistical software SPSS 26 and MS-Excel for the 'demography' table

Hypothesis Test Summary			
	Null Hypothesis	Test	Sig.	Decision
1	The distribution of ScorePEBscale is normal with mean 63 and standard deviation 7.607.	One-Sample Kolmogorov-Smirnov Test	.187ª	Retain the null hypothesis.

Asymptotic significances are displayed. The significance level is .050.

a. Lilliefors Corrected

Figure 8.9 Hypothesis test summary – PEB scale
Source: Derived after the data analysis conducted on the statistical software SPSS 26 and MS-Excel for the 'demography' table

One-Sample Kolmogorov-Smirnov Normal Test

ScorePEBScale

One-Sample Kolmogorov-Smirnov Normal Test Summary		
Total N		115
Most Extreme Differences	Absolute	.073
	Positive	.073
	Negative	-.050
Test Statistic		.073
Asymptotic Sig. (2-sided test)		.187ª

a. Lilliefors Corrected

Figure 8.10 One-Sample Kolmogorov-Smirnov Normal test – PEB scale
Source: Derived after the data analysis conducted on the statistical software SPSS 26 and MS-Excel for the 'demography' table

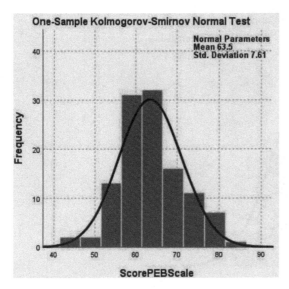

Figure 8.11 One-Sample Kolmogorov-Smirnov Normal test – PEB scale – histogram
Source: Derived after the data analysis conducted on the statistical software SPSS 26 and MS-Excel
for the 'demography' table

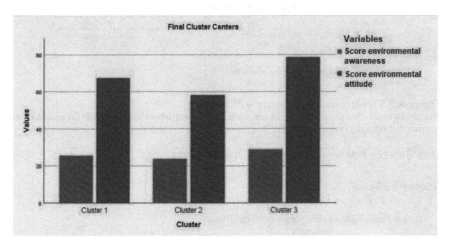

Figure 8.12 Cluster analysis – Score environmental awareness and score environmental
attitude
Source: Derived after the data analysis conducted on the statistical software SPSS 26 and MS-Excel
for the 'demography' table

K Means Cluster Analysis –PEB

In figures 8.14 and 8.15, it has been noted that three clusters have been formed and
the highest score cluster is number 2 which has 45 cases. The lowest scoring cluster
is number 1 with 54 cases.

ANOVA

	Cluster		Error			
	Mean Square	df	Mean Square	df	F	Sig.
ScoreEnvAwareness	155.102	2	6.336	112	24.481	.000
ScoreEnvAttitude	2680.833	2	11.284	112	237.584	.000

The F tests should be used only for descriptive purposes because the clusters have been chosen to maximize the differences among cases in different clusters. The observed significance levels are not corrected for this and thus cannot be interpreted as tests of the hypothesis that the cluster means are equal.

Number of Cases in each Cluster

Cluster	1	54.000
	2	45.000
	3	16.000
Valid		115.000
Missing		.000

Figure 8.13 ANOVA – Score environmental awareness and score environmental attitude
Source: Derived after the data analysis conducted on the statistical software SPSS 26 and MS-Excel for the 'demography' table

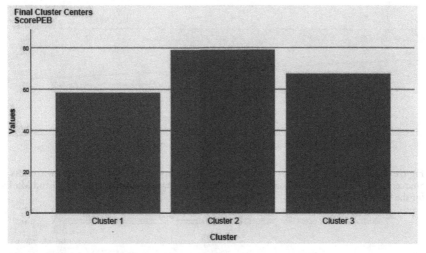

Figure 8.14 Cluster analysis – Score PEB
Source: Derived after the data analysis conducted on the statistical software SPSS 26 and MS-Excel for the 'demography' table

Spearman's correlation

In figure 8.16, Spearman's correlation coefficient has been found out between PEB and awareness and it has been noted that there is no significant correlation and data is hence fit for multiple regression analysis.

In figure 8.17, Spearman's correlation coefficient has been found out between PEB and attitude and it has been noted that there is no significant correlation and data is hence fit for multiple regression analysis.

ANOVA

	Cluster		Error			
	Mean Square	df	Mean Square	df	F	Sig.
ScoreEnvAwareness	155.102	2	6.336	112	24.481	.000
ScoreEnvAttitude	2680.833	2	11.284	112	237.584	.000

The F tests should be used only for descriptive purposes because the clusters have been chosen to maximize the differences among cases in different clusters. The observed significance levels are not corrected for this and thus cannot be interpreted as tests of the hypothesis that the cluster means are equal.

Number of Cases in each Cluster

Cluster	1	54.000
	2	45.000
	3	16.000
Valid		115.000
Missing		.000

Figure 8.15 ANOVA – Score PEB
Source: Derived after the data analysis conducted on the statistical software SPSS 26 and MS-Excel for the 'demography' table

Correlations

			ScorePEB	ScoreEnvAwareness
Spearman's rho	ScorePEB	Correlation Coefficient	1.000	.303**
		Sig. (2-tailed)	.	.001
		N	115	115
	ScoreEnvAwareness	Correlation Coefficient	.303**	1.000
		Sig. (2-tailed)	.001	.
		N	115	115

**. Correlation is significant at the 0.01 level (2-tailed).

Figure 8.16 Spearman's correlation – Score PEB and score environment awareness
Source: Derived after the data analysis conducted on the statistical software SPSS 26 and MS-Excel for the 'demography' table

Correlations

			ScorePEB	ScoreEnvAttitude
Spearman's rho	ScorePEB	Correlation Coefficient	1.000	.249**
		Sig. (2-tailed)	.	.007
		N	115	115
	ScoreEnvAttitude	Correlation Coefficient	.249**	1.000
		Sig. (2-tailed)	.007	.
		N	115	115

**. Correlation is significant at the 0.01 level (2-tailed).

Figure 8.17 Spearman's correlation – Score PEB and score environment attitude
Source: Derived after the data analysis conducted on the statistical software SPSS 26 and MS-Excel for the 'demography' table

Multiple linear regression

Multiple linear regression analysis has been conducted to check the predictability between PEB and Environmental awareness and attitude taken together but it has been found that the model is not robust with an adjusted r square value of 14.4.

Two other multiple regression analyses were then conducted –

- To check the predictability of Environmental attitude by age of the employee, industry and environmental awareness.
- The PEB has been divided into habit and intention and it has been attempted to check the dependency of PEB on age of employee, industry, habit, intention and the organisation policy.

Dependent variable: ScoreEnvAttitude

In figure 8.22, it has been noted that the there is no problem of multicollinearity. The figure 8.18 denotes the correlation between the variables which shows that there is no significant correlation. The data has been found suitable for multiple regression because the variance inflation factors are below 10 in figure 8.25. The assumption of homoscedasticity has also been checked and from the scatter plots in figures 8.19, 8.20, and 8.21, and the distribution of data it has been found that the assumption of homoscedasticity is valid. In figure 8.23, it can be seen that the adjusted r square value is 0.251. With significance 0.000 in the ANOVA table in figure 8.24, it has been inferred in this model that environmental attitude is determined by age and environmental awareness and a regression equation is derived in equation 1.

Correlations

		Age	Industry	ScoreEnvAwareness
Age	Pearson Correlation	1	-.016	.124
	Sig. (2-tailed)		.864	.186
	N	115	115	115
Industry	Pearson Correlation	-.016	1	-.040
	Sig. (2-tailed)	.864		.671
	N	115	115	115
ScoreEnvAwareness	Pearson Correlation	.124	-.040	1
	Sig. (2-tailed)	.186	.671	
	N	115	115	115

Figure 8.18 Correlation – Age, industry ScoreEnvAwareness
Source: Derived after the data analysis conducted on the statistical software SPSS 26 and MS-Excel for the 'demography' table

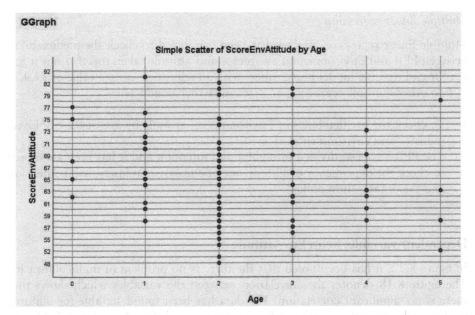

Figure 8.19 Scatter plot –ScoreEnvAttitude by age
Source: Derived after the data analysis conducted on the statistical software SPSS 26 and MS-Excel
for the 'demography' table

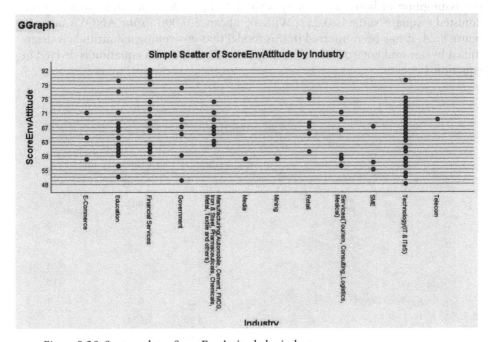

Figure 8.20 Scatter plot – ScoreEnvAttitude by industry
Source: Derived after the data analysis conducted on the statistical software SPSS 26 and MS-Excel
for the 'demography' table

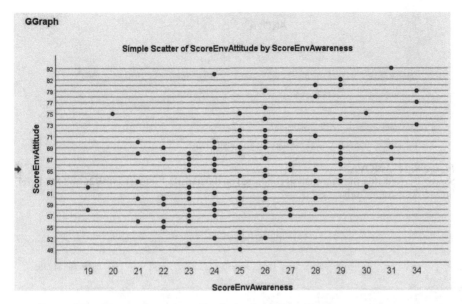

Figure 8.21 Scatter plot – ScoreEnvAttitude by ScoreEnvAwareness
Source: Derived after the data analysis conducted on the statistical software SPSS 26 and MS-Excel for the 'demography' table

Collinearity Diagnostics[a]

Model	Dimension	Eigenvalue	Condition Index	(Constant)	Age	Industry	ScoreEnvAwareness
					Variance Proportions		
1	1	3.586	1.000	.00	.01	.02	.00
	2	.290	3.517	.00	.13	.84	.00
	3	.117	5.525	.02	.86	.12	.02
	4	.007	23.145	.98	.00	.02	.97

a. Dependent Variable: ScoreEnvAttitude

Figure 8.22 Collinearity diagnostics
Source: Derived after the data analysis conducted on the statistical software SPSS 26 and MS-Excel for the 'demography' table

Model Summary[b]

Model	R	R Square	Adjusted R Square	Std. Error of the Estimate	R Square Change	F Change	df1	df2	Sig. F Change	Durbin-Watson
					Change Statistics					
1	.521[a]	.271	.251	6.597	.271	13.750	3	111	.000	1.937

a. Predictors: (Constant), ScoreEnvAwareness, Industry, Age
b. Dependent Variable: ScoreEnvAttitude

Figure 8.23 Model summary
Source: Derived after the data analysis conducted on the statistical software SPSS 26 and MS-Excel for the 'demography' table

ANOVA^a

Model		Sum of Squares	df	Mean Square	F	Sig.
1	Regression	1795.078	3	598.359	13.750	.000^b
	Residual	4830.365	111	43.517		
	Total	6625.443	114			

a. Dependent Variable: ScoreEnvAttitude

b. Predictors: (Constant), ScoreEnvAwareness, Industry, Age

Figure 8.24 ANOVA
Source: Derived after the data analysis conducted on the statistical software SPSS 26 and MS-Excel for the 'demography' table

Coefficients^a

Model		Unstandardized Coefficients		Standardized Coefficients	t	Sig.	Collinearity Statistics	
		B	Std. Error	Beta			Tolerance	VIF
1	(Constant)	40.807	5.434		7.509	.000		
	Age	-1.783	.591	-.246	-3.014	.003	.984	1.016
	Industry	-.283	.162	-.142	-1.754	.082	.998	1.002
	ScoreEnvAwareness	1.180	.208	.463	5.663	.000	.983	1.017

a. Dependent Variable: ScoreEnvAttitude

Figure 8.25 Coefficients
Source: Derived after the data analysis conducted on the statistical software SPSS 26 and MS-Excel for the 'demography' table

The regression equation is as follows:

$$y = 40.807 - 0.246 \times \text{age} + 0.463 \times \text{ScoreEnvAwareness} \tag{1}$$

Dependent variable: ScorePEBNew
Figure 8.26 shows that there is no significant correlation between the variables. In figure 8.33, a robust model has been derived with an adjusted r square value of 0.554. It means that 55.4% of the variation in PEB is described by the independent variables. In figure 8.35, the data has been found suitable for multiple regression because the variance inflation factors are below 10 and none of the scores of the variance proportion are greater than 0.9. In figures 8.27, 8.28, 8.29, 8.30, and 8.31 the assumption of homoscedasticity has also been checked and has been found valid. Figure 8.32 shows that there is no multicollinearity between the variables. Figure 8.34 shows that significance is 0.000. The following regression equation has been derived in equation 2.

$$y = 2.901 + 0.284 \times \text{ScoreHabit} + 0.507 \times \text{ScoreIntention} \tag{2}$$

Correlations

		Age	Industry	ScoreHabit	ScoreIntention	ScoreOrgPolicy
Age	Pearson Correlation	1	-.016	.110	.117	-.073
	Sig. (2-tailed)		.864	.243	.213	.440
	N	115	115	115	115	115
Industry	Pearson Correlation	-.016	1	-.079	.055	.195[*]
	Sig. (2-tailed)	.864		.403	.561	.036
	N	115	115	115	115	115
ScoreHabit	Pearson Correlation	.110	-.079	1	.564[**]	.208[*]
	Sig. (2-tailed)	.243	.403		.000	.026
	N	115	115	115	115	115
ScoreIntention	Pearson Correlation	.117	.055	.564[**]	1	.224[*]
	Sig. (2-tailed)	.213	.561	.000		.016
	N	115	115	115	115	115
ScoreOrgPolicy	Pearson Correlation	-.073	.195[*]	.208[*]	.224[*]	1
	Sig. (2-tailed)	.440	.036	.026	.016	
	N	115	115	115	115	115

*. Correlation is significant at the 0.05 level (2-tailed).

**. Correlation is significant at the 0.01 level (2-tailed).

Figure 8.26 Correlations – Age, industry, ScoreHabit, ScoreIntention, ScoreOrgPolicy
Source: Derived after the data analysis conducted on the statistical software SPSS 26 and MS-Excel
for the 'demography' table

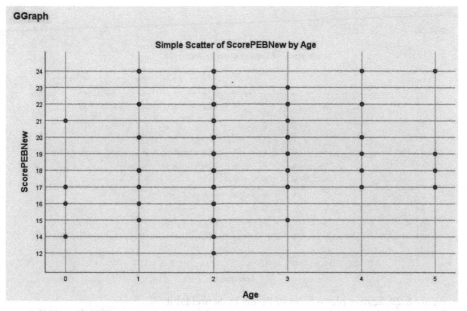

Figure 8.27 Scatter plot – ScorePEBNew by age
Source: Derived after the data analysis conducted on the statistical software SPSS 26 and MS-Excel
for the 'demography' table

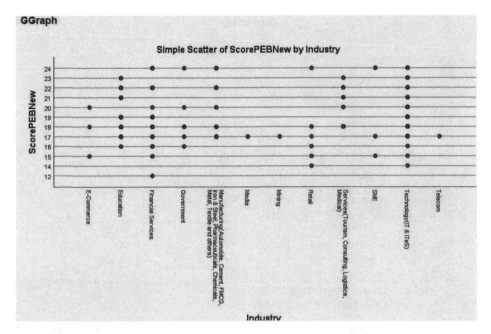

Figure 8.28 Scatter plot – ScorePEBNew by industry
Source: Derived after the data analysis conducted on the statistical software SPSS 26 and MS-Excel for the 'demography' table

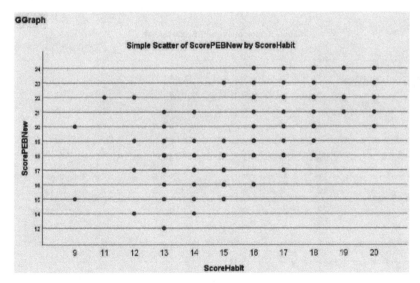

Figure 8.29 Scatter plot – ScorePEBNew by ScoreHabit
Source: Derived after the data analysis conducted on the statistical software SPSS 26 and MS-Excel for the 'demography' table

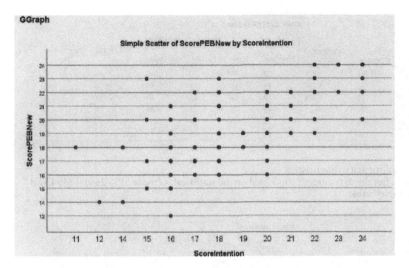

Figure 8.30 Scatter plot – ScorePEBNew by ScoreIntention
Source: Derived after the data analysis conducted on the statistical software SPSS 26 and MS-Excel for the 'demography' table

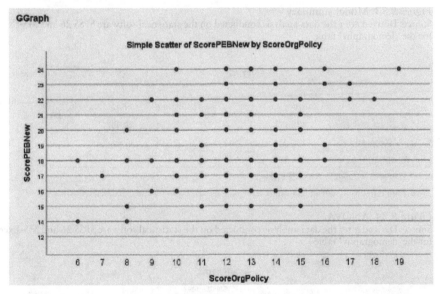

Figure 8.31 Scatter plot – ScorePEBNew by ScoreOrgPolicy
Source: Derived after the data analysis conducted on the statistical software SPSS 26 and MS-Excel for the 'demography' table

Findings
In the context of our study,

- The highest Environmental awareness scores have been of the 'technology' industry followed by 'services' and 'financial services' and 'education' sector following suit.

Collinearity Diagnostics[a]

Model	Dimension	Eigenvalue	Condition Index	(Constant)	Age	Industry	ScoreHabit	ScoreIntention	ScoreOrgPolicy
								Variance Proportions	
1	1	5.505	1.000	.00	.01	.01	.00	.00	.00
	2	.300	4.287	.00	.07	.95	.00	.00	.00
	3	.150	6.055	.00	.87	.07	.01	.00	.02
	4	.026	14.591	.00	.04	.03	.08	.08	.86
	5	.010	22.928	.99	.01	.01	.15	.12	.12
	6	.009	24.247	.00	.00	.02	.75	.79	.00

a. Dependent Variable: ScorePEBNew

Figure 8.32 Collinearity diagnostics
Source: Derived after the data analysis conducted on the statistical software SPSS 26 and MS-Excel for the 'demography' table

Model Summary[b]

Model	R	R Square	Adjusted R Square	Std. Error of the Estimate	R Square Change	F Change	df1	df2	Sig. F Change	Durbin-Watson
					Change Statistics					
1	.758[a]	.574	.554	1.807	.574	29.357	5	109	.000	1.539

a. Predictors: (Constant), ScoreOrgPolicy, Age, Industry, ScoreIntention, ScoreHabit
b. Dependent Variable: ScorePEBNew

Figure 8.33 Model summary
Source: Derived after the data analysis conducted on the statistical software SPSS 26 and MS-Excel for the 'demography' table

ANOVA[a]

Model		Sum of Squares	df	Mean Square	F	Sig.
1	Regression	479.171	5	95.834	29.357	.000[b]
	Residual	355.820	109	3.264		
	Total	834.991	114			

a. Dependent Variable: ScorePEBNew
b. Predictors: (Constant), ScoreOrgPolicy, Age, Industry, ScoreIntention, ScoreHabit

Figure 8.34 ANOVA
Source: Derived after the data analysis conducted on the statistical software SPSS 26 and MS-Excel for the 'demography' table

Coefficients[a]

Model		Unstandardized Coefficients B	Std. Error	Standardized Coefficients Beta	t	Sig.	Collinearity Statistics Tolerance	VIF
1	(Constant)	2.901	1.439		2.017	.046		
	Age	.025	.163	.010	.154	.878	.972	1.029
	Industry	-.014	.046	-.020	-.316	.753	.938	1.066
	ScoreHabit	.323	.088	.284	3.677	.000	.655	1.526
	ScoreIntention	.497	.075	.507	6.587	.000	.659	1.517
	ScoreOrgPolicy	.164	.074	.148	2.227	.028	.890	1.123

a. Dependent Variable: ScorePEBNew

Figure 8.35 Coefficients
Source: Derived after the data analysis conducted on the statistical software SPSS 26 and MS-Excel for the 'demography' table

- The highestEnvironmental attitude scores have been found to be that of the "technology' industry followed by 'financial services' and the 'education' sectors with "manufacturing' trailing behind while "mining' and "media' finished last with same scores.
- PEB scores are highest for the "technology' industry followed by 'financial services' and "education' followed by "manufacturing' and 'services' and 'mining', "telecom' and "media' with similar scores finishing last.
- In the highest scores cluster 3 for awareness and attitude, it has been found that 'financial services' industry constitutes 37.5% and IT industry constitutes 25%.
- In the highest scores cluster 2 for PEB, it has been found that 'IT' industry constitutes 37% and 'financial services' 32%.
- Null hypothesis (H_O) is rejected and has been concluded that 'PEB' is determined by 'EA and EA' taken together in the context of our study but the model was found to be not very robust and hence PEB was divided further into "habit' and ' 'intention'.
- A multiple regression model has been formed to find the predictability of PEB by 'habit', 'intention', 'age', and type of industry. This was found to be a robust model with r square value of 0.554.
- A multiple regression model has also been formed to find the predictability of EA by age, type of industry and EA. The results were significant and it was found that age and EA were significant contributors.

Discussion

A comprehensive and detailed study has been conducted to assess the 'environmental awareness', 'environmental attitude', and ' 'PEB' of the workforce across industries in India. The scores indicate that in the context of our study, the professionals of the 'technology' industry are highly aware of the environmental perspectives (awareness and attitude) and also translate well their awareness and attitude into their behaviour at the workplace. The cluster analysis also affirms the same in a way. It has been found that age of an employee plays a significant role to form environmental attitude of a person. The habit and intention of an employee translates well into PEB. It has also been found that organisation policy is not a significant factor to determine the PEB of an employee.

Practical implications

The practical implications of our study indicate the following:

- Create healthy and safe work environment which would increase employee morale.
- Enhance organisation's image in a growing environmentally conscious business world.
- By adopting and practicing environmentally friendly behaviour, employees would contribute to building a healthy and sustainable environment in the present and for the future.

- Help employees make appropriate environment-related choices and act more responsibly towards the environment.

Conclusion

Knowledge and awareness need not always translate into behaviour. For e.g. even when waste bins are available and a person is aware that waste should be thrown in it, she/he might not actually use it. One must discipline herself/himself and inculcate the habit and intention to choose environmentally friendly ways. Strong organisation policies towards environment also need not result into positive behaviour on the ground. Thus, organisation training plays a crucial role in promoting a positive outlook towards the environment. Awareness and attitude somewhat correspond with highest scoring industries. Although the findings of our study are practical and encouraging, there is still a long way to go as far as environmental sustainability is concerned. With new initiatives by the government and new regulation in place; alignment of awareness, attitude, and behaviour is expected in future. A supportive and positive green workforce can go a long way in overcoming the resistance from individuals towards acting in favour of the environmental benefits. It is thus suggested that organisations should encourage pro-environmental behaviour at work which can result in reduction of environmental problems and because an employee spends a large time of the day in an office setting, she/he is expected to influence the environment positive behaviour also in other sections of the society. We are living in the world of a dramatic climate change. We need to conserve our fossil fuels, water, manage e-wastes, find alternate sources of energy, reduce our carbon footprint and take many more actions towards environment sustainability. Any environment friendly action, however small or big as an individual or as a group, has the potential to go a long way to sustain our environment for the benefit of our future generation.

The limitation of this study lies in the cross-sectional data used for study.

References

Bacsi, Z. (2020). Environmental awareness in different European cultures. *Visegr. J. Bioecon. Sustain. Dev.* 9(2);47–54.

Blok, V., Wesselink, R., Studynka, O., and Kemp, R. (2015). Encouraging sustainability in the workplace: A survey on the pro-environmental behaviour of university employees. J. Clean. Prod. 106:55–67.

Crane, A. (2000). Corporate greening as amoralization. *Organization Studies*, 21(4), 673–696.

Do Prado, N. B., & Moraes, G.H.S.M.d. (2020). Environmental awareness, consumption of organic products and gender. *Revista de Gestão*, 27(4):353–368.

Dunphy, D.(2003). Corporate sustainability: challenge to managerial orthodoxies. *Journal of the Australian and New Zealand Academy of Management*, 19:2–11.

Duroy, Q. M. (2005). The determinants of environmental awareness and behavior. J. Environ. Dev.

Fairfiled. K. D., Harmon J., & Beheson, S. J. (2011). Influences on the organizational implementation of sustainability: an integrative model. *Organization Management Journal*, 8(1), 4–20.

Linnenluecke, M. K., & Griffiths, A. (2010). Corporate sustainability and organizational culture. *Journal of World Business*, 45(4): 357–366.

Milfont, T. L. and Duckitt, J. (2010). The environmental attitudes inventory: A valid and reliable measure to assess the structure of environmental attitudes J. Environ. Psy. 30(1):80–94.

Ones, D., & Dilchert, S. (2012). Environmental Sustainability at Work: A Call to Action. *Industrial and Organizational Psychology*, 5(4): 444–466. doi:10.1111/j.1754-9434. 2012.01478.x

Putra, M. A. H., Mutiani, M., Jumriani, J., and Handy, M. R. N. (2020). The Development of a Waste Bank as a Form of Community Participation in Waste Management. KSSJ. 2(1):22–30.

Purser, R. E. (1994). Guest editorial: "Shallow" versus "deep" organizational development and environmental sustainability. *Journal of Organizational Change Management*, 7(4): 4–14.

Sanyal, U. and Pal, D. (2017). Effect of organizational culture in environmental awareness on pro-environmental behaviour at workplace: A new perspective on organizational sustainability. IMS Business School Presents Doctoral Colloquium–ISBN (pp. 978–93).

Schein, E. (2004). The concept of organizational culture. *Organizational culture and leadership* (3rd ed.). San Fransisco: Josey Bass, 3–23.

Škatarić, G., Vlahović, B., Užar, D., Spalevic, V., & Novićević, R. (2021). The influence of green marketing on consumer environmental awareness. *Agriculture & Forestry/ Poljoprivreda i Sumarstvo*, 67(2): 21–36.

Stern, P. (2000). Toward a Coherent Theory of Environmentally Significant Behavior. *The Journal of Social Issues*, 56:407–424.

Sun, Y., & Sun, H. (2021). Executives' Environmental Awareness and Eco-Innovation: An Attention-Based View. *Sustainability*, 13(8): 4421.

Unsworth, K. L., Dmitrieva, A., & Adriasola, E. (2013). Changing behaviour: Increasing the effectiveness of workplace interventions in creating pro-environmental behaviour change. *Journal of Organizational Behavior*, 34(2):211–229. ISSN 0894-3796

Yusliza, M. Y., Faezah, J. N., Mat, N. H. N., Saputra, J., Muhammad, Z., Muhamad, A. S., & Ramayah, T. (2021). Modelling Pro-environmental Behaviour in the Workplace: A Preliminary Study. *Proceedings of the 11th Annual International Conference on Industrial Engineering and Operations Management*, 3953–3963.

9 Prediction of bankruptcy of Indian manufacturing companies (construction) using Zmijewski model and Altman Z score

Nithya Shree[1] and Joseph Durai Selvam[2]

[1]Student – MBA, School of Business Management CHRIST (Deemed to be University), India

[2]Associate Professor – School of Business Management CHIRST (Deemed to be University), India

Abstract

Prediction of bankruptcy is one of the major concerns with regard to the classification of firms. Bankruptcy prediction of the firms gives investors and management an idea about the exact condition of the firms in a precise manner so the sudden adverse situations can be avoided. The stakeholders of the firms such as owners, shareholders, debtors, creditors, managers, partners, and other institutions etc. have always shown a keen interest in understanding the financial position of the firms they are related to, whether financial or non-financial. To provide an aid to these stakeholders, different models have been developed to predict bankruptcy. The purpose of this thesis is to predict the bankruptcy of 104 manufacturing companies located in India listed in Bombay Stock Exchange that come under construction sector using 2 models, ie…, Zmijewski model and Altman Z Score and then, comparing the results obtained from both the models. Zmijewski model and Altman Z Score are used to predict bankruptcy. For the study, the data was collected for two years, that is 2019 and 2020. The data was collected from Prowess IQ and Yahoo finance. The Z score obtained from the Altman model is used to predict bankruptcy to two years preceding the happening of the event. Altman Z Score can be applied to the manufacturing companies in India but it does not have an accuracy of 100%. Previous studies have shown that Altman Z Score can be applied and can predict proper results but the rest of the studies have shown that it has given the opposite results. As a result, there is a need to check whether the variables in the Altman Z Score affect Altman model in prediction of bankruptcy. Wilcoxon rank model is used for the hypothesis to find out if there is any significant difference between the models used to predict the bankruptcy – Zmijewski model and Altman Z Score. The values obtained from Zmijewski model and Altman Z Score is used in testing the hypothesis. The mean is either found from the positive ranks or negative ranks whichever is smaller. After obtaining the mean, zigma is calculated and then the z score is obtained through which z value is found out with the help of the z table. The secondary data of those 104 companies was taken. The results obtained from Zmijewski model showed that all the companies were safe and will not become bankrupt in the next two years. This means that all the companies under Zmijewski model are healthy. The results from Altman Z Score showed that only three companies were safe and the rest of the companies had to be on alert or they would reach bankruptcy in two years. Pattern of Bankruptcy differs in both the models. Zmijewski model uses three ratios and Altman Z Score uses 5 ratios. The financial indicators used in both these models are profitability, liquidity, and leverage. Exploratory form of research has been used here. The dependant variable is bankruptcy and the independent variables are the five ratios used in both the models. They are Net profit/total assets, total assets/total liabilities, current assets/

current liabilities, working capital/total assets, retained earnings/total assets, Earnings before interest and tax/total assets, market value of equity/total liabilities, and sales/total assets.

Introduction

The word bankruptcy means the process which is conducted legally in which entities or people who cannot repay the loans taken or any other form of debt may seek to get relief for a part or for whole of their debt. It is initiated by a debtor who is not able to repay the debts and is imposed by courts. On filing for bankruptcy, the initiator gets a stay where their creditors cannot deduct money from the bank account, go after any assets that are secured, etc. The different types of bankruptcies are: (1) Liquidation (2) Repayment plan (3) Large reorganisation (4) Family farmers (5) Used in foreign cases (6) Municipalities. The process of filing bankruptcy in India is first to file a petition saying that you have gone insolvent. Then submit the petition to the authority and you will be declared insolvent. You also have an option to file for insolvency resolution using Sec 9 of IBC 2016. The insolvency and bankruptcy code 2015 were introduced in Lok Sabha on 21 December 2015. The maximum time allotted to either accept or reject the plea submitted to the adjudicating authority is 14 days. Within 180 days, the tribunal must appoint an Interim resolution professional. The directors will be suspended during that time. The insolvency and bankruptcy code are believed to solve the banking issues in the country.

The ultimate aim of every business is to make profit. This is the main aim of the businesses. But at the same time, they should give due importance to the society also and also to the stakeholders of the firms. The stakeholders of every firm would wish to know the current performance and the predicted future performance of the firms they are into as they have invested their time and money in the companies. Keeping an eye on the company whether they will do well in the future or go bankrupt is one of the major areas of concern of the stakeholders. Different models and theories have come up with regard to this matter. The reason for developing of different models and coming up of various theories is the failure of the businesses due to various reasons. Stakeholders will have a negative impact in case of negative bankruptcies. Companies get the benefit if they are able to predict bankruptcy at an early stage as they can take necessary steps accordingly. As a result, necessary marketing strategies can also be created. Companies that give anticipating signals of bankruptcy should act in such a way that their conditions get improved.

Bankruptcy is a legal status provided to a person who is not in a situation to pay back his/her loans or other obligations to the creditors. Under Insolvency and Bankruptcy code 2016, Bankruptcy has been defined as the state of being bankrupt. The Insolvency and Bankruptcy code, 2016 defines bankrupt as:

a) A debtor who has been adjudged as bankrupt order under section 126
b) Each of the partners of a firm, where bankruptcy order under section 126 has been made against the fire. Or
c) Any person adjudged as an undischarged insolvent

In this thesis, two models (a) Altman Z Score and (b) Zmijewski model have been used, for bankruptcy prediction and the results of both have been compared.

Edward I Altman agreed to the approach of predicting bankruptcy using industrial characteristics. He said that models for predicting bankruptcy should also contain data from financial statements. This can be used for those companies that have similar business. Prediction of bankruptcy can be analysed and measured through the financial statements of a firm with the help of ratio analysis (Adnan and Kurniasih 2000). The main content of bankruptcy prediction models is financial ratios. Beaver suggested that financial ratios can be used to predict bankruptcy. This was the start for financial ratios being used in predicting bankruptcy. For example, the usage of the Altman model developed by Edward I Altman in the year 1968 – this model can be used to predict bankruptcy prior to two years before the happening of the event. It has an accuracy of 72% in the prediction prior to two years of happening of the event and 80% to 90% accuracy for one year prior to the event.

The second model used here is Zmijewski model. It is used to predict bankruptcy within two years prior to the happening of the event. The ratios used in this model were determined by probit analysis. In this model, if the scores are less than 0.5, then there is a higher chance for the company to go into a state of bankruptcy. The major criticism faced was that the other models used for predicting bankruptcy had more distressed firms and had situations which provided with a complete list of data. Zmijewski model was earlier found using 800 non-bankrupt and 40 bankrupt firms.

Ratio analysis is divided into five parts. They are solvency ratios, activity or turnover ratios, liquidity ratios, market ratios, and profitability ratios. Each ratio has a different role in assessing the financial condition/stability of the firm. The combination of these ratios gives rise to a bankruptcy prediction model.

In order to survive the competition after the opening of the markets, this would be a great opportunity to the manufacturing firms. This can be used for the anticipation of the disclosure of the firms at an early stage (Shezad et al., 2014).

Bankruptcy prediction of an organisation can be done with the help of ratios embedded in the model that had been developed since 1968. Altman Z Score uses five ratios whereas Zmijewski model uses three ratios. Different conclusions can be derived from different models.

Services are in vogue in the manufacturing sector. Providing products with value additions will show the way to earn profits when customers ask for customisation of products and innovative goods. Manufacturing firms earn competitive advantage when they provide after-sales services to the products manufactured by them. Such manufacturing companies have the least chance of falling bankrupt. After-sales services are considered to be a source of income and contribute to profit margin. Researchers in this field have always insisted upon providing services to increase satisfaction among the customers which would help in building a strong customer bond. Manufacturing companies have to cut their costs in order to compete in developing countries. In order to survive in developing countries, it is not easy the manufacturing firms to stay as pure manufacturing firms all along. That is the reason they started providing services, too. Recent developments in technology help the firms build new business models that help them to exploit the potential of the products they provide to the customers.

Bankruptcy can be due to different reasons, for instance lack of skills in marketing and management and the inability to compete. These can be visualised from the performance of the company. Due to this, accounting data from the financial statements of the company is mostly used to analyse the performance of the firms. Different models like Altman Z Score, Springate, Ohlson model, and Zmijewski models are built upon accounting ratios. The major problem with Altman Z Score and Zmijewski models are they ignore the time factor.

Construction sector was the worst hit by bankruptcy under manufacturing firms followed by leather and textile companies in Fiscal Year 2020. The number had doubled to 3774 in the manufacturing sector out of which 1604 cases have been settled by tribunals in and around the country. The main reason was the outbreak of coronavirus and the lockdown followed by it. The condition was the same for the manufacturing sector in FY 19. There were about 772 cases under Insolvency and Bankruptcy Code 2016 from the manufacturing sector. It was around 41% of the total cases. Most of the times, a major part of India's bankrupt cases come from the manufacturing sector. As per the statistics, two out of five filed cases for bankruptcy were from the manufacturing sector. Under construction, the basic metal category seems to be worst affected. The number of cases filed is increasing under IBC.

This thesis follows a specific structure. The major content is the abstract followed by the introduction to the study, then the literature review, that focuses on bankruptcy prediction of manufacturing firms focusing on different models like Altman Z Score, Zmijewski model, Springate model, Ohlson model, Decision trees, logit model etc. Next is the data methodology followed by analysis and interpretation and then come the findings, conclusions, and annexure respectively.

Literature review

Models used for predicting bankruptcy have come into tplay after the model developed by Edward I Altman. The models compare firms after getting the results, and classify the firms into bankrupt and non-bankrupt. As per Hanafi and Halim (2007), early warning signals for bankruptcy can be obtained by an analysis with the available variables. If the organisations are able to detect the signs of bankruptcy, then they are able to make necessary changes and make improvements in their decisions. Not only the management, but the lenders, creditors, debtors, and investors etc. can also take necessary decisions on the analysis. The warning signals can be received after the analysis with different models. The slightest problem with a firm starts by liquidity issues and the biggest problem for a firm is when the firm is declared bankrupt. This is the most severe problem faced by the firms. Financial difficulties can be either small or very huge depending upon the situations prevailing within the company.

Most of the US and European firms have not received enough attention in the literature review for bankruptcy. Those firms are either small companies or mid-sized companies. The liquidation rate was found for 72 small firms in Finland that had filed for bankruptcy code during 1982–92 and comparison was made between American and Finnish code. Dummy variables were introduced for retail, manufacturing, and construction industries. Type and size of the business affects the liquidation process for firms in Finland and US. The type of business that the organisation is engaged in and the size of the firm are the main characteristics for liquidation (Ravid and Sundgren, 1998).

The purpose of the paper was to find a model using economic variables along with results of financial ratios for a model superior to traditional model that includes financial ratios alone. Every observation for 78 failed and non-failed firms consisted of six financial ratios. The results showed that models that used logit analysis are significant with reference to likelihood ratio tests and index in distinguishing between firms that have failed and non-failed for five years prior to the date of failure. The factors such as financial ratios and market variables are important to predict the likelihood of bankruptcy (Darayseh et al., 2003). More bankruptcy related firms from the construction, trade, and manufacturing firms were found in East Germany. Firms that are not efficient, have no market success, and less productivity file for financial distress. Taking the start-ups into consideration, the entrepreneur specific characteristics are more related to bankruptcy. There has been an effect of education on the risk of voluntary liquidation for new firms in West and East Germany. In East Germany, start-ups have the highest share in filing for liquidations related to bankruptcy (Prantl, 2003).

The paper had the data saying that US manufactures must cut production costs by 30% to compete with China. More firms that include both manufacturing and service go bankrupt than those firms that undertake only manufacturing (Neely, 2007).

The aim of the paper was to use multiple discriminant analysis (MDA), Altman Z Score to predict bankruptcy in the textile industry. The study concluded that the revised Altman Z Score predicts about the firms that go bankrupt one or two years before filing for bankruptcy (Cardwell et al., 2011). The Springate model is more conservative than Zmijewski model to predict bankruptcy. Industrially poor firms in the previous research were found to be bankrupt as per Zmijewski and Springate model (Imanzadeh et al., 2011). The problems of business failures are due to financial and non-financial causes. The author also stated that Altman Z score was formulated for public manufacturing companies. Models that use artificial intelligence are still not used by many as they have not received much recognition and hence are not widely used. Most of the recognition is received by Altman Z Score model. Some authors have shown support saying that Altman Z Score model is the best model while some say that adjustments must be made as different authors interpret it in different ways. The ratios that are used widely are profit before tax and assets ratio, sale of assets and revenue from sales, working capital and assets ratio as well as income earned from the revenue from operations and monetary relations (Kiyak and Labanauskaitė, 2012).

The author has tried to develop a statistical model to predict the risk of bankruptcy In Romanian circle, principle component analysis is applied to manufacturing sector. The two groups of companies selected for the article are listed companies and the other group of companies that will be unlisted in next few years (Achim et al., 2012). The aim of the paper was to evaluate the validity of potential practical application of the models to predict bankruptcy and the conceptual economic principles. The author found that the greatest number of bankruptcies declined in manufacturing on comparing 2010 and 2009. Later he pointed that most of the bankrupt companies are from the sectors of manufacturing, retail and wholesale, and construction (Kiyak and Labanauskaitė, 2012).

The aim of the paper was to find whether the model used might deviate from the original observation due to differences. Multiple discriminant analysis was developed for 132 public manufacturing companies in Japan. The author also pointed to predict bankruptcy as early as possible. Shareholders have focused on reducing their risks. The shareholders have started to find ways to predict bankruptcy as they feel that bankruptcy has a negative impact on the economy. Early warning of bankruptcy gained importance because financial distress can lead to bankruptcy. Both the investors and management can gain from prediction of bankruptcy (Gurau and Sar, 2013). The study is about the testing of validity of Beneish M score and Altman Z Score as models for investment that can be used by stakeholders in analysis of financial statements of entity. The models used save the investors from incurring losses while making the investments. The study was undertaken for the manufacturing companies in Zimbabwe (Othman, 2013). The probability of the bankruptcy is predicted using Business failure prediction models. These can be done using capital turnover and financial ratios etc. Different stakeholders like investors, creditors, lenders, and the government are showing keen interest in the area of bankruptcy prediction of the corporates. The sample consisted of companies listed in Taiwan stock exchange. Business failure protection models have been used which help the lenders not to lend to businesses that are likely to fail. The manufacturing companies in Taiwan stock exchange were randomly selected. The model was constructed using valuation, leverage, and efficiency and profitability ratios. The statistical models help to categorise whether the business or the organisations will fall into the category of success or failure (Lee, 2014). The objective of the study was to check whether Z model can be used to classify accurately for the manufacturing companies situated in Lebanon. Based on the findings, the author said that though Altman Z Score can be used to classify manufacturing companies, to have more level of accuracy it is better to apply and use subsamples where firms are sharing business conditions which are almost the same and performing same business activity (Rim and Roy, 2014).

The paper examined the percentage that the model used will fit to Thailand Stock Exchange that applies EM Z-Score model and Altman Z Score model. The results showed that higher the ratios used such as operating efficiency, liquidity ratio, and retained earnings more is the capital efficiency of the firm. The author also recommended that to predict bankruptcy stakeholders must use variables which are not mentioned in Altman Z Score model, like ratios from Statement of cash flow. When bankruptcy is predicted, the investors can secure their organisations and take necessary steps to minimise risks and losses. This might also lead to avoidance of bankruptcy. The authors also recommended the usage of other variables other than those mentioned in the models, from the cash flow statement (Meeampol, 2014). The paper aimed to create prediction on bankruptcy models using neural networks and logistic regression of Estonian manufacturing firms. Neural networks include 14 variables and logistic regression had 3 variables. The time between declaration of bankruptcy and last annual report would be same for all the companies (for the data). The results showed that the models that use different methods do not have the ability to predict one year before the prediction of bankruptcy but can predict two or three years before the occurrence of bankruptcy. The performance of the models was not up to the mark on taking the information that took place during the time of economic recession. The prediction was better for the neural network model than for the logit regression model (Grünberg and Lukason, 2014).

The information that is not taken from balance sheet may show risk factors and improve the power of logit estimates. The paper also suggests that in order to eliminate the specificity in samples caused by uncertainty in the expected scenario in the field of macroeconomics, it is important to find ratios which resume financial and real causes of risk in bankruptcy (Zeshan, 2000). The issue of bankruptcy should be taken seriously by the companies. There will be a negative impact of bankruptcy on the shareholders of that company. The prediction of bankruptcy helps to detect the possibility of bankruptcy in the company and helps the shareholders and the investors to take decisions accordingly. Other financial ratios can be included to get a more accurate model. Altman model is good enough to predict bankruptcy for the companies listed in the stock exchange of Indonesia. The partial test done for retained earnings to total assets, EBIT to total assets, working capital/ total assets were able to classify the bankruptcy of the firms listed in Indonesian Stock Exchange (Matturungan et al., 2017).

The purpose is to study the suitability for manufacturing companies in India by using major prediction models for bankruptcy. The study also showed that KMV Merton cannot say when it can exactly predict the occurrence of bankruptcy but the Altman Z Score model is able to predict at least two years prior to the happening of the bankruptcy (Hughes, 2008). The author provides a methodological analysis of risk in credit in manufacturing sector firms by using Data Envelopment Analysis and traditional Discriminant Approach. The financial performance of the firms is important as it speaks about the future decisions and actions thereafter affect the growth at the company and economy levels. Defaults of the bankrupt firms were able to predict whose balance sheet was used in discriminant analysis. An accurate separation between unsound and sound firms was done using GLM regression method which also suggested that the usage of the model can be used to find the creditworthiness of the organisations (Bartoloni and Baussola, 2014).

The paper provides a comparison for manufacturing firms by standard discriminant approach based on logistic regression model and a Robust Bayesian Approach. By using robust GLM regression methodology helped to provide a proper separation between unsound and sound firms. The study of financial performance of a firm is very much important when the economy is in downturn. The results reached a conclusion that it is not proper to predict a rare event like bankruptcy as it is needed to select the required proportion of firms that have failed in the final sample (Baussola et al., 2015). The study used Springate, Zmijewski and Altman Z Score models to determine the health level for manufacturing and metal companies listed in Indonesia stock exchange. T-test and linear regression are used to test hypothesis. Accounting data is used to check the signs of bankruptcy. The conclusions of the three models showed that there was a significance difference to the approach of Springate with Zmijewski and Z score with Zmijewski, but there is no significance difference between Z Score with Springate. Zmijewski model affects bankruptcy prediction in such a way that it has components that contribute to the prediction purpose (Sinarti and Sembiring, 2015). The author has explored the quantifiable characteristics of the potential bankrupt companies and the utility of ratio analysis (Sukma, 2015). Since 2010, the bankruptcy rate has increased in the manufacturing French food industry. The pattern of risk in bankruptcy is different for manufacturing firms and firms in food industry. The productivity for the firms starts deteriorating three years before failure happens. There is a significant impact on probability of bankruptcy that is dependent by cost in credit. In the manufacturing sector, the food industry is more resistant to risks in bankruptcy. One-third of the companies that file for bankruptcy are from food manufacturing firms. The firms filing for bankruptcy includes big firms. The age and size of the firms are taken as the factors that mainly affect the risks in bankruptcy (Aleksanyan and Huiban, 2016).

Multivariate discriminant analysis and bootstrapping method was used to find the determinants for bankruptcy in certain industries and to compare the errors of industry and general models. The results show that industry based models do not have an error in lower average prediction on comparing with general models. Companies become bankrupt in developed economies, too. The author has also said that it is important to prepare industry based bankruptcy prediction model though it does not always show models that have got high probability for predicting bankruptcy. Different financial ratios can be used to predict bankruptcy in different industries (Herman, 2017).

The study tries to implement Altman Z Score from 2011 to 15 listed in NSE&BSE and the companies are selected from both manufacturing and non-manufacturing companies. The research revealed that for a few years some companies were in the safe zone. Most of the firms were in distress zone which says that it might go bankrupt in the upcoming years (Murthy et al., 2018). Previous research was about preparation of models for bankruptcy for companies in manufacturing sector. The study has examined whether financial ratios are suitable indicators of bankruptcy for manufacturing and construction industry. For manufacturing industry, asset structure, ROA and inventory turnover ratio are important predictors (Karas and Režňáková, 2017). Financial distress leads to bankruptcy that will leave an impact on the micro and macro environment of a country. Both the internal and external stakeholders are in a need to evaluate the financial strength of the companies. The manufacturer of commercial vehicles is in the verge of financial distress which might cause them to file for bankruptcy. The Altman Z Score model can be used to help the management to analyse the problems to take actions to avoid bankruptcy. The demand from middle income groups for motorcycles made them stay away from being bankrupt. Firms should take decisions so that optimum utilisation of resources is achieved (Shilpa and Amulya, 2017). Increase in debt to assets ratio increases the chance for bankruptcy. The main part of successful prediction of bankruptcy is taking proper samples of bankrupt firms which should be almost same and total quantitative and qualitative features of the financial information from financial statements (Arnis et al., 2018). Asian firms have more bankruptcy risk, high net profit margin, high inventory turnover and sales growth rate and less liquidity risk than European firms. Manufacturing firms in European countries take less time to collect money from their debtors. There has not been much difference in the case of Return on Equity between Asian and European firms. Higher net profit margins and less manufacturing costs are a result of having less labour costs for Asian firms. Asian firms have more financial risk (Meric et al., 2018).

Bankruptcy prediction and financial risks is connected to finding financial problems. Bankruptcy prediction models can be divided into intelligence techniques, theoretical models and statistical techniques. Bankruptcy of firms in manufacturing sector increased mainly due to recession (Klepáč and Hampel, 2018).

Bankruptcy happens due to market situations, not utilising the resources optimally, inefficient management, and decline in sales etc. Prediction of bankruptcy is useful to everyone who is connected to a firm. This is for taking the right action at the right time. The problem of bankruptcy can be due to improper forecasting in sales, fraud, changes in tastes and preferences of the customers, poor management, etc. The financial soundness of a firm is in one way judged by the ability of the firm to pay interest and principal regularly. Failures in business are caused both by non-financial and financial causes. Altman Z Score analysis, working capital ratios, solvency ratios, and liquidity ratios were used to understand the problem of bankruptcy (Venkataramana et al., 2012). Real net worth of the firm will turn to be negative when bankruptcy arises. From the 19 manufacturing companies selected and listed in stock exchange of Colombo, only four firms were under safer zone for the entire study period (Lecturer and Lanka, 2017). A company can be declared bankrupt if the firm is in the distress zone which means that the finances of the company are weak. Altman Z Score can be used by the interested parties of a company so that they can land safely by taking wise decisions. Altman Z Score is used to predict bankruptcy two years before the events happened. Bankruptcy of seven selected companies in India could be predicted three years before the event happened. Though Altman Z Score is not 100% accurate, it can still be applied to predict bankruptcy. The financial interests of the investors can be saved by using the Altman Z Score. The study showed that Altman Z Score model can be used to predict three years prior to the occurrence of bankruptcy and has an accuracy of 85% (Apoorva et al., 2019). The measurement of risk for bankruptcy is a great challenge for the firms as the consequences are huge and has a negative impact on the firm. Static models can't be used to differentiate between companies that have low ratios that worsen each year and firms that have low financial ratios and improve every year. But dynamic models can help to differentiate this. Fuzzy sets model had more effectiveness during the ten year study period. Decision trees, multilayer and recurrent artificial neural network, and fuzzy sets will tell whether the deviation in the values of the organisations are important in predicting the financial crisis (Korol, 2019). Altman Z Score does not enumerate how the discrete variables behave in the last two years of bankruptcy. The activity ratio did not have a significant relationship with Altman Z Score. Relationship between Altman Z Score and Independent Altman variables was significant two years before bankruptcy (Ka, 2019).

The models for bankruptcy are taken from non-random samples with the proportion of bankrupt companies differing from that in the population which creates bias in estimated probabilities for bankruptcy for individual companies. Many issues discussed which were neglected while applying in the models for bankruptcy was discussed in the study. The author has gone tried find the reason for the usage of unbalanced samples for bankruptcy models that generate biased bankruptcy probabilities and give ways to calibration to unbiased probabilities. The cases of bankruptcy are not common in the group of active companies. It is less than 1 percent (Gruszczyński, 2019). There is no significant impact of the change in econometric

methods of default prediction models on its predictive performance when significant indicators of bankruptcy are found out. A little accounting information like
turnover, leverage, and profitability ratios can be used in default prediction (Singh
and Mishra, 2019). Financial health of the companies needs to be taken care of
when the number of bankrupt companies increases or financial failures occur. The
company will become insolvent when the reserves of the company become negative. Altman Model 1, Altman model 2 and Springate model can be used to predict
bankruptcy successfully (Amarasiri, 2019). The problem of sampling bias has to
be taken care while assembling the database for models for bankruptcy prediction
which might lead to a worsening of the performance of the model. The prediction for bankruptcy became possible in ex-socialist countries twenty years later in
Western countries. The prediction of bankruptcy will not work independently without space, time, and economic environment. The inclusion of inputs will lead to a
better prediction of the models for predicting bankruptcy. The problem of bias in
sampling has to be dealt with care. Cross validation can be used to handle problems
with small databases (Kristóf and Virág, 2020). The problems of business failures
are due to financial and non-financial causes. The author also stated that Altman Z
score was formulated for public manufacturing companies. Models that use artificial intelligence are still not used by many as it has not received much recognition
and hence not widely used. Most of the recognition is received by Altman Z Score
model. Some authors have come in support saying that Altman Z Score model is
the best model while some say that adjustments must be made as different authors
interpret it in different ways. The ratios that are used widely are profit before tax
and assets ratio, sale of assets and revenue from sales, working capital and assets
ratio as well as income earned from the revenue from operations and monetary
relations (Kiyak and Labanauskaitė, 2012).

The study found that Altman model performs well for manufacturing companies where the mean accuracy rate was 87.88% for three years before bankruptcy.
For bankrupt and non-bankrupt US manufacturing firms Altman is better than
Springate and Ohlson model. The larger values for the Springate and Ohlson model
showed it was fit for the model. The models that are used for the prediction of bankruptcy which are market based have received more popularity. Springate (1978),
Ohlson (1980), and Altman (2000), are models used to predict bankruptcy that
are accounting related. All the three models have varying bankruptcy prediction
power in the manufacturing firms of United States of America. It was also found
that Altman was able to classify the firms that are not bankrupt in a much better
way than Springate (1978) and Ohlson (1980) models (Laurila, 2020). Different
factors affect bankruptcy. The author has thrown light on how the performance of
the financial factors deteriorates as approached by bankruptcy relative to Altman
Indices. Bankruptcy is preceded by financial distress. There is a high accuracy for
bankruptcy prediction in manufacturing firms using the original Altman Z Score.
Young firms have more chance to fall in the category of financial distress that will
make them file for bankruptcy. The accuracy of Altman Z Score reduces as lead
time ascends (Ka, 2019). The issue of bankruptcy should be taken seriously by the
companies. There will be a negative impact of bankruptcy on the shareholders of
that company. The prediction of bankruptcy helps to detect the possibility of bankruptcy in the company and helps the shareholders and the investors take decisions

accordingly. Other financial ratios can be included to get a more accurate model. Altman model is good enough to predict bankruptcy for the companies listed in the stock exchange of Indonesia. The partial test done for retained earnings to total assets, EBIT to total assets, working capital/ total assets were able to classify the bankruptcy of the firms listed in Indonesian Stock Exchange (Matturungan et al., 2017).

The study has looked into the relationship between service provision and internal and external risks of bankruptcy of companies that do manufacturing business. Service business has more internal risks and hence more probability for bankruptcy. The risks and weakness faced by firms, and wealth of the organisations, are also analysed while looking into bankruptcy. It is assumed that the manufacturing firms that provide services also have less chance for being bankrupt. The innovation in services in manufacturing sector is backed up by technology. Having a service strategy makes a firm to engage in different activities and expand their portfolio. The weakness of managers in manufacturing areas is that they have less skills that are required to deal with the demand when it is high (*Examining the Influence of Service Additions on Manufacturing Firms ' Bankruptcy Likelihood Ornella Benedittini , Morgan Swink and Andy Neely Paper Accepted for Publication in Industrial and Marketing Management Examining the Influence of Service Addition*, n.d.). Real net worth of the firm will turn to be negative when bankruptcy arises. From the 19 manufacturing companies selected and listed in stock exchange of Colombo, only four firms were under safer zone for the entire study period (Lecturer and Lanka, 2017).

Research Gap

One of the widely used methods for predicting bankruptcy is Altman Z Score. Accounting ratios are being used in Altman Z Score, Zmijewski model, Ohlson model, Springate model to predict bankruptcy. Different studies have been conducted onAltman Z Score and Zmijewski model. But there are no existing studies which specifically predict bankruptcy with a combination of Altman Z Score and Zmijewski model. Comparison of both Altman Z Score and Zmijewski model needs to be done.

Objectives and methodology

Objectives
Following are the objectives of the study:

- To find whether the companies will go bankrupt or not
- To check the credit worthiness of the firm
- To give insights to the investors on whether to buy the stock of the firm or not

On getting the Z score from Altman model, it can also be used to check the credit worthiness of the firm, whether they are well and good in paying their debts or obligations or loans. The same Z score is useful to investors also to know whether they can invest in that particular firm or not. This means if the company is not performing well, then they will go bankrupt or might have the chance of being bankrupt. As a result it is not advisable to invest in those companies. It is better to invest in those companies that are considered to be safe.

The aim of the research is to develop an understanding between Zmijewski model and Altman Z Score and to know the companies that will go bankrupt in two years from 2019. Knowledge about the accounting ratios has provided a valid framework in understanding both the models used to predict bankruptcy.

Methodology

Research methodology includes the design of the data collection, calculation, and data analysis processes to be done to attain the research objectives. The researcher uses the research methodology as a guide to arrive at the results for a given data either primary or secondary and thus make inferences. The data collection methods are chosen by the researcher, either primary or secondary.

The data was actually collected for more than 700 companies from prowess for construction industry under manufacturing sector. Whole information required for calculating the Z Scores of both the models were not available for all companies. Filtering was done to take only those companies which had every information to calculate the accounting ratios used in Zmijewski model and Altman Z Score.

The two models used to predict bankruptcy are Altman Z Score and Zmijewski model.

The data required for every ratio in both the models were taken from Prowess IQ. The data for market value of equity was taken from Yahoo Finance. The data is solely collected from secondary source of data. The data analysis is carried out in MS Excel for both prediction purpose and testing hypothesis. The data was taken for two years – 2019 and 2020. The reason behind taking the data for two years was both the models can predict bankruptcy two years prior to happening of the event. Specific criteria were not followed in selection of the company. It was chosen on a random basis as the main aim was to predict bankruptcy in construction sector.

1. **ZMIJEWSKI MODEL**

   $Z = -4.3 - 4.5X1 + 5.7 X2 + 0.004 X3$

   X1 stands for Net profit/total assets

   X2 stands for Total liabilities/total assets

   X3 stands for Current assets/current liabilities

   The firm will go bankrupt if the Z score obtained from Zmijewski model is less than 0.5 and the company will be safe or will not be bankrupt in two years if the Z score is more than 0.5.

   The ratio used in this model was determined by probit analysis. The model actually looks upon liquidity, leverage, or debt of the company. Zmijewski ME is the founder of this model. During the process of building up of the model, he used 800 non-bankrupt and 40 bankrupt companies as a sample. He developed the model using liquidity, leverage and return on assets.

2. **ALTMAN MODEL**

   $Z = 1.2 A + 1.4 B + 3.3 C + 0.6 D + 1 E$

   A stands for working capital/total assets

B stands for retained earnings/total assets
C stands for earnings before interest and tax/total assets
D stands for market value of equity/total liabilities
E stands for sales/total assets

Altman Z score was developed by Edward I Altman in the year 1968. Altman Z Score uses 5 accounting ratios. It is used to measure financial health of a company. It can be used for prediction whether the companies will go bankrupt prior to two years of the happening of the event. The value received is known as Z score. The lower the value, higher the chance for the company to go bankrupt. The accuracy of this model is more than 95% one year prior to the happening of the event.

If the Z score is less than 1.8, then there is a high chance for the company to go bankrupt, if the z score is between 1.8 and 2.7, then the firm will go bankrupt in two years, if the z score is between 2.7 and 2.99, then the firms should be very alert and if the score is 3 or more than 3, then the firms are very safe. There is least or no chance for the company to go bankrupt. This means those companies are safe. This model was actually developed for manufacturing companies that are listed.

Models and Variables

Each research needs to define each of its variables. Variables are classified into two groups. They are dependant and independent variables.

a) Independent variable
    An independent variable stands on its own. It is not dependant on any other value or factor. The independent variable in this case is the three ratios used in Zmijewski model and five ratios used in Altman Z Score. They are net profit/total assets, total liabilities/total assets, current assets/current liabilities, working capital/total assets, retained earnings/total assets, earnings before interest and tax/total assets, market value of equity/total liabilities, sales/total assets.

b) Dependent variable
    The value of the dependant variable is based upon another independent value or variable. The dependant variable in this case will be whether the firm will go bankrupt or not.

The financial indicators used here are profitability, liquidity, and leverage.

Hypothesis Testing

Hypothesis testing is done using Wilcoxon rank model. It is a non-parametric test. There will be two pairs. It is used to check if there is a significant difference between the two pairs.

In this case, both the models have the same dependant variable.

The hypothesis can be done using MS Excel also. An important step that should be noted is the presence of tied ranks. If the excel shows the presence of tied ranks, additional steps have to be followed. The hypothesis testing can be done with the help of few steps:

Framing of hypothesis

a) Difference of the values should be calculated from the models for all the 104 companies.
b) Next step is to place the differences in order and to give them ranks. In this step, the sign of the differences are ignored.
c) In the next column to the differences, the signs of the differences are noted
d) The sum of the ranks of both positive and negative differences has to be calculated separately. W+ will be denoted as sum of the ranks for positive differences and W− will be denoted as sum of the ranks for negative differences. Smaller of W+ or W− should be noted
e) Calculate mean: n (n+1)/4
f) Calculate sigma: square root of n (n + 1) (2n + 1)/24
g) If there is tied ranks, for each tied ranks it should be reduced by ($t^3 - t$)/48
h) Z score = smaller of {(W+ or W−) − mean}/sigma
i) Check the value for z score in z table and interpret accordingly

Hypothesis Testing

Null Hypothesis: H0 – There is no significance difference between Zmijewski model and Altman Model in predicting bankruptcy of 104 manufacturing companies in the construction sector.

Alternate Hypothesis: H1 – There is significance difference between Zmijewski model and Altman Model in predicting bankruptcy of 104 manufacturing companies in the construction sector.

With regard to the hypothesis, after taking into consideration the different variables, z value was calculated for both Zmijewski model and Altman model for 104 firms. The aim of doing hypothesis testing was to compare and contrast the results of Zmijewski model and Altman model in predicting bankruptcy of the above said firms. Wilcoxon signed rank test was used to examine the existence of a relationship between the two models. In this test, if the table value is greater than 0.05, the null hypothesis of the researcher is accepted or vice versa.

Here, the table value obtained is 0.0268. This is less than 0.05 and this shows that null hypothesis will be rejected that says there is significance difference between Zmijewski model and Altman model.

Sum of positive ranks	3327
Sum of negative ranks	2133
Mean	2730
Sigma	308.3748
Z score	−1.93
Z value	0.0268

Data Analysis and Interpretation

Zmijewski Model

Prediction of bankruptcy using Zmijewski model provided the results stating that all the 104 companies are safe and they will not fall into bankruptcy within two years from 2020. The model was used to calculate Z score for two years – 2019 and 2020. In 2019, except two companies – Graphite India Limited and HEG Limited – the rest of the companies are in the safe zone. The situation of those two companies has improved which can be seen from Zmijewski value as the values were more than 0.5. For 2020, all companies are safe which can be seen from the results. Each company can be said to be in good condition. The minimum score in this model to classify as non-bankrupt companies is 0.5 and here every company has crossed that mark. The Zmijewski value can be seen resulting from any average company in small numbers or negative numbers which means the company can be classified as safe company.

The financial performance of Graphite India Limited was very poor for the year ending 2018–19. Their profit reduced by 98% from 2018 to 2019. Its stock price will bounce back only when the demand for graphite is increases. The share price of Graphite India Limited has reduced drastically from 2018 to February 2020. The share price of Graphite India Limited was around Rs 1100 on August 2018 but it reduced to Rs 283 on February 14, 2020. The balance sheet in terms of total assets and total liabilities has reduced for Graphite India Limited from 2019 to 2020.

Though in 2018, the growth of HEG Limited improved, it was not easy to maintain the same rate in future. The share price HEG Limited reduced by 51%. Both the sales and profit of HEG Limited reduced by 9.1% and 23.3% respectively for the year ended March 2020.

Score	<0.5	≥0.5
Interpretation	High chance for bankruptcy	Safe
Number of companies (2019)	2	102
Number of companies (2020)	0	104

Altman Model

Prediction of bankruptcy using Altman Z Score for 104 companies which were listed in Bombay Stock Exchange (BSE) showed the results that only 5 companies will not reach bankruptcy two years from 2019. They are ARL Infratech Limited, Aakash Manufacturing Company Private Limited, Ador Cements Limited, Aryan Enterprises private limited, HEG Limited. 35 companies had the score between 1.8 and 2.7. That means they are likely to fall into the category of bankruptcy in two years from 2019. Two companies need to be very alert. Their scores are between 2.77 and 2.99. Those two companies are Archidply Industries Limited and Zigma paints private limited. Rest of the 62 companies had a high chance to be bankrupt within two years from 2019, as their z scores were less than 1.8.

Considering the year 2020, only three companies had the z score of more than 3 which said that those three companies will not be bankrupt within two years from 2020. Those three companies are ARL Infratech limited, Aryan Enterprises Limited, Zigma paints Limited. The situation of Zigma paints limited has improved as they reached 2020 because they were in the category of Alert Zone in 2019 and have come to the safe zone in 2020. Four companies have to be alert as their z score is between 2.77 and 2.99. Those four companies are Acer Granito Private Limited, Ador Cermaics Private Limited, and Maithan Ceramic Limited. Ador Ceramics Private Limited which was earlier in the category of safe zone is now in alert zone. 36 companies have the chance of falling into the category of bankruptcy in two years from 2020. Rest 61 companies had a high likelihood to be bankrupt within two years from 2020, as their z scores were less than 1.8.

Score	>1.8	1.8–2.77	2.77–2.99	≥3
Interpretation	High chance for bankruptcy	In 2 years	Alert	Safe
Number of companies (2019)	62	35	2	5
Number of companies (2019)	61	36	4	3

In Altman Model, only two companies were safe for both the years. It is better to invest in those companies that are safe. Safe companies also depict that their credit worthiness is good.

Conclusion

Bankruptcy is a situation where the individuals or the company is not in a situation to pay off its debts or obligations. Bankruptcy prediction is very much needed so that the organisation can take decisions accordingly that help the organisation to be on a safer side. Different models are used to predict bankruptcy like Altman Z Score, Zmijewski model, Ohlson model, Springate model, decision trees etc. In this study, both Zmijewski model and Altman Z Score are being used. Both these models are based on accounting ratios. The study period taken was two years – 2019 and 2020 as both models help in predicting bankruptcy prior to two years to the happening of the event. Hypothesis was framed to check significance difference between the models. The dependant variable used is Bankruptcy and the independent variables are net profit/total assets, total liabilities/total assets, current assets/current liabilities, working capital/total assets, retained earnings/total assets, earnings before interest and tax/total assets, market value of equity/total liabilities, sales/total assets. From the study, it was found that in Zmijewski model, majority of the companies were safe for both the years. It was also found that, each company will be safe from two years since 2020, whereas in 2021, majority of the companies will fall into the category of bankruptcy in 2019 and 2020. This says that there is huge difference between both the models. This was also proved with the hypothesis using Wilcoxon ranked test with the data and scores of 2020 for both the models. Majority of the companies that were classified as safe in Zmijewski model were considered to be bankrupt in Altman model. The advantage of Altman is that it uses both qualitative and quantitative aspects. Investors mainly use this model to decide whether to invest in a company or not. On considering this use of the model, from the study, we can conclude that it is advisable for investors to invest in companies that are safe, here it will be ARL Infratech limited, Aryan Enterprises Limited, Zigma paints Limited. Considering 2019, it was safe for the investors to invest in ARL Infratech Limited, Aakash Manufacturing Company Private Limited, Ador Cements Limited, Aryan Enterprises private limited, HEG Limited. Those companies that fall into the category 'safe', have a better financial stability and their credit worthiness is also good. It is strange to see that HEG limited that was classified into the category of bankruptcy under Zmijewski model is safe in the Altman model.

References

Achim, M. V., Mare, C., and Borlea, S. N. (2012). A statistical model of financial risk bankruptcy applied for Romanian manufacturing industry. Procedia Econ. Finac. 3(12):132–137. https://doi.org/10.1016/s2212-5671(12)00131-1

Aleksanyan, L. and Huiban, J. P. (2016). Economic and financial determinants of firm bankruptcy: Evidence from the French food industry. Rev. Agri. Food Env. Stud. 97(2):89–108. https://doi.org/10.1007/s41130-016-0020-7

Apoorva, D. V, Prasad, S., and Namratha, C. (2019). Application of Altman Z Score Model on Selected Indian Companies to Predict Bankruptcy. 8(01):77–82.

Arnis, N. I., Chytis, E. T., and Kolias, G. D. (2018). Bankruptcy prediction and homogeneity of firm samples: The case of Greece. J. Account. Taxation. 10(9):110–125. https://doi.org/10.5897/jat2018.0321

Bartoloni, E. and Baussola, M. (2014). Financial performance in manufacturing firms: A comparison between parametric and non-parametric approaches. Bus. Econ. 49(1):32–45. https://doi.org/10.1057/be.2013.31

Baussola, M., Bartoloni, E., and Corbellini, A. (2015). *Business Failure Prediction in Manufacturing: A Robust Bayesian Approach to Discriminant Scoring*. Advances in Latent Variables: Methods, Models and Applications, Ed.: Carpita, Maurizio and Brentari, Eugenio and Qannari, El Mostafa, Springer International Publishing, pp. 277–285.

Cardwell, P. M., McGregor, C. C., and Synn, W. J. (2011). Bankruptcy prediction in the textile industry. Int. Bus. Eco. Res. J. 2(8):31–40. https://doi.org/10.19030/iber.v2i8.3829

Darayseh, M., Waples, E., and Tsoukalas, D. (2003). Corporate failure for manufacturing industries using firms specifics and economic environment with logit analysis. Manag. Financ. 29(8):23–36. https://doi.org/10.1108/03074350310768409

Grünberg, M. and Lukason, O. (2014). Predicting bankruptcy of manufacturing firms. Int. J. Trade, Econ. Financ. 5(1):93–97. https://doi.org/10.7763/ijtef.2014.v5.347

Herman, S. (2017). Industry specifics of joint-stock companies in Poland and theirbankruptcy prediction. *11Th Professor Aleksander Zelias International Conference on Modellingand Forecasting of Socio-Economic Phenomena*, October, 93–102.

Hughes, R. (2008). 済無No title no title. J. Chem. Inf. Model. 53(9): 287. https://doi.org/10.1017/CBO9781107415324.004

Imanzadeh, P., Maran-Jouri, M., and Sepehri, P. (2011). A study of the application of springate and zmijewski bankruptcy prediction models in firms accepted in tehran stock exchange. Aust. J. Basic appl. Sci. 5(11):1546–1550.

Karas, M. and Režňáková, M. (2017). The stability of bankruptcy predictors in the construction and manufacturing industries at various times before bankruptcy. E a M: Ekonomie a Management, 20(2):116–133. https://doi.org/10.15240/tul/001/2017-2-009

Klepáč, V. and Hampel, D. (2018). Predicting bankruptcy of manufacturing companies in EU. E a M: Ekonomie a Management. 21(1):159–174. https://doi.org/10.15240/tul/001/2018-1-011

Korol, T. (2019). Dynamic bankruptcy prediction models for European enterprises.J. Risk financ. Manag. 12(4):185. https://doi.org/10.3390/jrfm12040185

Kristóf, T. and Virág, M. (2020). A comprehensive review of corporate bankruptcy prediction in Hungary. J. Risk Financ. Manag. 13(2):35. https://doi.org/10.3390/jrfm13020035

Laurila, K. (2020). *Accuracy comparison of accounting-based bankruptcy prediction models of Springate (1978), Ohlson (1980) and Altman (2000) to US manufacturing companies 1990-2018 Master's Thesis Aalto University School of Accounting, 1978.*

Lee, M. C. (2014). Business bankruptcy prediction based on survival analysis approach. Int. J. Comput. Sci. Inf. Technol. Res. 6(2):103–119. https://doi.org/10.5121/ijcsit.2014.6207

Matturungan, N. H., Purwanto, B., and Irwanto, A. K. (2017). Manufacturing company bankruptcy prediction in Indonesia with Altman Z-score model. J. Apl. Manaj. 15(1):18–24. https://doi.org/10.18202/jam23026332.15.1.03

Meric, G., Welsh, C., Scarpa, R., & Meric, I. (2018). A comparison of the financial characteristics of European and Asian manufacturing firms Stud. Bus. Econ. 12(3):112–125. https://doi.org/10.1515/sbe-2017-0040

Murthy, B. S. R., Sravanth, K. R. S., Kethan, M., and Ravikumar, M. (2018). International Journal of Business and Management Invention (IJBMI). Predicting bankruptcy of heritage foods company by applying Altman's Z-score model. 4(12):105–107.

Neely, A. (2007). The servitization of manufacturing : An analysis of global trends: The servitization of manufacturing : Further evidence. *14th European Operations Management Association Conference*, pp. 1–10.

Prantl, S. (2003). Bankruptcy and voluntary liquidation: Evidence for new firms in East and West Germany after unification. ZEW Discussion Papers.0372:03. Retrieved from http://www.econstor.eu/handle/10419/24022

Ravid, S. A. and Sundgren, S. (1998). The comparative efficiency of small-firm bankruptcies: A study of the US and Finnish bankruptcy codes. Financ. Manag. 27(4):28. https://doi.org/10.2307/3666411

Rim, E. K. and Roy, A. B. (2014). Classifying manufacturing firms in Lebanon: An application of Altman's model.Procedia Soc Behav Sci. 109:11–18. https://doi.org/10.1016/j.sbspro.2013.12.413

Shilpa, N. C. and Amulya, M. (2017). Corporate financial distress: Analysis of Indian automobile industry. SDMIMD J. Manage. 8(1):85. https://doi.org/10.18311/sdmimd/2017/15726

Singh, B. P. and Mishra, A. (2019). Sensitivity of bankruptcy prediction models to the change in econometric methods.J. Theor. Appl. Econ. , 26(3):71–86.

Venkataramana, N., Azash, S. M., & Ramakrishnaiah, K. (2012). Financial performance and predicting the risk of bankruptcy: A case of selected cement companies in India. Int.J. Pub. Admin. Manag. Res. 1(1): 40–56. Retrieved from www.rcmss.org/ijpamr/Vol.1/No.1/.pdf

Annexure

S.No	Title
1	A model for bankruptcy prediction: Calibration of Altman's score for Japan
2	A study of the application of Springate and Zmijewski bankruptcy prediction models in firms accepted in Tehran stock Exchange
3	A comparison of the financial characteristics of European and Asian manufacturing firms
4	A study of efficacy of Altman's Z Score to predict bankruptcy of speciality retail firms doing business in contemporary times
5	Accuracy comparison of accounting-based bankruptcy prediction models of Springate (1978), Ohlson (1980), and Altman (2000) to US manufacturing companies 1990–2018
6	Analysis of bankruptcy prediction models and their effectiveness: An Indian perspective
7	Applicability of financial distress prediction models to Sri Lankan manufacturing firms
8	Application of Altman Z Score model on selected Indian companies to predict bankruptcy
9	Applying emerging market score model to predict bankruptcy in Thailand stock Exchange
10	Assessment of the practical application of corporate bankruptcy prediction model
11	A statistical model for financial risk bankruptcy applied for Romanian manufacturing industry
12	Bankruptcy and voluntary liquefaction: Evidence from new firms in East and West Germany after unification
13	Bankruptcy prediction of manufacturing companies listed in Indonesia
14	Bankruptcy prediction and homogeneity of firm samples: The case of Greece – Journal of Accounting and Taxation
15	Bankruptcy prediction in the construction industry: Financial ratio analysis
16	Bankruptcy prediction in textile industry
17	Business failure prediction in manufacturing: A Robust Bayesian approach to Discriminant scoring
18	Business bankruptcy prediction based on survival analysis approach
19	Classifying manufacturing firms in Lebanon: An application of Altman Z Score
20	A comparative efficiency of small firm bankruptcies: A study of US and Finnish Bankruptcy codes
21	Comprehensive review of corporate bankruptcy prediction in Hungary
22	Corporate failure of manufacturing industries using firm specifics and economic environment with logit analysis
23	Corporate financial distress: Analysis of Indian automobile industry
24	Determinants of financial distress among manufacturing companies in Malaysia
25	Dynamic bankruptcy prediction models for European enterprises
26	Economic and financial determinants of firm bankruptcy in French food industry

S.No	Title
27	Effects of bankruptcy procedures on firm restructuring evidence from Italy
28	Examine the influence of service additions on manufacturing firm's bankruptcy likelihood
29	Explanatory and predictive values of the drivers of corporate bankruptcy
30	Financial performance and predicting the risk of bankruptcy – A case of selected cement companies in India
31	Financial performance in manufacturing firms: A comparison between parametric and non-parametric approaches
32	Industry specifics of Joint stock companies in Poland and their bankruptcy
33	Manufacturing company bankruptcy prediction in Indonesia
34	Predicting bankruptcy of certain firms by applying Altman Z Score
35	Predicting bankruptcy of firms in Colombo stock exchange
36	Predicting bankruptcy of manufacturing firms
37	Predicting financial distress of revisiting z-score and zeta models
38	Predicting bankruptcy of manufacturing companies in EU
39	Sensitivity of bankruptcy prediction model due to change in econometric systems
40	Predicting corporate bankruptcy and earnings manipulation using Altman Z Score and Beneish M Score: The case of manufacturing firms in Zimbabwe
41	The servitisation of manufacturing: An analysis of global trends
42	The stability of bankruptcy prediction in the construction industry
43	On unbalanced sampling in bankruptcy prediction

Results 2019

Company Name	Zmijewski model	Interpretation	Altman z score	Interpretation
A C C Ltd.	0.989922267	Safe	1.731730516	High chance- bankruptcy
A Infrastructure Ltd.	1.230525207	Safe	2.186897154	In 2 years
A K Lumbers Ltd.	1.371076452	Safe	2.348251436	In 2 years
A R L Infratech Ltd.	0.828146565	Safe	3.140187358	Safe
Aakaash Manufacturing Co. Pvt. Ltd.	0.822122158	Safe	3.177877122	Safe
Acer Granito Pvt. Ltd.	1.297024464	Safe	2.463369337	In 2 years
Acrysil Ltd.	1.195530124	Safe	1.495733111	High chance- bankruptcy
Adhunik Cement Ltd.	1.920362801	Safe	0.723412093	High chance- bankruptcy
Ador Ceramics Pvt. Ltd.	1.308995661	Safe	3.376403823	Safe
Akash Ceramics Pvt. Ltd.	1.439685108	Safe	1.75316128	High chance- bankruptcy
Akzo Nobel India Ltd.	1.14123306	Safe	1.502480543	High chance- bankruptcy
Amazon Wood Pvt. Ltd.	1.262094036	Safe	2.238099137	In 2 years
Amazoone Ceramics Ltd.	1.102018387	Safe	1.752362846	High chance- bankruptcy
Ambuja Cements Ltd.	1.145599805	Safe	0.932321972	High chance- bankruptcy
Amora Tiles Pvt. Ltd.	1.640613791	Safe	2.400334928	In 2 years
Andhra Cements Ltd.	2.076030076	Safe	0.082811179	High chance- bankruptcy
Anjani Portland Cement Ltd.	1.128120124	Safe	2.112886557	In 2 years
Anjani Tiles Ltd.	1.210512048	Safe	1.451208808	High chance- bankruptcy
Antique Marbonite Pvt. Ltd.	1.320591893	Safe	1.475448919	High chance- bankruptcy
Aparna Enterprises Ltd.	1.447598604	Safe	1.397567514	High chance- bankruptcy
Archidply Decor Ltd.	1.573145587	Safe	0.590962561	High chance- bankruptcy
Archidply Industries Ltd.	1.234968655	Safe	2.742705419	Alert
Aro Granite Inds. Ltd.	1.279878679	Safe	1.370872576	High chance- bankruptcy
Aryan Enterprises Pvt. Ltd.	1.160178101	Safe	3.046983051	Safe
Ashok Granites Ltd.	1.393035783	Safe	1.935146018	In 2 years
Asian Paints Indl. Coatings Ltd.	1.496621341	Safe	2.49200816	In 2 years
Barak Valley Cements Ltd.	1.336951888	Safe	1.159802124	High chance- bankruptcy
Berger Paints India Ltd.	1.034470242	Safe	1.70465177	High chance- bankruptcy
C I C O Technologies Ltd.	1.3770951	Safe	1.283110531	High chance- bankruptcy
Calcom Cement India Ltd.	0.822242161	Safe	1.553342755	High chance- bankruptcy
Carborundum Universal Ltd.	0.930369663	Safe	2.077001038	In 2 years
Century Plyboards (India) Ltd.	1.010228007	Safe	2.230717645	In 2 years
Darshan Boardlam Ltd.	1.346111915	Safe	1.91103654	In 2 years
Deccan Cements Ltd.	1.07780935	Safe	2.0808367	In 2 years
Ecoboard Industries Ltd.	1.853933288	Safe	0.508780828	High chance- bankruptcy
Elantas Beck India Ltd.	0.716477988	Safe	2.248653374	In 2 years
Everest Industries Ltd.	1.138610909	Safe	2.173705937	In 2 years
Graphite India Ltd.	-0.69469386	High chance- bankruptcy	2.692064699	In 2 years
Greenlam Industries Ltd.	1.077336795	Safe	2.362534254	In 2 years
Greenpanel Industries Ltd.	1.270920524	Safe	0.688817976	High chance- bankruptcy
Greenply Industries Ltd.	1.121848332	Safe	2.302013156	In 2 years
Grindwell Norton Ltd.	0.90257333	Safe	1.914878067	In 2 years
Gujarat Sidhee Cement Ltd.	1.448507563	Safe	1.240880487	High chance- bankruptcy
H E G Ltd.	-1.287548914	High chance- bankruptcy	3.302120911	Safe
Heidelberg Cement India Ltd.	1.062102573	Safe	1.295011525	High chance- bankruptcy
Himadri Speciality Chemical Ltd.	0.96435738	Safe	1.485962772	High chance- bankruptcy
I F G L Refractories Ltd.	1.237552055	Safe	1.361163579	High chance- bankruptcy
Inani Marbles & Inds. Ltd.	1.355438035	Safe	1.379907063	High chance- bankruptcy
India Cements Ltd.	1.376680961	Safe	1.082909166	High chance- bankruptcy
J K Cement Ltd.	1.208205435	Safe	1.456535852	High chance- bankruptcy
J K Lakshmi Cement Ltd.	1.329170967	Safe	1.410368577	High chance- bankruptcy
J S W Cement Ltd.	1.308526383	Safe	0.903734507	High chance- bankruptcy
K C P Ltd.	1.280128491	Safe	1.412339225	High chance- bankruptcy
Kajaria Ceramics Ltd.	0.873188259	Safe	2.186487627	In 2 years
Kakatiya Cement Sugar & Inds. Ltd.	1.343181031	Safe	0.814887307	High chance- bankruptcy
Kesoram Industries Ltd.	1.600796318	Safe	0.788981929	High chance- bankruptcy
Lexus Granito (India) Ltd.	1.397659246	Safe	1.829946096	In 2 years
Madhav Marbles & Granites Ltd.	1.2897022	Safe	1.107779902	High chance- bankruptcy
Madhucon Granites Ltd.	1.361963747	Safe	0.763209146	High chance- bankruptcy
Maithan Ceramic Ltd.	1.117659498	Safe	1.714350797	High chance- bankruptcy
Mangalam Cement Ltd.	1.431825212	Safe	1.26765292	High chance- bankruptcy
Mangalam Timber Products Ltd.	1.980456205	Safe	0.352053314	High chance- bankruptcy
Milestone Global Ltd.	1.360481588	Safe	1.991389432	In 2 years
Murudeshwar Ceramics Ltd.	1.362000302	Safe	1.224538768	High chance- bankruptcy
N C L Industries Ltd.	1.213981321	Safe	1.538091155	High chance- bankruptcy
Navkar Builders Ltd.	1.47040953	Safe	1.125030189	High chance- bankruptcy
Nexion International Pvt. Ltd.	1.606100777	Safe	0.952656985	High chance- bankruptcy
Nihon Parkerizing (India) Pvt. Ltd.	1.140017374	Safe	1.700512529	High chance- bankruptcy

Company Name	Zmijewski	Interpretation	Altman z score	Interpretation
Nitco Ltd.	1.574700062	Safe	1.010817734	High chance- bankruptcy
O C L India Ltd. [Merged]	1.156414914	Safe	1.534378785	High chance- bankruptcy
Orient Abrasives Ltd.	1.215326811	Safe	2.010852201	In 2 years
Orient Bell Ltd.	1.319869908	Safe	2.255836633	In 2 years
Orient Cement Ltd.	1.337158854	Safe	1.491810988	High chance- bankruptcy
Pacific Industries Ltd.	1.378558468	Safe	1.293140649	High chance- bankruptcy
Patil Rail Infrastructure Pvt. Ltd.	1.20111645	Safe	1.895877504	In 2 years
Pokarna Ltd.	1.270587699	Safe	1.273854135	High chance- bankruptcy
Prism Johnson Ltd.	1.262576509	Safe	2.105163597	In 2 years
Rain Cements Ltd.	1.283399864	Safe	1.518092612	High chance- bankruptcy
Ramco Cements Ltd.	1.130375145	Safe	1.254116029	High chance- bankruptcy
Ramco Industries Ltd.	1.126637607	Safe	1.563805005	High chance- bankruptcy
Ravileela Granites Ltd.	1.250122917	Safe	1.731937836	High chance- bankruptcy
Rushil Decor Ltd.	1.29373416	Safe	1.146519591	High chance- bankruptcy
Sagar Cements (R) Ltd.	1.479908124	Safe	0.90989437	High chance- bankruptcy
Sagar Cements Ltd.	1.329524697	Safe	1.011843344	High chance- bankruptcy
Sahyadri Industries Ltd.	0.901683483	Safe	2.153455306	In 2 years
Sanghi Industries Ltd.	1.320257755	Safe	1.259546425	High chance- bankruptcy
Saurashtra Cement Ltd.	1.437391098	Safe	1.627581508	High chance- bankruptcy
Shalimar Paints Ltd.	1.964172801	Safe	0.478275804	High chance- bankruptcy
Shree Cement Ltd.	1.126551642	Safe	2.19494889	In 2 years
Shree Digvijay Cement Co. Ltd.	1.380325422	Safe	1.684722215	High chance- bankruptcy
Somany Fine Vitrified Pvt. Ltd.	1.307340403	Safe	2.396716693	In 2 years
Somany Fine Vitrified Pvt. Ltd.	1.307340403	Safe	2.396716693	In 2 years
Srichakra Cements Ltd.	1.537215643	Safe	2.083866321	In 2 years
Star Cement Ltd.	0.730007732	Safe	1.883554138	In 2 years
Star Cement Meghalaya Ltd.	1.052405394	Safe	2.59677961	In 2 years
Ultratech Cement Ltd.	1.251595073	Safe	1.108944209	High chance- bankruptcy
Ultratech Nathdwara Cement Ltd.	1.712679726	Safe	0.521739898	High chance- bankruptcy
Umiya Wood Works Pvt. Ltd.	1.346565432	Safe	2.520417881	In 2 years
Uniply Decor Ltd.	1.367998361	Safe	0.559702689	High chance- bankruptcy
Vintage Tiles Pvt. Ltd.	1.552214761	Safe	1.803384233	In 2 years
Visaka Industries Ltd.	1.081187931	Safe	2.166121435	In 2 years
Welspun Wasco Coatings Pvt. Ltd.	2.153360679	Safe	0.030643642	High chance- bankruptcy
Western India Plywoods Ltd.	1.298053431	Safe	2.253828876	In 2 years
Zigma Paints Pvt. Ltd.	1.302442505	Safe	2.969590909	Alert
Zuari Cement Ltd.	1.326816436	Safe	1.087182485	High chance- bankruptcy

2020

Company Name	Zmijewski	Interpretation	Altman z score	Interpretation
A C C Ltd.	1.056234591	Safe	1.622139076	High chance- bankruptcy
A Infrastructure Ltd.	1.328635513	Safe	2.100469466	In 2 years
A K Lumbers Ltd.	1.367938469	Safe	2.423121001	In 2 years
A R L Infratech Ltd.	0.742452038	Safe	3.392451791	Safe
Aakaash Manufacturing Co. Pvt. Ltd.	1.255512044	Safe	2.206088221	In 2 years
Acer Granito Pvt. Ltd.	1.310666611	Safe	2.834928596	Alert
Acrysil Ltd.	1.193377147	Safe	1.544500037	High chance- bankruptcy
Adhunik Cement Ltd.	1.793209221	Safe	1.044024063	High chance- bankruptcy
Ador Ceramics Pvt. Ltd.	1.296560036	Safe	2.949099277	Alert
Akash Ceramics Pvt. Ltd.	1.733595024	Safe	1.582002736	High chance- bankruptcy
Akzo Nobel India Ltd.	1.127155302	Safe	1.420242956	High chance- bankruptcy
Amazon Wood Pvt. Ltd.	1.207260507	Safe	2.514765282	In 2 years
Amazoone Ceramics Ltd.	1.198483954	Safe	1.477662869	High chance- bankruptcy
Ambuja Cements Ltd.	1.156069329	Safe	0.95056082	High chance- bankruptcy
Amora Tiles Pvt. Ltd.	1.458668887	Safe	2.584519207	In 2 years
Andhra Cements Ltd.	2.049947979	Safe	0.009985848	High chance- bankruptcy
Anjani Portland Cement Ltd.	0.950807047	Safe	2.229754239	In 2 years
Anjani Tiles Ltd.	1.403672568	Safe	1.102729922	High chance- bankruptcy
Antique Marbonite Pvt. Ltd.	1.266828032	Safe	1.646770361	High chance- bankruptcy
Aparna Enterprises Ltd.	1.304562169	Safe	2.037368752	In 2 years
Archidply Decor Ltd.	1.467710447	Safe	1.513071676	High chance- bankruptcy
Archidply Industries Ltd.	1.31848378	Safe	2.52193445	In 2 years

Aro Granite Inds. Ltd.	1.364090403	Safe	1.154078841	High chance- bankruptcy
Aryan Enterprises Pvt. Ltd.	1.176600334	Safe	3.745507246	Safe
Ashok Granites Ltd.	1.390000933	Safe	1.747756196	High chance- bankruptcy
Asian Paints Indl. Coatings Ltd.	1.411038411	Safe	2.989759435	Alert
Barak Valley Cements Ltd.	1.317810894	Safe	1.145095204	High chance- bankruptcy
Berger Paints India Ltd.	0.864151943	Safe	1.773983923	High chance- bankruptcy
C I C O Technologies Ltd.	1.362923218	Safe	2.059056911	In 2 years
Calcom Cement India Ltd.	1.102910484	Safe	1.24428503	High chance- bankruptcy
Carborundum Universal Ltd.	0.87610394	Safe	2.048282461	In 2 years
Century Plyboards (India) Ltd.	0.981467473	Safe	2.440808421	In 2 years
Darshan Boardlam Ltd.	1.329859015	Safe	2.219366838	In 2 years
Deccan Cements Ltd.	1.048825575	Safe	1.741059549	High chance- bankruptcy
Ecoboard Industries Ltd.	0.383105067	Safe	1.933476097	In 2 years
Elantas Beck India Ltd.	0.940814904	Safe	1.875538843	In 2 years
Everest Industries Ltd.	1.344859459	Safe	1.982236726	In 2 years
Graphite India Ltd.	1.390571167	Safe	0.950805106	High chance- bankruptcy
Greenlam Industries Ltd.	1.005704039	Safe	2.259971022	In 2 years
Greenpanel Industries Ltd.	1.35578243	Safe	0.914063131	High chance- bankruptcy
Greenply Industries Ltd.	1.261248381	Safe	2.001693452	In 2 years
Grindwell Norton Ltd.	0.894137238	Safe	1.872825331	In 2 years
Gujarat Sidhee Cement Ltd.	1.134458748	Safe	1.550753022	High chance- bankruptcy
H E G Ltd.	1.355193302	Safe	1.002699334	High chance- bankruptcy
Heidelberg Cement India Ltd.	0.995539818	Safe	1.362084955	High chance- bankruptcy
Himadri Speciality Chemical Ltd.	1.280125654	Safe	1.101650087	High chance- bankruptcy
I F G L Refractories Ltd.	1.213673715	Safe	1.411937261	High chance- bankruptcy
Inani Marbles & Inds. Ltd.	1.422691162	Safe	1.174770142	High chance- bankruptcy
India Cements Ltd.	1.41655134	Safe	0.996404507	High chance- bankruptcy
J K Cement Ltd.	1.191030869	Safe	1.388521811	High chance- bankruptcy
J K Lakshmi Cement Ltd.	1.190288465	Safe	1.51010001	High chance- bankruptcy
J S W Cement Ltd.	1.296573822	Safe	1.01766907	High chance- bankruptcy
K C P Ltd.	1.424451598	Safe	1.296278075	High chance- bankruptcy
Kajaria Ceramics Ltd.	0.84298603	Safe	2.071615325	In 2 years
Kakatiya Cement Sugar & Inds. Ltd.	1.422882577	Safe	0.951126189	High chance- bankruptcy
Kesoram Industries Ltd.	1.980581661	Safe	0.587987694	High chance- bankruptcy
Lexus Granito (India) Ltd.	1.451323032	Safe	1.598744108	High chance- bankruptcy
Madhav Marbles & Granites Ltd.	1.363489517	Safe	0.957379223	High chance- bankruptcy
Madhucon Granites Ltd.	1.389319733	Safe	0.783177263	High chance- bankruptcy
Maithan Ceramic Ltd.	0.985434937	Safe	2.962456425	Alert
Mangalam Cement Ltd.	1.208001708	Safe	1.387434323	High chance- bankruptcy
Mangalam Timber Products Ltd.	1.947454727	Safe	0.302244393	High chance- bankruptcy
Milestone Global Ltd.	1.358789926	Safe	2.018440367	In 2 years
Murudeshwar Ceramics Ltd.	1.389513487	Safe	1.289021231	High chance- bankruptcy
N C L Industries Ltd.	1.205962655	Safe	1.474186127	High chance- bankruptcy
Navkar Builders Ltd.	1.276290132	Safe	1.339481615	High chance- bankruptcy
Nexion International Pvt. Ltd.	1.34560828	Safe	1.399041932	High chance- bankruptcy
Nihon Parkerizing (India) Pvt. Ltd.	1.158275552	Safe	1.81203044	In 2 years
Nitco Ltd.	1.672257795	Safe	1.225712904	High chance- bankruptcy
O C L India Ltd. [Merged]	1.054512724	Safe	1.557121702	High chance- bankruptcy
Orient Abrasives Ltd.	1.154743005	Safe	2.108864782	In 2 years
Orient Bell Ltd.	1.33379283	Safe	2.166581708	In 2 years
Orient Cement Ltd.	1.281245152	Safe	1.591847297	High chance- bankruptcy
Pacific Industries Ltd.	1.406300863	Safe	1.123111381	High chance- bankruptcy
Patil Rail Infrastructure Pvt. Ltd.	1.288055655	Safe	1.987332895	In 2 years
Pokarna Ltd.	1.503969991	Safe	0.826045182	High chance- bankruptcy
Prism Johnson Ltd.	1.355463218	Safe	1.761360205	High chance- bankruptcy
Rain Cements Ltd.	1.010109777	Safe	1.924921699	In 2 years
Ramco Cements Ltd.	1.139368684	Safe	1.089126242	High chance- bankruptcy
Ramco Industries Ltd.	1.181313337	Safe	1.368323754	High chance- bankruptcy
Ravileela Granites Ltd.	1.378671757	Safe	0.99653206	High chance- bankruptcy
Rushil Decor Ltd.	1.272729192	Safe	0.89332367	High chance- bankruptcy
Sagar Cements (R) Ltd.	1.438078302	Safe	1.146445349	High chance- bankruptcy
Sagar Cements Ltd.	1.316909418	Safe	0.887263455	High chance- bankruptcy
Sahyadri Industries Ltd.	1.031056306	Safe	1.831250238	In 2 years
Sanghi Industries Ltd.	1.317102715	Safe	1.098047153	High chance- bankruptcy

Saurashtra Cement Ltd.	1.060638866	Safe	2.235958054	In 2 years
Shalimar Paints Ltd.	1.682753605	Safe	0.915165284	High chance- bankruptcy
Shree Cement Ltd.	1.043919494	Safe	1.864511113	In 2 years
Shree Digvijay Cement Co. Ltd.	0.803881984	Safe	2.27540349	In 2 years
Somany Fine Vitrified Pvt. Ltd.	1.321644645	Safe	2.370750693	In 2 years
Srichakra Cements Ltd.	1.673274048	Safe	1.263569862	High chance- bankruptcy
Star Cement Ltd.	0.818927068	Safe	1.810563291	In 2 years
Star Cement Meghalaya Ltd.	1.060662801	Safe	2.683422841	In 2 years
Ultratech Cement Ltd.	1.069946044	Safe	1.28719404	High chance- bankruptcy
Ultratech Nathdwara Cement Ltd.	9.880963549	Safe	-7.512566953	High chance- bankruptcy
Umiya Wood Works Pvt. Ltd.	1.339473412	Safe	2.502398778	In 2 years
Uniply Decor Ltd.	1.295226352	Safe	0.856557789	High chance- bankruptcy
Vintage Tiles Pvt. Ltd.	1.354043869	Safe	2.517457334	In 2 years
Visaka Industries Ltd.	1.172694755	Safe	2.058948487	In 2 years
Welspun Wasco Coatings Pvt. Ltd.	3.593492736	Safe	-1.703121718	High chance- bankruptcy
Western India Plywoods Ltd.	1.318827597	Safe	2.203064316	In 2 years
Zigma Paints Pvt. Ltd.	1.283003166	Safe	3.265869074	Safe
Zuari Cement Ltd.	1.288309517	Safe	1.161170011	High chance- bankruptcy

Hypothesis testing

	2020			
Company Name	Zmijewski	Altman z score	Difference	Sign
Pokarna Ltd.	1.056235	1.622139076	-0.5659	-
Inani Marbles & Inds. Ltd.	1.328636	2.100469466	-0.77183	-
Aparna Enterprises Ltd.	1.367938	2.423121001	-1.05518	-
Sanghi Industries Ltd.	0.742452	3.392451791	-2.65	-
J K Lakshmi Cement Ltd.	1.255512	2.206088221	-0.95058	-
Pacific Industries Ltd.	1.310667	2.834928596	-1.52426	-
Aro Granite Inds. Ltd.	1.193377	1.544500037	-0.35112	-
C I C O Technologies Ltd.	1.793209	1.044024063	0.749185	+
I F G L Refractories Ltd.	1.29656	2.949099277	-1.65254	-
Ramco Cements Ltd.	1.733595	1.582002736	0.151592	+
K C P Ltd.	1.127155	1.420242956	-0.29309	-
Murudeshwar Ceramics Ltd.	1.207261	2.514765282	-1.3075	-
Ultratech Cement Ltd.	1.198484	1.477662869	-0.27918	-
Rushil Decor Ltd.	1.156069	0.95056082	0.205509	+
Orient Cement Ltd.	1.458669	2.584519207	-1.12585	-
Antique Marbonite Pvt. Ltd.	2.049948	0.009985848	2.039962	+
Mangalam Cement Ltd.	0.950807	2.229754239	-1.27895	-
Barak Valley Cements Ltd.	1.403673	1.102729922	0.300943	+
Madhav Marbles & Granites Ltd.	1.266828	1.646770361	-0.37994	-
Saurashtra Cement Ltd.	1.304562	2.037368752	-0.73281	-
Gujarat Sidhee Cement Ltd.	1.46771	1.513071676	-0.04536	-

Ambuja Cements Ltd.	1.318484	2.52193445	-1.20345	-
Heidelberg Cement India Ltd.	1.36409	1.154078841	0.210012	+
Rain Cements Ltd.	1.1766	3.745507246	-2.56891	-
Zuari Cement Ltd.	1.390001	1.747756196	-0.35776	-
Anjani Tiles Ltd.	1.411038	2.989759435	-1.57872	-
J K Cement Ltd.	1.317811	1.145095204	0.172716	+
Vintage Tiles Pvt. Ltd.	0.864152	1.773983923	-0.90983	-
India Cements Ltd.	1.362923	2.059056911	-0.69613	-
Acrysil Ltd.	1.10291	1.24428503	-0.14137	-
Shree Digvijay Cement Co. Ltd.	0.876104	2.048282461	-1.17218	-
Akash Ceramics Pvt. Ltd.	0.981467	2.440808421	-1.45934	-
Sagar Cements Ltd.	1.329859	2.219366838	-0.88951	-
N C L Industries Ltd.	1.048826	1.741059549	-0.69223	-
Navkar Builders Ltd.	0.383105	1.933476097	-1.55037	-
Akzo Nobel India Ltd.	0.940815	1.875538843	-0.93472	-
O C L India Ltd. [Merged]	1.344859	1.982236726	-0.63738	-
J S W Cement Ltd.	1.390571	0.950805106	0.439766	+
Lexus Granito (India) Ltd.	1.005704	2.259971022	-1.25427	-
Ramco Industries Ltd.	1.355782	0.914063131	0.441719	+
Ravileela Granites Ltd.	1.261248	2.001693452	-0.74045	-
Himadri Speciality Chemical Ltd.	0.894137	1.872825331	-0.97869	-
Kakatiya Cement Sugar & Inds. Ltd.	1.134459	1.550753022	-0.41629	-
Ashok Granites Ltd.	1.355193	1.002699334	0.352494	+
Srichakra Cements Ltd.	0.99554	1.362084955	-0.36655	-
Nihon Parkerizing (India) Pvt. Ltd.	1.280126	1.101650087	0.178476	+
Nitco Ltd.	1.213674	1.411937261	-0.19826	-
Darshan Boardlam Ltd.	1.422691	1.174770142	0.247921	+
Sagar Cements (R) Ltd.	1.416551	0.996404507	0.420147	+
Greenpanel Industries Ltd.	1.191031	1.388521811	-0.19749	-
Maithan Ceramic Ltd.	1.190288	1.51010001	-0.31981	-
Madhucon Granites Ltd.	1.296574	1.01766907	0.278905	+
Milestone Global Ltd.	1.424452	1.296278075	0.128174	+
Amazoone Ceramics Ltd.	0.842986	2.071615325	-1.22863	-
Nexion International Pvt. Ltd.	1.422883	0.951126189	0.471756	+
Berger Paints India Ltd.	1.980582	0.587987694	1.392594	+
Patil Rail Infrastructure Pvt. Ltd.	1.451323	1.598744108	-0.14742	-
Calcom Cement India Ltd.	1.36349	0.957379223	0.40611	+
A C C Ltd.	1.38932	0.783177263	0.606142	+
Amora Tiles Pvt. Ltd.	0.985435	2.962456425	-1.97702	-
Orient Abrasives Ltd.	1.208002	1.387434323	-0.17943	-
Uniply Decor Ltd.	1.947455	0.302244393	1.64521	+

Kesoram Industries Ltd.	1.35879	2.018440367	-0.65965	-
Prism Johnson Ltd.	1.389513	1.289021231	0.100492	+
Orient Bell Ltd.	1.205963	1.474186127	-0.26822	-
Western India Plywoods Ltd.	1.27629	1.339481615	-0.06319	-
A Infrastructure Ltd.	1.345608	1.399041932	-0.05343	-
Amazon Wood Pvt. Ltd.	1.158276	1.81203044	-0.65375	-
A K Lumbers Ltd.	1.672258	1.225712904	0.446545	+
Archidply Decor Ltd.	1.054513	1.557121702	-0.50261	-
Anjani Portland Cement Ltd.	1.154743	2.108864782	-0.95412	-
Asian Paints Indl. Coatings Ltd.	1.333793	2.166581708	-0.83279	-
Deccan Cements Ltd.	1.281245	1.591847297	-0.3106	-
Grindwell Norton Ltd.	1.406301	1.123111381	0.283189	+
Everest Industries Ltd.	1.288056	1.987332895	-0.69928	-
Shree Cement Ltd.	1.50397	0.826045182	0.677925	+
Visaka Industries Ltd.	1.355463	1.761360205	-0.4059	-
Somany Fine Vitrified Pvt. Ltd.	1.01011	1.924921699	-0.91481	-
Carborundum Universal Ltd.	1.139369	1.089126242	0.050242	+
Star Cement Ltd.	1.181313	1.368323754	-0.18701	-
Acer Granito Pvt. Ltd.	1.378672	0.99653206	0.38214	+
Umiya Wood Works Pvt. Ltd.	1.272729	0.89332367	0.379406	+
Greenply Industries Ltd.	1.438078	1.146445349	0.291633	+
Ultratech Nathdwara Cement Ltd.	1.316909	0.887263455	0.429646	+
Adhunik Cement Ltd.	1.031056	1.831250238	-0.80019	-
Century Plyboards (India) Ltd.	1.317103	1.098047153	0.219056	+
Sahyadri Industries Ltd.	1.060639	2.235958054	-1.17532	-
Greenlam Industries Ltd.	1.682754	0.915165284	0.767588	+
Kajaria Ceramics Ltd.	1.043919	1.864511113	-0.82059	-
Ecoboard Industries Ltd.	0.803882	2.27540349	-1.47152	-
Shalimar Paints Ltd.	1.321645	2.370750693	-1.04911	-
Archidply Industries Ltd.	1.673274	1.263569862	0.409704	+
Elantas Beck India Ltd.	0.818927	1.810563291	-0.99164	-
Star Cement Meghalaya Ltd.	1.060663	2.683422841	-1.62276	-
Mangalam Timber Products Ltd.	1.069946	1.28719404	-0.21725	-
Zigma Paints Pvt. Ltd.	9.880964	-7.512566953	17.39353	+
Aryan Enterprises Pvt. Ltd.	1.339473	2.502398778	-1.16293	-
Andhra Cements Ltd.	1.295226	0.856557789	0.438669	+
Ador Ceramics Pvt. Ltd.	1.354044	2.517457334	-1.16341	-
Welspun Wasco Coatings Pvt. Ltd.	1.172695	2.058948487	-0.88625	-
A R L Infratech Ltd.	3.593493	-1.703121718	5.296614	+
Aakaash Manufacturing Co. Pvt. Ltd.	1.318828	2.203064316	-0.88424	-
Graphite India Ltd.	1.283003	3.265869074	-1.98287	-
H E G Ltd.	1.28831	1.161170011	0.12714	+

Sum of negative ranks	3327
Sum of positive ranks	2133
	5460
Smaller	2133
Mean	2730
	95095
Sigma	308.3748
z score	−1.93596
z value from z table	0.0268

10 Impact of ESG on financial performance: An Indian perspective

Vidhi S[1] and Joseph Durai Selvam[2]

[1]Student, School of Business and Management, CHRIST (Deemed to be University), Bengaluru, India

[2]Associate Professor, School of Business and Management, CHRIST (Deemed to be University), Bengaluru, India

Abstract

The research tries to find a link between environmental, social, and governance (ESG) performance and financial performance in the Indian context. Research on the topic of ESG in India has been chiefly from an investor perspective. This research tries to shift the focus and start a conversation about looking at ESG from a company perspective. The impact on financial performance is measured in two different ways accounting- based financial performance and market-based financial performance. Return on Assets was taken as a variable for the accounting-based measure, and Tobin's Q was used for the market-based measure. A correlation and regression analysis helped in determining the link between the variables under study. The research will help in creating awareness among Indian companies about the interdependence of ESG and financial performance to increase the shareholders' value.

Keywords: ESG India, ESG performance, financial performance, shareholder value

Introduction

Environmental, social and governance (ESG) is a non-financial factor which is gaining attraction among the investors for some time now. Investors around the world are increasingly looking into this performance criterion to take investment decisions in the market. This has especially become a source for a new product in the mutual funds world. It is said that if a company doesn't work on its ESG factors it might pose a threat to its financial performance in the long run. This non-financial factor is supposed to have long term financial implications and thus, this paper tries to find the impact of ESG on the financial performance of the company.

ESG investing is also referred to as sustainable investing and responsible investing practices.

Review of Literature

This paper evaluates the impact of environmental, social and governance performance as a whole and individually, on the financial performance of companies (Velte, P. 2017). Post the financial crisis, the European Commission wanted companies to take governance and sustainability factors more seriously and think about the long term effects of every strategic decision that they were taking. The commission also claimed that a better environment, social and governance performance of the companies would impact their financial performance. This paper largely tries to validate this statement. The author undertakes this study by selecting companies listed on the German Prime Standard for the years 2010–2014. To measure the financial performance of the companies' two variables were considered: Accounting based – return on assets and market based-Tobin's Q. A correlation and regression analysis was carried out to evaluate the link between these variables. It was concluded that there was a positive relationship between ESG and ROA but there was no significant impact of ESG on Tobin's Q. Further, it was found that the impact on financial performance was stronger by the governance performance of the company.

The authors examine the impact of considering ESG while allocation of an equity portfolio (Spiegeleer et al., 2021). To measure the ESG performance of the companies' two different variables were considered. One variable was the ESG rating and the other variable was the GHG emission intensity. The study was performed with companies in both STOXX Europe 600 and the companies in the Russell 1000 index. Two strategies were considered green strategy and the brown strategy. The brown strategy referred to the portfolio strategy of assigning more weight to poor ESG companies, while the green strategy was the portfolio strategy to assign more weights to companies that have a higher ESG score. The returns of both the portfolio strategies were calculated for the years December 2009 to December 2019. It was found that the brown strategy generated larger returns in the first few years of the period under study and the green strategy generated better returns in the later years of the study. It was also concluded that the green strategy was much more profitable and less risky in the STOXX Europe 600 companies while it was the opposite in the Russell 1000 companies. It was also concluded in the study that shifting to low GHG emission intensity did not add to the companies' investment risk and also did not invite any losses for the investors, either.

Higher risk means high volatility is the conventional dialogue (Ashwin Kumar et al., 2016). The author tries to go against the conventional statement and prove that less risk can also lead to higher return. To prove this statement, he shows that ESG companies show lower volatility in stock performance against their peers in the same industries. The study also proves that the ESG companies generate higher returns. The gap that is addressed in the study was the ESG risk factor. All the studies during that period were related to the financial performance of sustainable investments. To undertake the study 157 companies from the DJSI and 809 randomly selected companies were considered. These companies were divided into twelve different industries. After analysis it was found that the ESG listed companies showed lower stock return volatility when compared to the other randomly selected companies. Each industry was affected by the ESG factors at different levels of intensity. The author also proved that ESG companies have low risk but they are able to generate higher returns. Only a few industries in the study, Automobiles, Durables, and Banks, showed that the ESG factor did not have high intensity as both the ESG companies and the randomly selected industries were performing almost similarly.

Sustainability has been valued more than ever, especially after the Covid-19 (Ferriani & Filippo Natoli, 2020). The way to look at ESG has also shifted after the Morningstar's ESG risk ratings first published in the year 2019. The study conducts a regression analysis and finds whether the scores could tell anything about the various different fund flows during January 2020 to May 2020. The study analyses whether investors consider the ESG risk during the shock time. The regression model results showed that there has been a significant impact of the ESG risk score during the Covid-19 crisis. Since the crash during February 2020, more and more investors are willing to deal with stocks of companies who have a lower ESG risk. Under the ESG factors, more preference seemed to be given to the governance and environment risk of the company. The author tells us that during the crisis period investors usually prefer to invest in sustainable stocks; this was proved by stating the results of Nofsinger and Varma (2014), who showed investor preference towards sustainable assets during the great financial crisis.

The exploratory research sheds light upon the investor perceptions towards ESG criteria for investing in the emerging economy of Tunisia (Khemir, 2019). Tunisia is a very small developing economy in North Africa, the research on ESG criteria up until then were conducted usually in developed nations, this research gives a viewpoint of the investors of a developing nation. The research data collection was from primary sources – the investors. The data collection method was focus groups and semi structured interviews with finance professionals. The finance professionals included 19 financial analysts and 4 portfolio managers. The study concluded that the ESG criterion is not the top most criterion that is considered while planning to invest in any company. The foremost criterion is the financials of the company, and the second criterion is the ESG criteria. Further, it was also found that the importance to ESG elements is ranked in the order, first of all corporate governance, second of all social criteria and third of all the environment criteria. From the interview conducted the author concluded that ESG criteria is something the investors look into before taking the final decision but it only supports their decision, it is never a primary determinant to take an investment decision.

Research Methodology

Objective

- To determine the link between ESG performance and accounting based financial performance.
- To determine the link between ESG performance and market based financial performance.
- To find the impact of each ESG component on accounting based financial performance.
- To find the impact of each ESG component on market based financial performance.

Methodology

The methodology used in the study is a regression model to understand the relationship between the variables. The variables in the study are independent variables: ESG disclosure score, environmental disclosure score, social disclosure score, and governance disclosure score. The dependent variables include return on assets and Tobin's Q ratio. Return on assets was taken to give an accounting perspective of the financial performance of the company and Tobin's Q ratio from the perspective of market side financial performance of the company.

The variables data was collected from a secondary source – Bloomberg. The data was collected for five different industries. Under each industry three Indian origin companies were chosen. The industries under study include: Automobile, cement, FMCG, IT, and p0ower. The industry is divided based on India Brand Equity Foundation (IBEF) division which is a government-owned resource centre.

Hypothesis

1. H0- There is no relationship between ESG performance and accounting based financial performance.
   H1-There exists a relationship between ESG performance and accounting based financial performance.
2. H0- There is no relationship between ESG performance and market based financial performance.
   H1-There exists a relationship between ESG performance and market based financial performance.

Data Analysis

Regression between AUTOMOBILE ESG and ROA

The R value is 0.653 which is a positive regression. The R square of the model is 42.6%, which tells that 42.6% of the data fits the regression model. The p value in the ANOVA table is 0.609 which is >0.05 significance level. Hence we reject the alternate hypothesis and accept the null hypothesis.

Model Summary - Return on Assets

Model	R	R^2	Adjusted R^2	RMSE
H_0	0.000	0.000	0.000	4.006
H_1	0.653	0.426	−0.147	4.291

ANOVA

Model		Sum of Squares	df	Mean Square	F	p
H_1	Regression	54.758	4	13.690	0.744	0.609
	Residual	73.637	4	18.409		
	Total	128.395	8			

Note. The intercept model is omitted, as no meaningful information can be shown.

Coefficients

Model		Unstandardized	Standard Error	Standardized	t	p
H_0	(Intercept)	10.614	1.335		7.948	< .001
H_1	(Intercept)	51.210	35.699		1.435	0.225
	ESG Disclosure Score	−216.106	925.997	−272.723	−0.233	0.827
	Environmental Disclosure Score	115.300	493.654	198.604	0.234	0.827
	Social Disclosure Score	50.616	218.129	57.969	0.232	0.828
	Governance Disclosure Score	49.424	214.152	47.858	0.231	0.829

Source: Data collected from Bloomberg Database and processed through IBM SPSS Software

Regression between AUTOMOBILE ESG and Tobin's Q ratio

The R value is 0.686 which is a positive regression, and the R squared value is 0.471 which shows that 47.1% of the model can be interpreted from the data. The 9 value is 0.543> 0.05, hence we reject the alternate hypothesis.

Model Summary - Tobin's Q Ratio

Model	R	R²	Adjusted R²	RMSE
H₀	0.000	0.000	0.000	0.594
H₁	0.686	0.471	−0.058	0.611

ANOVA

Model		Sum of Squares	df	Mean Square	F	p
H₁	Regression	1.330	4	0.333	0.891	0.543
	Residual	1.493	4	0.373		
	Total	2.823	8			

Note. The intercept model is omitted, as no meaningful information can be shown.

Coefficients

Model		Unstandardized	Standard Error	Standardized	t	p
H₀	(Intercept)	2.740	0.198		13.838	< .001
H₁	(Intercept)	8.479	5.084		1.668	0.171
	ESG Disclosure Score	91.686	131.865	780.267	0.695	0.525
	Environmental Disclosure Score	−48.863	70.298	−567.585	−0.695	0.525
	Social Disclosure Score	−21.630	31.062	−167.052	−0.696	0.525
	Governance Disclosure Score	−21.297	30.496	−139.065	−0.698	0.523

Source: Data collected from Bloomberg Database and processed through IBM SPSS Software

Regression between CEMENT ESG and ROA

The model has a positive regression as the R value is 0.967 which is very close to 1. The R square value is 0.936. We accept the alternate hypothesis.

Model Summary - Return on Assets ▼

Model	R	R²	Adjusted R²	RMSE
H₀	0.000	0.000	0.000	2.276
H₁	0.967	0.936	0.872	0.814

ANOVA

Model		Sum of Squares	df	Mean Square	F	p
H₁	Regression	38.795	4	9.699	14.624	0.012
	Residual	2.653	4	0.663		
	Total	41.448	8			

Note. The intercept model is omitted, as no meaningful information can be shown.

148   *Advances in Management Research*

Coefficients

Model		Unstandardized	Standard Error	Standardized	t	p
H_0	(Intercept)	6.984	0.759		9.205	< .001
H_1	(Intercept)	21.985	7.383		2.978	0.041
	ESG Disclosure Score	−193.305	197.198	−342.165	−0.980	0.382
	Environmental Disclosure Score	102.690	105.085	280.406	0.977	0.384
	Social Disclosure Score	45.403	46.536	54.256	0.976	0.384
	Governance Disclosure Score	44.928	45.634	57.643	0.985	0.381

Source: Data collected from Bloomberg Database and processed through IBM SPSS Software

Regression between CEMENT ESG and Tobin's Q ratio

The R value shows the regression is positive. The r square value is low at 49.7%. The p value is significantly higher than the significance level at 0.505. Therefore, we accept the null hypothesis.

Model Summary - Tobin's Q Ratio

Model	R	R^2	Adjusted R^2	RMSE
H_0	0.000	0.000	0.000	0.354
H_1	0.705	0.497	−0.007	0.355

ANOVA

Model		Sum of Squares	df	Mean Square	F	p
H_1	Regression	0.498	4	0.125	0.987	0.505
	Residual	0.505	4	0.126		
	Total	1.003	8			

Note. The intercept model is omitted, as no meaningful information can be shown.

Coefficients

Model		Unstandardized	Standard Error	Standardized	t	p
H_0	(Intercept)	2.212	0.118		18.745	< .001
H_1	(Intercept)	7.239	3.220		2.248	0.088
	ESG Disclosure Score	−23.194	86.013	−263.935	−0.270	0.801
	Environmental Disclosure Score	12.357	45.836	216.927	0.270	0.801
	Social Disclosure Score	5.402	20.298	41.503	0.266	0.803
	Governance Disclosure Score	5.346	19.905	44.092	0.269	0.802

Source: Data collected from Bloomberg Database and processed through IBM SPSS Software

Regression between FMCG ESG and ROA

The regression relation is positive as the r value is 0.844. The R square is 71.3%. The significance level is 0.05 and the p value is 0.123 which is more than the significance level. Hence, we reject the alternate hypothesis.

Model Summary - Return on Assets

Model	R	R^2	Adjusted R^2	RMSE
H_0	0.000	0.000	0.000	3.609
H_1	0.844	0.713	0.483	2.595

ANOVA

Model		Sum of Squares	df	Mean Square	F	p
H₁	Regression	83.540	4	20.885	3.101	0.123
	Residual	33.670	5	6.734		
	Total	117.210	9			

Note. The intercept model is omitted, as no meaningful information can be shown.

Coefficients

Model		Unstandardized	Standard Error	Standardized	t	p
H₀	(Intercept)	19.030	1.141		16.676	< .001
H₁	(Intercept)	25.048	10.874		2.304	0.069
	ESG Disclosure Score	-915.849	502.556	-689.721	-1.822	0.128
	Environmental Disclosure Score	487.883	267.698	279.575	1.823	0.128
	Social Disclosure Score	215.400	118.423	369.569	1.819	0.129
	Governance Disclosure Score	212.174	116.365	323.785	1.823	0.128

Source: Data collected from Bloomberg Database and processed through IBM SPSS Software

Regression between FMCG ESG and Tobin's Q ratio

There is a positive regression relationship among the variables. 50.1% of the variability can be predicted by the model. The p value is higher than the significance level and thus we accept the null hypothesis.

Model Summary - Tobin's Q Ratio

Model	R	R²	Adjusted R²	RMSE
H₀	0.000	0.000	0.000	1.144
H₁	0.708	0.501	0.101	1.084

ANOVA

Model		Sum of Squares	df	Mean Square	F	p
H₁	Regression	5.895	4	1.474	1.253	0.397
	Residual	5.880	5	1.176		
	Total	11.776	9			

Note. The intercept model is omitted, as no meaningful information can be shown.

Coefficients

Model		Unstandardized	Standard Error	Standardized	t	p
H₀	(Intercept)	6.942	0.362		19.192	< .001
H₁	(Intercept)	14.670	4.544		3.228	0.023
	ESG Disclosure Score	-187.151	210.021	-444.664	-0.891	0.414
	Environmental Disclosure Score	99.299	111.872	179.522	0.888	0.415
	Social Disclosure Score	44.108	49.490	238.758	0.891	0.414
	Governance Disclosure Score	43.359	48.629	208.754	0.892	0.413

Source: Data collected from Bloomberg Database and processed through IBM SPSS Software

Regression between IT ESG and ROA

The regression relationship is a highly positive relation as the R value is 0.958. 91.8% of the variability can be predicted by the model. The p value is less than the significance level which is 0.05 thus we accept the alternate hypothesis and reject the null hypothesis.

Model Summary - Return on Assets

Model	R	R²	Adjusted R²	RMSE
H₀	0.000	0.000	0.000	1.687
H₁	0.958	0.918	0.853	0.647

ANOVA

Model		Sum of Squares	df	Mean Square	F	p
H₁	Regression	23.531	4	5.883	14.041	0.006
	Residual	2.095	5	0.419		
	Total	25.626	9			

Note. The intercept model is omitted, as no meaningful information can be shown.

Coefficients

Model		Unstandardized	Standard Error	Standardized	t	p
H₀	(Intercept)	20.316	0.534		38.074	< .001
H₁	(Intercept)	17.886	1.404		12.741	< .001
	ESG Disclosure Score	463.327	120.805	2384.158	3.835	0.012
	Environmental Disclosure Score	−246.735	64.381	−1191.846	−3.832	0.012
	Social Disclosure Score	−109.293	28.450	−492.364	−3.842	0.012
	Governance Disclosure Score	−107.209	27.964	−879.022	−3.834	0.012

Source: Data collected from Bloomberg Database and processed through IBM SPSS Software

Regression between IT ESG and Tobin's Q ratio

The regression relationship is not very positive at 0.373. The R square is also very low at just 13.9%. The p value is way higher than the significance level at 0.927 thus we reject the alternate hypothesis.

Model Summary - Tobin's Q Ratio

Model	R	R²	Adjusted R²	RMSE
H₀	0.000	0.000	0.000	0.760
H₁	0.373	0.139	−0.550	0.946

ANOVA

Model		Sum of Squares	df	Mean Square	F	p
H₁	Regression	0.723	4	0.181	0.202	0.927
	Residual	4.477	5	0.895		
	Total	5.201	9			

Note. The intercept model is omitted, as no meaningful information can be shown.

Coefficients

Model		Unstandardized	Standard Error	Standardized	t	p
H₀	(Intercept)	4.189	0.240		17.428	< .001
H₁	(Intercept)	4.205	2.052		2.049	0.096
	ESG Disclosure Score	153.127	176.614	1749.078	0.867	0.426
	Environmental Disclosure Score	−81.619	94.123	−875.164	−0.867	0.426
	Social Disclosure Score	−36.068	41.594	−360.686	−0.867	0.426
	Governance Disclosure Score	−35.439	40.883	−644.996	−0.867	0.426

Source: Data collected from Bloomberg Database and processed through IBM SPSS Software

Regression between POWER ESG and ROA

There is a regression relationship among the variables. The R square is low at 48.5% and the p value also suggests that the regression relation is insignificant. Therefore, we accept the null hypothesis.

Model Summary - Return on Assets

Model	R	R^2	Adjusted R^2	RMSE
H_0	0.000	0.000	0.000	1.019
H_1	0.697	0.485	−0.029	1.034

ANOVA

Model		Sum of Squares	df	Mean Square	F	p
H_1	Regression	4.031	4	1.008	0.943	0.522
	Residual	4.273	4	1.068		
	Total	8.304	8			

Note. The intercept model is omitted, as no meaningful information can be shown.

Coefficients

Model		Unstandardized	Standard Error	Standardized	t	p
H_0	(Intercept)	2.183	0.340		6.428	< .001
H_1	(Intercept)	1.388	4.044		0.343	0.749
	ESG Disclosure Score	−270.569	382.370	−3050.618	−0.708	0.518
	Environmental Disclosure Score	144.132	203.810	1754.352	0.707	0.518
	Social Disclosure Score	63.737	90.025	992.020	0.708	0.518
	Governance Disclosure Score	62.667	88.585	495.741	0.707	0.518

Source: Data collected from Bloomberg Database and processed through IBM SPSS Software

Regression between POWER ESG and Tobin's Q ratio

The regression relationship is highly positive at 0.969 R value. The R square value is 94% and the p value is less than 0.05. Hence, we accept the alternate hypothesis. But, when we see the coefficient table no variable has a significance less than 0.05. Therefore, the model is significant but we cannot accept the alternate hypothesis.

Model Summary - Tobin's Q Ratio ▼

Model	R	R^2	Adjusted R^2	RMSE
H_0	0.000	0.000	0.000	0.075
H_1	0.969	0.940	0.880	0.026

ANOVA

Model		Sum of Squares	df	Mean Square	F	p
H_1	Regression	0.042	4	0.011	15.633	0.010
	Residual	0.003	4	6.794e−4		
	Total	0.045	8			

Note. The intercept model is omitted, as no meaningful information can be shown.

Coefficients

Model		Unstandardized	Standard Error	Standardized	t	p
H_0	(Intercept)	1.148	0.025		45.823	< .001
H_1	(Intercept)	0.818	0.102		8.026	0.001
	ESG Disclosure Score	5.324	9.643	813.540	0.552	0.610
	Environmental Disclosure Score	−2.836	5.140	−467.884	−0.552	0.610
	Social Disclosure Score	−1.261	2.270	−266.011	−0.555	0.608
	Governance Disclosure Score	−1.221	2.234	−130.905	−0.546	0.614

Source: Data collected from Bloomberg Database and processed through IBM SPSS Software

Conclusion

Based on the analysis it was found that the hypothesis held true in the IT industry which means there is an impact of ESG performance on the ROA of Indian origin IT sector companies, Cement ESG on ROA, and in the Power industry there is an impact of ESG performance on the Tobin's Q ratio. All other alternate hypothesis had to be rejected. This shows that there is further study required in the area to motivate the companies to be more conscious and work towards ESG factors. The ROA is an accounting metric, but Tobin's Q ratio is a market based metric. There is so much talk about ESG investing but it doesn't seem to hold true when we do our analysis. If the market and people do not consider ESG performance while investing, the companies will reduce/limit their ESG consciousness. Another factor which can be blamed for ESG investing choices is the availability of ESG scores to the investors. The ESG scores of Indian companies can only be found in paid data resource centres like Bloomberg, Thompson Reuters, etc. They are not freely accessible to the investors. They can only see the ESG index and see the companies which are a part of the index. Investors can't see the change in their ESG performances or the actual score for that matter. Thus to conclude, there is a lot of work remaining on the ESG front in our country and more recognition required to push the companies to be better in a more wholesome manner.

References

Al-Hiyari, A and Kolsi, M. C. (2021). How do stock market participants value ESG performance? Evidence from Middle Eastern and North African countries. Glob. Bus. Rev. https://doi.org/10.1177/09721509211001511

Ashwin Kumar, N. C., Smith, C., Badis, L., Wang, N., Ambrosy, P., and Tavares, R. (2016). ESG factors and risk-adjusted performance: A new quantitative model. J. Sustain. Finance Invest. 6(4):292–300. https://doi.org/10.1080/20430795.2016.1234909

Cornell, B. (2021). ESG preferences, risk and return. Eur. Financial Manag.27(1):12–19. https://doi.org/10.1111/eufm.12295

De Spiegeleer, J., Höcht, S., Jakubowski, D., Reyners, S., and Schoutens, W. (2021). ESG: A new dimension in portfolio allocation. J. Sustain. Finance Invest. https://doi.org/10.10 80/20430795.2021.1923336

El Khoury, R., Nasrallah, N., and Alareeni, B. (2021). ESG and financial performance of banks in the MENAT region: concavity–convexity patterns. J. Sustain. Finance Invest.. https://doi.org/10.1080/20430795.2021.1929807

Ferriani, F. and Natoli, F. (2021). ESG risks in times of Covid-19. Appl. Econ. Lett. 28(18): 1537–1541. https://doi.org/10.1080/13504851.2020.1830932

Friede, G., Busch, T., and Bassen, A. (2015). ESG and financial performance: Aggregated evidence from more than 2000 empirical studies. J. Sustain. Finance Invest. 5(4):210–233. https://doi.org/10.1080/20430795.2015.1118917

Gregory, R. P., Stead, J. G., and Stead, E. (2021). The global pricing of environmental, social, and governance (ESG) criteria. J. Sustain. Finance Invest. 11(4):310–329. https://doi.org/10.1080/20430795.2020.1731786

Jemel-Fornetty, H., Louche, C., and Bourghelle, D. (2011). Changing the dominant convention: The role of emerging initiatives in mainstreaming ESG. Crit. Stud. Corp. Responsib. Gov. Sustain. 2:85–117. https://doi.org/10.1108/S2043-9059(2011)0000002011

Kaiser, L. and Welters, J. (2019). Risk-mitigating effect of ESG on momentum portfolios. J. Risk Finance. 20(5):542–555. https://doi.org/10.1108/JRF-05-2019-0075

Khemir, S. (2019). Perception of ESG criteria by mainstream investors: Evidence from Tunisia. Int. J. Emerg. Mark. 14(5):752–768. https://doi.org/10.1108/IJOEM-05-2017-0172

Khemir, S., Baccouche, C., and Ayadi, S. D. (2019). The influence of ESG information on investment allocation decisions: An experimental study in an emerging country. J. Appl. Account. Res. 20(4): 458–480. https://doi.org/10.1108/JAAR-12-2017-0141

Landi, G. and Sciarelli, M. (2019). Towards a more ethical market: The impact of ESG rating on corporate financial performance. Soc. Responsib. J. 15(1):11–27. https://doi.org/10.1108/SRJ-11-2017-0254

Mandal, R. and Murthy, A. (2021). CSR in the post pandemic era: The dual promise of ESG investment and investor stewardship. Indian Law Rev. 5(2):229–249. https://doi.org/1 0.1080/24730580.2021.1899627

Schmidt, A. (2020). Optimal ESG portfolios: An example for the Dow Jones Index. J. Sustain. Finance Invest. 12(2):529-535. https://doi.org/10.1080/20430795.2020.1783180

Schramade, W. (2016). Integrating ESG into valuation models and investment decisions: The value-driver adjustment approach. J. Sustain. Finance Invest. 6(2):95–111. https://doi.org/10.1080/20430795.2016.1176425

Sherwood, M. W. and Pollard, J. L. (2018). The risk-adjusted return potential of integrating ESG strategies into emerging market equities. J. Sustain. Finance Invest. 8(1):26–44. https://doi.org/10.1080/20430795.2017.1331118

Steen, M., Moussawi, J. T., and Gjolberg, O. (2020). Is there a relationship between Morningstar's ESG ratings and mutual fund performance? J. Sustain. Finance Invest. 10(4): 349–370. https://doi.org/10.1080/20430795.2019.1700065

Velte, P. (2017). Does ESG performance have an impact on financial performance? Evidence from Germany. J. Glo. Respon. 8(2):169–178. https://doi.org/10.1108/jgr-11-2016-0029

Xu, J., Liu, F., and Shang, Y. (2021). R&D investment, ESG performance and green innovation performance: Evidence from China. Kybernetes. 50(3):737–756. https://doi.org/10.1108/K-12- 2019-0793

Young, S. (2013). Responsible investment, ESG, and institutional investors in Australia. Critical Studies on Corporate Responsibility, Governance and Sustainability. 5:61–80. https://doi.org/10.1108/S2043-9059(2013)0000005011

11 Effect of the pandemic on the selection of OTT platforms in the entertainment sector

Aarti Singh

FORE School of Management, New Delhi, India

Abstract

Streaming has always been a part of some of our lives. Others will recall a period when there were only a few TV networks and no cable television. Regardless of how you experienced the rise of over-the-top (OTT) streaming, we are all smack dab in the centre of it. What brought us here? And where do you think this technology will take us? As a subset of digital mediums, OTT is gaining momentum, and with the growth of data-connected smartphone users, this phenomenon is just getting started. Digital as an industry is expanding at a 25–30% CAGR, and with the digital revolution at its peak, it's just going to get bigger.

A distinguishing trend is that a growing number of families are opting for smart TVs, which provides a chance for OTT platforms to capture customers' attention. OTTs were once thought of as a platform that provided entertainment for smartphone users who wanted to watch content in the comfort of their own homes. However, like the television set gains in popularity and acceptability, it will be capable of playing a vast array of material, including cable TV, videos, the internet, OTT services. Netflix spent $17 billion on original programming alone last year. The technological infrastructure and content delivery platform are not included. It is costly to generate content, and it is much more costly to bring that content to customers in the quality they expect, on all of their preferred devices. As a result, further media consolidation is expected to occur in the future. Technically, the cable television experience is more regulated; there is a single bitrate, and programming is designed specifically for a particular device, thus there is only one delivery option. OTT is provided via the often-clogged public internet, adaptive bitrate is required, and material must be accessible across thousands of devices, resulting in over 150 million delivery possibilities. The potential for OTT content distribution is enormous. This implies that content producers need to be able to assess the quality of experience and comprehend the complete customer journey better than ever before.

Intrduction

Over-the-top (OTT) is a method of delivering television and cinema content over the internet at the consumer's request and tailored to their specific needs. The name itself means 'over-the-top,' implying that a content provider is building on top of already existing internet services.

The shift from IPTV to OTT

Let's begin with how we arrived here. Digital television content distribution through Internet Protocol (IPTV) has been the standard method for TV service providers to distribute material to clients since the mid-1990s. A TV subscription, a contract, a set-top box, and a technician to connect the array of hardware to high-speed internet services in each customer's home or workplace are often required for reception. As a result, content is delivered over private MPEG transport stream networks that are 'multicast' (meaning multiple streams are pushed to multiple consumer locations, like digital cable and satellite TV). This ties customers to one service provider (whatever is available in their location), and the content available is limited to channels available in their area.

The OTT advantage

While they both use IP technology, IPTV is delivered over a private cable network compared to OTT delivered over internet services. OTT systems overcome the limitations of the single operator set-top box (STB) technology required by IPTV. With OTT, content is only delivered upon request. Each connected device has a unique connection to the source of the content via the internet, making it 'unicast'- delivering one stream to one device. While they both employ IP technology, IPTV is supplied through a private cable network, whereas OTT is offered over the internet. OTT solutions get beyond the restrictions of IPTV's single-operator set-top box (STB) technology. OTT material is only supplied when it is requested. Each connected device has its internet connection to the content source, making it 'unicast,' or sending one stream to one device.

How does OTT work

One of the fundamental challenges of delivering TV programming over the internet is dealing with a broad range of network performance. The speed of the connection (e.g., fiber, Wi-Fi, LTE, DSL), the display device (e.g., phone, a streaming device like Roku, Apple TV, or Firestick, or laptop), and the number of network shop between the provider and the end-user all affect performance. At a high level, OTT systems and technologies are meant to reduce the influence of these factors by offering content with a 'best-effort' approach. That is, OTT technology will react in real-time to the network performance of the whole chain, ensuring that video and audio are transmitted without buffering interruptions. The audience will be irritated by these gaps, which may drive them to quit the content. It will scale down to lower bit rates on slower networks. It will scale up to give the greatest quality for faster networks. When connected to a high-speed network, the player should buffer more material to 'get ahead' and smooth out network slowdowns. This is accomplished using a technology known as ABR, which stands for Adaptive Bit Rate Streaming.

COVID-19 lockdown and change in media consumption

People's behavioural and lifestyle changes, including a shift in media intake, are reflecting the debilitating effect of the COVID-19 epidemic. According to Nielson, in the week ending March, there was an 18% rise in all types of television viewing in America, particularly among teens who were unable to attend school. In India, the Broadcast Audience Research Council (BARC) estimated a 38% increase in TV consumption before COVID-19, with people being entertained by fiction stories, historical pieces, mythological stories, and supernatural thrillers (Livemint, April 19, 2020). People's isolation and social distancing norms have boosted at-home digital consumption, resulting in a spike in demand for subscription-based streaming services.

The current study investigates the key important elements impacting customers' willingness to continue and subscribe (WCS) for streaming services in the future against the backdrop of this changing consumer behaviour. The study adds to the body of knowledge by examining the likelihood of 'habit' use of these services during the lockdown period, as well as its likely influence on the link between consumer satisfaction and future behaviour with regard to these services/service providers

Literature review

India is the fastest expanding entertainment and media industry internationally and is anticipated to retain that momentum, according to the article 'Global Entertainment & Media Outlook 2019–2023.' According to the study, India will witness a considerable increase in OTT, online gaming, and Internet advertising in the next five years (by 2023). Content makers and distributors are coming up with new strategies to entice customers. Marketers, on the other hand, are determining customer preferences and transforming them into potential purchasers. This is done by companies that utilise artificial intelligence to analyse people's specific interests and consumption patterns to deliver the most enticing information to them (Grewal et al., 2020).

This paper will discuss several factors related to satisfaction with OTT streaming platforms as mentioned in different articles. It concentrated on gaining a better grasp of consumer satisfaction, which is an important aspect of this study. Entertainment industry specifically OTT platforms is witnessing a paradigm shift in terms of viewership. The internet has opened up a whole new world of viewing possibilities. At the stroke of a button, a customer may access a lot of online content on his computer or phone.

There are a number of small elements that go into developing content on an OTT platform, and it is not easy. Many factors come into play while managing a digital platform, some of which may or may not be beneficial to the user. The purpose of this study is to determine whether such components exist, and if so, how they could impact consumer behaviour when watching content online.

The fact that over 60% of online viewers are between the ages of 13 and 35, is also the major demographic for OTT platform viewers. International companies are taking India more seriously as a result of increased demand.

The purpose of this research is to investigate the factors that impact a consumer's decision basically of a particular gender on which digital platform to watch content on. The preset aspects that were examined before finishing the study were price, video and audio quality, variety of content, customisation, ease of access across devices, and user interface.

To evaluate the available material, the focus was primarily on Netflix and Amazon Prime, with all other future players being overlooked. This research deviated a little when the analysis included examining the gender role in viewing these platforms, as it had previously claimed to illustrate the influence of all the elements that the researchers had stated beforehand (Prashant Akhare and Sachin Nayak, 2019).

OTT video streaming is becoming a key influence in the digital environment. The increased accessibility owing to faster internet speed, increased broadband rollout, and competent devices to display such films is the cause for this amazing surge. Another motivation is improved user experience, such as improved recommendations for what to watch next based on a systematic customer data trend (Udovita, 2020). OTT streaming is altering the face of media, which explains why it's so appealing as a choice. The reasons are:

a. High value, low-cost model
b. The original content of various OTT platforms
c. Multiple devices supported. (Harvey, 2019)

In India, the media and entertainment sectors are developing, even though the pace of change was slower than in many other countries. The author (Moochala, 2018) identifies this shift based on primary and secondary research data and characteristics such as age, attraction to OTT, gender and genre, brand, and recognition. The study showed that content quality, smartphone, and smart TV users are the primary drivers for this shift among younger age groups (18–35). India's consumption of digital media material has increased dramatically in recent years. India is one of the world's fastest developing internet nations, thanks to its use of digital media platforms to obtain information on news, health, and other issues, as well as entertainment and e-commerce. This movement in consumer preference toward digital media has piqued marketers' interest and compelled them to update their traditional advertising channels (Bhavsar, 2018). The elements that have contributed to the rise of OTT in India are discussed in a recent blog. It has been narrowed down to the region›s mobile device prevalence. This increase is due to improved internet access and the increasing number of people who own smartphones. Data traffic in the Asia Pacific is anticipated to grow at a CAGR of 58% between 2014 and 2019. This is critical because a developing economy like India is seeing rapid growth. The sheer size of the nation aids firms greatly in catering to diverse customer groups (Ekpo et al., 2015). Consumers were first perplexed by the variety of options and recommendations, but this has now been simplified via the application of AI, which simplifies the use of OTT in a much more straightforward manner. One of the main reasons why consumers like the new platform are because of this. Although most publications argue that TV and OTT will coexist, advancements in 5G technology will be a key driver driving OTT content to be seen by the general public. This allows advertisers to concentrate on customised advertisements and 'hyper' target their ads to maximize consumer experience and value. Even if the customer's choice to reveal data remains a key obstacle in this targeting, data is the oil that allows these customised advertisements and hyper-targeting to function (Boehm et al., 2018). Advertisers are looking for ways to advertise their businesses on OTT platforms to reach a larger audience. Targeting and retargeting become more simplified when data from consumer browsing is used (Yun et al., 2020). The paper titled 'UNDERSTANDING ADOPTION FACTORS OF OVER-THE-TOP VIDEO SERVICES AMONG MILLENNIAL CONSUMERS' stated the difficulty for marketers, according to them, to understand how customers watch OTT (over-the-top) content. The development of OTT platforms by individual media firms has been noticed as a trend in television content watching. The results were based on 35 respondents who were interviewed and probed, with the questions primarily mapping their usage patterns, content preferences, and perceptions of OTT platforms, as well as a comprehensive comparison with other video media service providers such as television and downloaded content. With internet and mobile penetration rising by the day, the future of OTT appears bright, according to the publication. OTT services have attracted a lot of attention and money, but it's hard to claim that they will ever replace television as the major video consumption medium. Almost all OTT platforms' pricing methods are now significantly higher for the Indian consumer, resulting in a high level of dissuasion from becoming a regular paying client (Dasgupta, 2019).

In research on Indian OTT platforms, the global media and entertainment sector has experienced rapid changes over the years. The digital revolution has altered how we consume material. Print, radio, television, cinema, video games, live events, and music are all undergoing digital transformations. And, because all of these sectors' content distribution and consumption are shifting to digital platforms, the resulting convergence is unparalleled. It was decided that India has become the ideal market for OTT providers. The rivalry in the OTT market is heating up, with a mix of local, national, and international competitors making their impact. The country has begun to move in the direction of digitally enabled entertainment outlets. The future of OTT will be determined by several factors, including consumption patterns, content creation costs, revenue models, and connectivity. Though the digital domain saw the largest percentage increase in 2017–2018, the trend is expected to continue in the future years, with new entrants bringing novel content and subscription models (Dwivedi et al., 2021). Technology plays a critical part in today's worldwide economy in almost everything we do according to the paper titled 'Video on Demand Industry: Challenges and Opportunities in the Indian Market'. Video on demand (VOD) is another business that has benefited from technological developments in recent years. To have a better knowledge of the VOD industry, the researchers gathered data from a variety of trustworthy secondary sources. Primary data was also collected in the form of a questionnaire, which included questions to evaluate respondents' understanding of the industry, its problems, and the key factors that impact its growth. The conclusions were as follows: The worldwide VOD industry has experienced an exponential increase in the last several years. Europe, the United States, and China are the largest markets, accounting for 85.5% of the worldwide VOD market. In India, live video streaming is a booming sector, with young people and working people spending more and more time watching videos. Hotstar is India's most popular VOD service, with Netflix and YouTube Red coming in second and third, respectively. Other participants in the VOD industry in India include Voot, TVF Play, and Amazon Prime, with an increasing number of consumers ready to test out the different alternatives available in the VOD sector. The report concluded by stating that India's VOD industry was the primary emphasis. In India, the VOD business is still developing, with more and more individuals becoming aware of it. And as people's reliance on and exposure to technology grows, this trend will only continue. However, India still has a long way to go before becoming a major participant in the global VOD market. Poor internet access is one of the key factors impeding the expansion of VOD in India (Johny and Alukal, 2018).

The following research gaps were identified from the literature review

1. Concerning India, there hasn't been much study done based on gender
2. There hasn't been much study done to know about the shift in usage patterns because of the pandemic on OTT platforms based on the content streamed by each gender.

The research aims at understanding the impact of the pandemic on OTT platform selection in the entertainment industry based on gender, of how OTT players like Netflix, Amazon Prime, Sony LIV, Hotstar are bringing new content every day, and how viewership is constantly migrating to these OTT platforms and how they are becoming the major players in the industry.

The objectives of the project are

- To understand the shift in usage pattern during the pandemic in OTT platforms in the entertainment industry
- To know about the shift in usage pattern because of the pandemic on OTT platforms based on the content streamed by each gender

Research methodology

The methodology used in this research involves secondary research, which consists of collecting first-hand data with the help of a questionnaire that was floated on June 10, 2021 on various social media platforms. The aim was to gain information about the shift in usage patterns, vis-à-vis the pandemic, of the OTT platforms based on content streamed by each gender. The research design is a mixture of

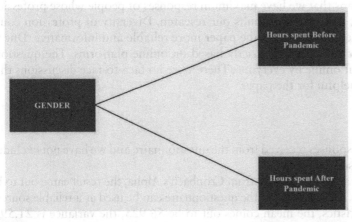

Figure 11.1 Research model
Source: Developed by author

qualitative and quantitative research which gives enough flexibility in the research while keeping it analytical at the same time. It thus provides an additional dimension to the research.

Data collection method

The primary data involves a questionnaire to understand the shift in usage patterns because of the pandemic on the OTT platform based on content streamed by each gender. It was floated on June 10, 2021, on various platforms and it was filled with people of diverse backgrounds. The questionnaire was kept open for 15 days and was filled out by 424 people. The questionnaire has been designed in such a manner to gain maximum knowledge while keeping the questions as simple as possible. The questionnaire has questions that help in deriving deep insights.

Sampling technique

The convenience sampling technique has been used so that people can fill out the questionnaire at their convenience and are not barred by anything. The aim was to get as diverse as possible. This technique was used so that people did not feel that they were under any burden or stress to complete the questionnaire and could do it when they were in peace of mind.

Sample size

The sample size for the research is 424. It was very well thought of beforehand that the questionnaire would be distributed to people of diverse backgrounds.

Limitations

The first limitation here is that our data lacks different age diversity. This means that we have data of mainly 20–30 years of age. We have little data of ages other than this that is below 20 and above 30. This gives a narrow perspective when seen from the research point of view. The second limitation is that we have student-centric data. This means that we have maximum responses of people whose profession is a student. This, too, in a way, limits our research. Diversity of profession could have been more helpful and made the paper more reliable and informative. Due to the pandemic, our research was strictly based on online platforms. The questionnaire was filled out online by everyone. There were no face-to-face discussions that could have been helpful for the paper.

Analysis

There were 424 responses received from the questionnaire and we have not excluded any of the responses received.

In the reliability analysis obtained from Cronbach's Alpha, the result came out to be 0.826 for 19 items. This shows that the questionnaire can be used as a reliable source

In the scale statistics, the mean comes out to be 56.925, the variance is 21.592, the standard deviation is only 4.6468 and the number of items is 19.

Case Processing Summary

		N	%
Cases	Valid	424	100.0
	Excluded[a]	0	.0
	Total	424	100.0

a. Listwise deletion based on all variables in the procedure.

Figure 11.2 Case processing summary
Source: SPSS Calculation

Reliability Statistics

Cronbach's Alpha	N of Items
.826	19

Figure 11.3 Reliability statics
Source: Calculated from SPSS

Scale Statistics

Mean	Variance	Std. Deviation	N of Items
56.925	21.592	4.6468	19

Figure 11.4 Scale statics
Source: SPSS Software

The percentage of people below 20 years is only 2.8, and the people above 30 years is only 3.8 whereas for the age group of 20–30 years it is 93.4%. It is also because more people in this age group are hooked to OTT platforms and people of the other age groups i. e., below 20 years and above 30 years are considerably less involved in OTT platforms.

The total number of female respondents is 132 which is 31.1% of the respondents and for the male respondents, it is 292 in number which is 68.9% of the overall respondents.

A total of 43.4% of the respondents have no annual income. People falling below Rs. 2,00,000 annual income are 44 in number which is 10.4% of the respondents. People falling in the category of earning between two lakhs and five lakhs per annum are 56 in number which is 13.2% of the respondents. People falling in the category of earning between 5 lakhs and 10 lakhs per annum are 64 in number which is 15.1% of the respondents. People falling in the category of earning more than 10 lakhs per annum are 76 in number which is 17.9% of the respondents.

The number of people involved in the private sector is 128 in number which is 30.2% of the respondents. The number of people involved in the public sector is 12 in number which is 2.8% of the respondents. The number of self-employed people is 28 in number which is 6.6% of the respondents. The student's respondents covered 59.4% of total respondents. The maximum numbers of respondents are students. The total number of unemployed people is nine in number and 0.9% of the total respondents.

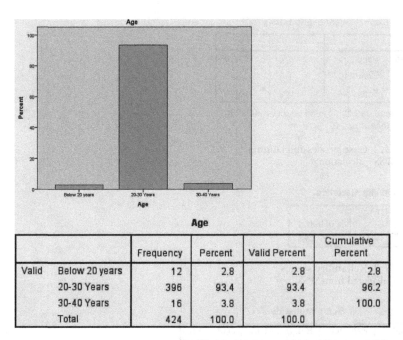

Age

		Frequency	Percent	Valid Percent	Cumulative Percent
Valid	Below 20 years	12	2.8	2.8	2.8
	20-30 Years	396	93.4	93.4	96.2
	30-40 Years	16	3.8	3.8	100.0
	Total	424	100.0	100.0	

Figure 11.5 Age groups hooked to OTT platforms
Source: SPSS Software

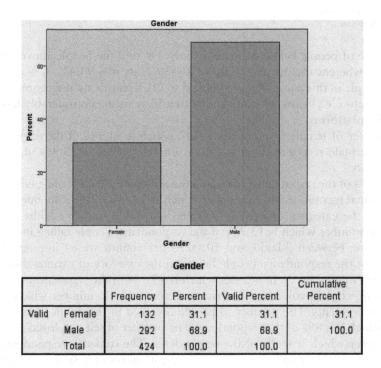

Gender

		Frequency	Percent	Valid Percent	Cumulative Percent
Valid	Female	132	31.1	31.1	31.1
	Male	292	68.9	68.9	100.0
	Total	424	100.0	100.0	

Figure 11.6 Demographic distribution of data
Source: SPSS Software

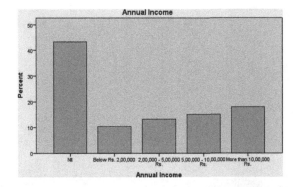

Annual Income				
		Frequency	Percent	Valid Percent	Cumulative Percent
Valid	NII	184	43.4	43.4	43.4
	Below Rs. 2,00,000	44	10.4	10.4	53.8
	2,00,000 - 5,00,000 Rs.	56	13.2	13.2	67.0
	5,00,000 - 10,00,000 Rs.	64	15.1	15.1	82.1
	More than 10,00,000 Rs.	76	17.9	17.9	100.0
	Total	424	100.0	100.0	

Figure 11.7 Annual income
Source: SPSS Software

The total number of subscribers of any OTT platform is 380 in number which is 89.6% of the respondents while the number of nonsubscribers is 44 in number which is 10.4% of the total respondents. This goes to show that the number of people involved in OTT platforms has considerably increased.

The number of people who use Amazon prime is 92 in number which is 21.7% of the respondents. The number of people who use HoiChoi is four in number which is 0.9% of the respondents. The number of people who use Hotstar is 20 in number which is 4.7% of the respondents. We have the maximum number of users of Netflix which is 260 in number which is 61.3% of the total respondents. The total number of respondents who use Sony LIV the most is eight in number which is 1.9% of the respondents. The total number of respondents who use YouTube is 36 in number which is 8.5% of the respondents.

For the duration spent on OTT platforms per day before the pandemic, we have divided it into four categories. The first category is below three hours, the second is three to five hours, the next being five to seven hours, and the last category is above seven hours. The number of people who spent less than three hours before the pandemic on OTT platforms is 368 in number which is 86.8%. The number of respondents who spent three to five hours is 48 which is 11.3%. no respondent spends five to seven hours. While eight respondents spent above seven hours which is 1.9% of the total respondents.

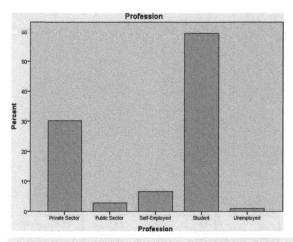

Profession				
		Frequency	Percent	Valid Percent	Cumulative Percent

		Frequency	Percent	Valid Percent	Cumulative Percent
Valid	Private Sector	128	30.2	30.2	30.2
	Public Sector	12	2.8	2.8	33.0
	Self-Employed	28	6.6	6.6	39.6
	Student	252	59.4	59.4	99.1
	Unemployed	4	.9	.9	100.0
	Total	424	100.0	100.0	

Figure 11.8   Respondent distribution as per their earnings
Source: SPSS Software

For the duration spent on OTT platforms per day after the pandemic, we have divided it into four categories. The first category is below three hours, the second is three to five hours, the next being five to seven hours, and the last category is above seven hours. The number of people who spent less than 3 hours before the pandemic on OTT platforms is 224 in number which is 52.8%. The number of respondents who spent three to five hours is 132 in number which is 31.1% of the respondents. 68 respondents spent above seven hours which is 16% of the total respondents.

We can see that the overall duration has increased. Earlier 368 people used to watch below three hours, now only 224 people are watching it below three hours. At the same time, the number of people watching between three to five hours before the pandemic was 48 but it has now increased to 132 which shows a significant increase. Also, the number of people who are watching above seven hours has increased enormously as earlier it was just 1.9% of the respondents there as now it is 16 % of the respondents.

Here we have asked the respondents to answer how satisfied they were with the price factor and we have broken it down into five categories which range from highly dissatisfied to highly satisfied. The percentage of people who are not satisfied

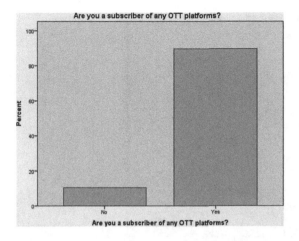

Are you a subscriber of any OTT platforms?				
		Frequency	Percent	Valid Percent	Cumulative Percent
Valid	No	44	10.4	10.4	10.4
	Yes	380	89.6	89.6	100.0
	Total	424	100.0	100.0	

Figure 11.9 Subscriber of OTT platforms
Source: SPSS Software

with the pricing is 5.7% of the respondents. In this, we have further broken it into two parts which are dissatisfied and highly dissatisfied 1.9% of respondents are dissatisfied and 3.8% of respondents are highly dissatisfied, while 73.6% of the respondents are satisfied with the pricing of the OTT platforms currently. In this, we have further broken it into two parts which are satisfied and highly satisfied and 43.4% of respondents satisfied and 30.2% of respondents are highly satisfied. There is 20.8% of the respondents who are neutral in this which means that they are neither satisfied nor dissatisfied with the pricing strategy.

Here we have asked the respondents to answer how satisfied they were with the content that is available on the respective OTT platforms and we have broken it down into five categories which range from highly dissatisfied to highly satisfied. The percentage of people who are satisfied with the pricing is 97.2% of the respondents. In this we have further broken it into two parts which are satisfied and highly satisfied and 14.2% of respondents are satisfied and 83.0% of respondents are highly satisfied, there is 2.8% of the respondents who are neutral in this which means that they are neither satisfied nor dissatisfied with the availability of the content there is. There are no respondents who were dissatisfied with the content available in the OTT platforms.

Here, we have asked the respondents to answer how satisfied they were with the promotional offers that they received for various OTT platforms and we have

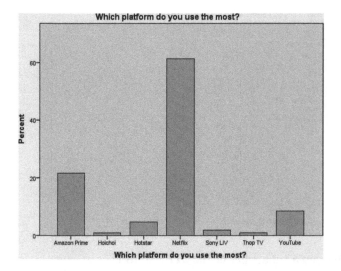

Which platform do you use the most?				
		Frequency	Percent	Valid Percent	Cumulative Percent
Valid	Amazon Prime	92	21.7	21.7	21.7
	Hoichoi	4	.9	.9	22.6
	Hotstar	20	4.7	4.7	27.4
	Netflix	260	61.3	61.3	88.7
	Sony LIV	8	1.9	1.9	90.6
	Thop TV	4	.9	.9	91.5
	YouTube	36	8.5	8.5	100.0
	Total	424	100.0	100.0	

Figure 11.10 Frequency of using specific OTT platform
Source: SPSS Software

broken it down into five categories which range from highly dissatisfied to highly satisfied. The percentage of people who are not satisfied with the pricing is 20.8% of the respondents. In this, we have further broken it into two parts which are dissatisfied and highly dissatisfied 8.5% of respondents are dissatisfied and 12.3% of respondents are highly dissatisfied, while 44.3% of the respondents are satisfied with the pricing of the OTT platforms currently. In this, we have further broken it into two parts which are satisfied and highly satisfied and 26.4% of respondents are satisfied and 17.9% of respondents are highly satisfied. There is 26.4% of the respondents who are neutral in this which means that they are neither satisfied nor dissatisfied with the promotional offers which were offered.

Here we have asked the respondents to answer how satisfied they were with the availability of regional content for various OTT platforms, and we have broken it down into five categories which range from highly dissatisfied to highly satisfied.

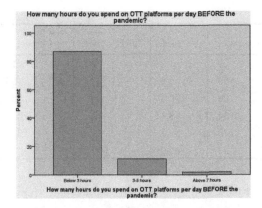

How many hours do you spend on OTT platforms per day BEFORE the pandemic?				
		Frequency	Percent	Valid Percent	Cumulative Percent
Valid	Below 3 hours	368	86.8	86.8	86.8
	3-5 hours	48	11.3	11.3	98.1
	Above 7 hours	8	1.9	1.9	100.0
	Total	424	100.0	100.0	

Figure 11.11 Frequency of spending time on OTT platform before the pandemic
Source: SPSS Software

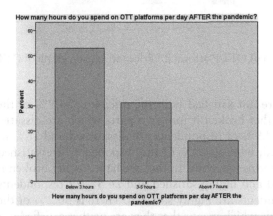

How many hours do you spend on OTT platforms per day AFTER the pandemic?				
		Frequency	Percent	Valid Percent	Cumulative Percent
Valid	Below 3 hours	224	52.8	52.8	52.8
	3-5 hours	132	31.1	31.1	84.0
	Above 7 hours	68	16.0	16.0	100.0
	Total	424	100.0	100.0	

Figure 11.12 Frequency of spending time on OTT platform after the pandemic
Source: SPSS Software

Price

		Frequency	Percent	Valid Percent	Cumulative Percent
Valid	STRONGLY DISAGREE	8	1.9	1.9	1.9
	DISAGREE	16	3.8	3.8	5.7
	NEUTRAL	88	20.8	20.8	26.4
	AGREE	184	43.4	43.4	69.8
	STRONGLY AGREE	128	30.2	30.2	100.0
	Total	424	100.0	100.0	

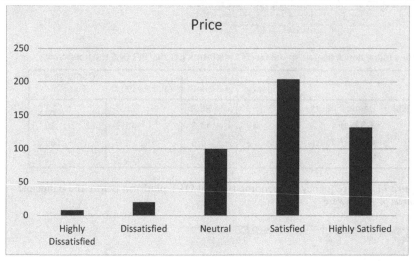

Figure 11.13 (a) Price satisfaction of OTT Platform (b) Price satisfaction graph of OTT platform
Source: SPSS Software

The percentage of people who are not satisfied with the pricing is 34.9% of the respondents. In this, we have further broken it into two parts which are dissatisfied and highly dissatisfied and 18.9% of respondents are dissatisfied and 16% of respondents are highly dissatisfied, while 34.9% of the respondents are satisfied with the pricing of the OTT platforms currently. In this, we have further broken it into two parts which are satisfied and highly satisfied and 24.5% of respondents are satisfied and 10.4% of respondents are highly satisfied. There is 30.2% of the respondents who are neutral in this which means that they are neither satisfied nor dissatisfied with the available regional content that each OTT platform has to offer right now.

Here we have asked the respondents to answer how satisfied they were with the availability of the mobile application to use these OTT platforms and we have broken it down into five categories which range from highly dissatisfied to highly satisfied. The percentage of people who are not satisfied with the pricing is 12.3% of the respondents. In this, we have further broken it into two parts which are dissatisfied and highly dissatisfied and 4.7% of respondents are dissatisfied and 7.5% of respondents are highly dissatisfied, while 68.9% of the respondents are satisfied with the pricing of the OTT platforms currently. In this, we have further broken it

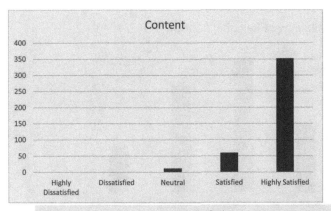

Content				
	Frequency	Percent	Valid Percent	Cumulative Percent
Valid NEUTRAL	12	2.8	2.8	2.8
AGREE	60	14.2	14.2	17.0
STRONGLY AGREE	352	83.0	83.0	100.0
Total	424	100.0	100.0	

Figure 11.14 Content satisfaction with respective OTT platforms
Source: SPSS Software

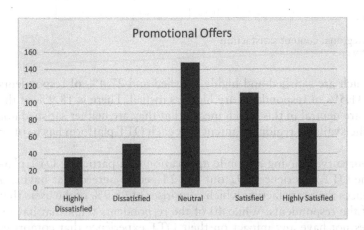

Promotional Offers				
	Frequency	Percent	Valid Percent	Cumulative Percent
Valid STRONGLY DISAGREE	36	8.5	8.5	8.5
DISAGREE	52	12.3	12.3	20.8
NEUTRAL	148	34.9	34.9	55.7
AGREE	112	26.4	26.4	82.1
STRONGLY AGREE	76	17.9	17.9	100.0
Total	424	100.0	100.0	

Figure 11.15 Promotional offers impact on customer
Source: SPSS Software

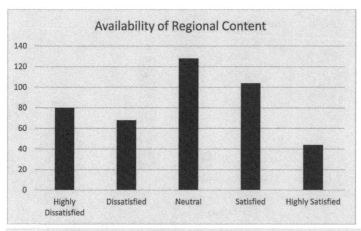

Availability of Regional Content				
		Frequency	Percent	Valid Percent	Cumulative Percent
Valid	STRONGLY DISAGREE	80	18.9	18.9	18.9
	DISAGREE	68	16.0	16.0	34.9
	NEUTRAL	128	30.2	30.2	65.1
	AGREE	104	24.5	24.5	89.6
	STRONGLY AGREE	44	10.4	10.4	100.0
	Total	424	100.0	100.0	

Figure 11.16 Regional content satisfaction
Source: SPSS Software

into two parts which are satisfied and highly satisfied and 27.4% of respondents are satisfied and 41.5% of respondents are highly satisfied. There is 18.9% of the respondents who are neutral in this which means that they are neither satisfied nor dissatisfied with the available regional content that each OTT platform has to offer right now.

According to our survey having a mobile application of a particular OTT platform enhances the OTT experience. 292 out of 424 people agreed that having a mobile app influences their satisfaction which comprises of 68.9% of the users that is the majority of the respondents. While 40 of the respondents think that having a mobile app does not have any impact on their OTT experience that comprises 9.4% of the total respondents. Whereas 92 of the respondents are not sure of this factor. They may or may not get influenced by a mobile app of a particular OTT platform which is 21.7% of the total respondents.

This pandemic has changed everyone's lives and everyone is dealing with it in their way. Many people start working on their hobbies again and others decided to be fit and started working out. Many of us binge-watch just to deal with our boredom. According to our survey 164 respondents strongly agree that they are more involved in these OTT platforms to deal with boredom which comprises 38.7% of the total survey. 128 people that is 30.2% agree that their screen time has also increased in this time. 80 people are neutral about it that it may or may not have affected their screen time and there could have been other reasons as well. While 44

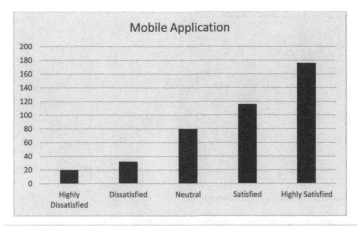

Mobile Application				
	Frequency	Percent	Valid Percent	Cumulative Percent
Valid STRONGLY DISAGREE	20	4.7	4.7	4.7
DISAGREE	32	7.5	7.5	12.3
NEUTRAL	80	18.9	18.9	31.1
AGREE	116	27.4	27.4	58.5
STRONGLY AGREE	176	41.5	41.5	100.0
Total	424	100.0	100.0	

Figure 11.17 Impact of the mobile application
Source: SPSS Software

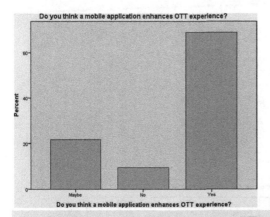

Do you think a mobile application enhances OTT experience?				
	Frequency	Percent	Valid Percent	Cumulative Percent
Valid Maybe	92	21.7	21.7	21.7
No	40	9.4	9.4	31.1
Yes	292	68.9	68.9	100.0
Total	424	100.0	100.0	

Figure 11.18 Performance impact of mobile application
Source: SPSS Software

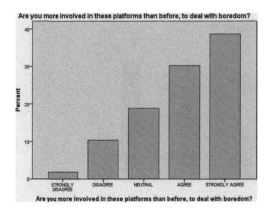

Are you more involved in these platforms than before, to deal with boredom?

		Frequency	Percent	Valid Percent	Cumulative Percent
Valid	STRONGLY DISAGREE	8	1.9	1.9	1.9
	DISAGREE	44	10.4	10.4	12.3
	NEUTRAL	80	18.9	18.9	31.1
	AGREE	128	30.2	30.2	61.3
	STRONGLY AGREE	164	38.7	38.7	100.0
	Total	424	100.0	100.0	

Figure 11.19 Pre-Pandemic impact of OTT platforms to deal with boredom
Source: SPSS Software

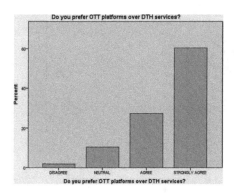

Do you prefer OTT platforms over DTH services?

		Frequency	Percent	Valid Percent	Cumulative Percent
Valid	DISAGREE	8	1.9	1.9	1.9
	NEUTRAL	44	10.4	10.4	12.3
	AGREE	116	27.4	27.4	39.6
	STRONGLY AGREE	256	60.4	60.4	100.0
	Total	424	100.0	100.0	

Figure 11.20 Preference of OTT platforms over DTH services
Source: SPSS Software

people disagree with this that is 10.4%. Eight people disagree with this and their screen time didn't increase to deal with the boredom.

According to our survey, 256 out of 424 respondents strongly agree that they prefer OTT platforms over DTH services, whatever reasons or circumstances may be and that comprises 60.4% of the total respondents that results in the majority. 116 respondents agree that they prefer OTT over DTH which results in 27.4% in total. Forty four respondents that are 10.4% of the people are neutral about it. They don't have any particular opinion about it. They will go wherever they will find good offers or content. 8 people disagree about it that is they will prefer DTH services over OTT platforms which comprise of 1.9% of the total respondents.

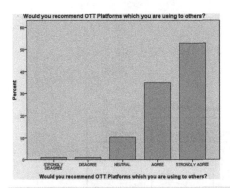

		Frequency	Percent	Valid Percent	Cumulative Percent
Valid	STRONGLY DISAGREE	4	.9	.9	.9
	DISAGREE	4	.9	.9	1.9
	NEUTRAL	44	10.4	10.4	12.3
	AGREE	148	34.9	34.9	47.2
	STRONGLY AGREE	224	52.8	52.8	100.0
	Total	424	100.0	100.0	

Source: SPSS Software

According to our survey 224 respondents strongly agree that they would recommend their OTT platforms to other people as well which comprises of 52.8% which is the majority. A total of 148 of the people agree that they would recommend that is 34.9%. 44 of them are neutral about it that they might or might not recommend that is 10.4%. Four people disagree that they won't and the other 4 strongly disagree that will never recommend it to others.

According to our survey, 176 out of 424 respondents strongly agree that they are fully satisfied with their current OTT platform, whatever reasons or circumstances may be and that comprises 41.9% of the total respondents. 208 respondents agree that they are satisfied for now which results in 49.1 in total. 32 respondents that are 7.5% of the people are neutral about it. They don't have any particular opinion about it. They'll go wherever they will find good offers or content. 8 people disagree about it that is they are satisfied with their current OTT platform which comprises 1.9%of the total respondents.

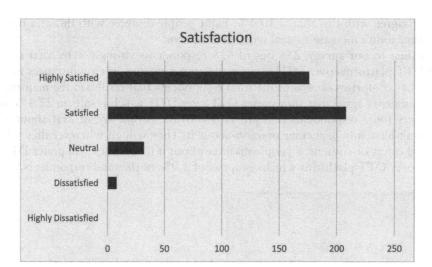

How would you rate your satisfaction with your current OTT Platform				
	Frequency	Percent	Valid Percent	Cumulative Percent
Valid DISAGREE	8	1.9	1.9	1.9
NEUTRAL	32	7.5	7.5	9.4
AGREE	208	49.1	49.1	58.5
STRONGLY AGREE	176	41.5	41.5	100.0
Total	424	100.0	100.0	

Source: SPSS Software

Chi-square test for variables

Gender and number of hours a person spent on OTT Platforms per day before the pandemic

> H0: there is no significant relationship between gender and number of hours a person spent on OTT platforms before the pandemic
> H1: there is a significant relationship between gender and number of hours a person spent on OTT platforms before the pandemic

Descriptive Statistics					
	N	Mean	Std. Deviation	Minimum	Maximum
How many hours do you spend on OTT platforms per day BEFORE the pandemic?	424	1.151	.4078	1.0	3.0
Gender	424	1.689	.4636	1.0	2.0

Source: SPSS Software

The total number of observation (N) is 424. The mean number of hours spent on OTT platforms per day before the pandemic is 1.151 and the mean for Gender is

1.689. The Standard deviation for a number of hours spent on OTT platforms per day before the pandemic is 0.4078 and for gender is 0.4636.

How many hours do you spend on OTT platforms per day BEFORE the pandemic?			
	Observed N	Expected N	Residual
Below 3 hours	368	141.3	226.7
3-5 hours	48	141.3	-93.3
Above 7 hours	8	141.3	-133.3
Total	424		

Source: SPSS Software

According to our survey, it was observed that 368 of the people spend less than three hours on the OTT platform where the expected value was 141.3. While 48 of them spend between three to five hours on it while the expected value was 141.3. It was also noticed that eight of them spend above seven hours while the expected value was 141.3

Gender			
	Observed N	Expected N	Residual
Female	132	212.0	-80.0
Male	292	212.0	80.0
Total	424		

Source: SPSS Software

In gender, the observed value for females is 132 and for males, it is 292. The expected value for males is 212 and it is 212 for females, which is the same for both.

Test Statistics		
	How many hours do you spend on OTT platforms per day BEFORE the pandemic?	Gender
Chi-Square	550.943[a]	60.377[b]
df	2	1
Asymp. Sig.	.000	.000

a. 0 cells (0.0%) have expected frequencies less than 5. The minimum expected cell frequency is 141.3.

b. 0 cells (0.0%) have expected frequencies less than 5. The minimum expected cell frequency is 212.0.

Source: SPSS Software

Degree of freedom (hours spent on OTT platforms before pandemic) = 2
Degree of freedom (gender) = 1
As the level of significance (p-value) =<0.001, it implies that H1 is accepted
Gender and no. of hours a person spent on OTT Platform per day after a pandemic

H0: There is no significant relationship between gender and number of hours
a person spent on OTT platforms after a pandemic
H1: There is a significant relationship between gender and number of hours a
person spent on OTT platforms after a pandemic

Descriptive Statistics

	N	Mean	Std. Deviation	Minimum	Maximum
How many hours do you spend on OTT platforms per day AFTER the pandemic?	424	1.632	.7447	1.0	3.0
Gender	424	1.689	.4636	1.0	2.0

Figure 11.21 Post Pandemic time impact on OTT platforms
Source: SPSS Software

The total number of observation (N) is 424. The mean number of hours spent
on OTT platforms per day after the pandemic is 1.632 and the mean for Gender is
1.689. The standard deviation for a number of hours spent on OTT platforms per
day after the pandemic is 0.7447 and for Gender is 0.4636.

How many hours do you spend on OTT platforms per day AFTER the pandemic?

	Observed N	Expected N	Residual
Below 3 hours	224	141.3	82.7
3-5 hours	132	141.3	-9.3
Above 7 hours	68	141.3	-73.3
Total	424		

Source: SPSS Software

According to our survey, it was observed that 224 of the people spend less than
three hours on the OTT platform where the expected value was 141.3. While 132
of them spend between—three to five hours on it while the expected value was
141.3. It was also noticed that 68 of them spend above seven hours while the
expected value was 141.3.

We can see that the number of hours in total has increased. The number of
people who watched for less than three hours has decreased from before the pandemic and after the pandemic while the number of people who watched for three
to five hours has increased from 48 respondents who watched before the pandemic to 132 respondents after the pandemic. Also, the number of respondents
has increased who watch more than seven hours from eight respondents who used
to watch above seven hours before pandemic to 68 respondents who watch above
seven hours after the pandemic.

Gender			
	Observed N	Expected N	Residual
Female	132	212.0	-80.0
Male	292	212.0	80.0
Total	424		

Source: SPSS Software

In gender, the observed value for females is 132 and for males, it is 292. The expected value for males is 212 and it is 212 for females, which is the same for both.

Test Statistics		
	How many hours do you spend on OTT platforms per day AFTER the pandemic?	Gender
Chi-Square	87.019[a]	60.377[b]
df	2	1
Asymp. Sig.	.000	.000

a. 0 cells (0.0%) have expected frequencies less than 5. The minimum expected cell frequency is 141.3.

b. 0 cells (0.0%) have expected frequencies less than 5. The minimum expected cell frequency is 212.0.

Source: SPSS Software

Degree of freedom (hours spent on OTT platforms after pandemic) = 2
Degree of freedom (gender) = 1
As the level of significance (p-value) =<0.001, it implies that H1 is accepted
Hence it can be said that there exists a significant relationship between gender and time a person spent on OTT platforms before the pandemic and after the pandemic.

Discussion and conclusion

COVID-19 has changed our world drastically and people are dealing with it in their ways. People are focusing on their hobbies trying to cope in any way possible. In this particular study, we have discussed how OTT platforms have changed the lives of people and how the pandemic has affected the OTT platforms. We have also studied the growth of the platforms in the last few years and how people are

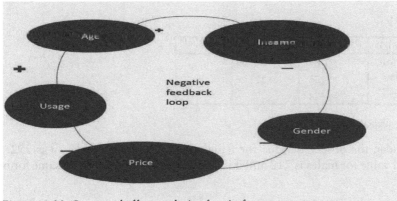

Figure 11.22 Cause and effect analysis of main factors
Source: i-think software

switching from DTH services to OTT platforms. There is a whole new set of content available now on these platforms of all genres. People of all age groups enjoy these platforms. There has been no boundary related to age or gender or language. We can now watch anything and everything with just a single click.

Conclusion

There has been an immense increase in the number of users on OTT platforms. The major portion of the users on these platforms are from between 20–30 years of age followed by 3040. Gender diversity is less as there is a majority of males who watch on OTT platforms which comprise 69% of the total respondents. It was concluded that the majority of viewers were students as a profession with no earning at this point followed by the private sector with a salary of more than 10 lakh per annum. Out of the total respondent 94.8% of the people use these OTT platforms and out of the 88% have subscribed to these platforms majority of the respondents use Netflix followed by Amazon prime and YouTube. 70% of the people prefer the thriller/mystery genre the most, followed by comedy, and then action. There has been diversity in this area as people prefer different kinds of genres rather than sticking to just a single one. It was observed that before the pandemic more people watched Amazon Prime but after the pandemic, the shift was to Netflix and people subscribed more to Netflix than to Amazon. Before the pandemic majority of people spent less than 3 hours on OTT platforms but after the pandemic, this percentage was decreased, and people started spending more time on it. The content was the major issue for subscribing to these particular OTT platforms followed by the ease of watching and the price for them. About 51% of people are satisfied with the price that they are paying for their OTT platform. People are highly satisfied with the content available on the platforms. People are not fully satisfied with the promotional offers or the availability of regional content on the OTT platforms. The mobile application plays a major role in switching to these platforms and people prefer them most because they can watch it anytime they want. Convenience is the word that they mostly describe these platforms and they would recommend it to their friends and family.

Recommendations

Based on our questionnaire and the observations, we found some things that need some improvement so that the users are more satisfied with the OTT platform that they are using.

1. There can be more content available for different age and generations. So, that everyone is equally satisfied.
2. There can be more promotional offers or discounts or other offers to attract potential users or to sustain the existing ones.
3. There should be a package for 15 days or less so that more people can afford it and find it feasible.
4. There can be more shows keeping different regional languages in mind concerning the diversity in our country.
5. There can be more content that includes documentaries or other shows that helps in enhancing knowledge.

References

Aggarwal, V. (2019). Nearly 20 million viewers opt-out of DTH services as bills start to pinch. Available at https://www.thehindubusinessline.com/info- tech/nearly-20-million-viewers-opt-out-of-dth-services-as-bills-start-to- pinch/article29568206.ece retrieved on1/6/21

Bhavsar, R. (2018). Digital Media: Rise of on-demand content. (Deloitte, 2015). Available at https://www2.deloitte.com/content/dam/Deloitte/in/Documents/technology-media-telecommunications/in-tmt-rise-of-on-demand-content.pdf retrievedon10/4/20

Mark Casey, Partner and Global Telecoms, Media & Entertainment Lead, Deloitte Patrick Steemers, Partner and Telecom, Media & Technology Lead, Deloitte Netherlands Jean-Charles Ferreri, Partner, Monitor Deloitte France (2018). The future of the TV and Video landscape by 2030. Deloitte. Available at https://www2.deloitte.com/content/dam/Deloitte/global/Documents/Technology-Media-Telecommunications/de-future-tv-and-video.pdf Retrieved on 10/5/21.

Chawla, P. R., (2020). OTT apps on India Top 10s per App Annie 2020: Only Netflix, Hotstar on consumer spends; MX Player, Hotstar on MAU. Available at https://www.mediabrief.com/mx-player-netflix-hotstar-on-app-annie-2020-india-lists/ Retrieved on20/6/21

Dasgupta, P. (2021). The Rise of Over-the-Top Content: Implications for Television Advertising in a Direct-to-Consumer World. Available at https://www.tcs.com/content/dam/tcs/pdf/Industries/communication-media-and-technology/Abstract/Over-d-Top-Content.pdf.

Dwivedi, Y. K., Ismagilova, E., Hughes, D. L., Carlson, J., Filieri, R., Jacobson, J., . . . & Wang, Y. (2021). Setting the future of digital and social media marketing research: Perspectives and research propositions. *International Journal of Information Management, 59*, 102168.

Ekpo, A. E., Riley, B. K., Thomas, K. D., Yvaire, Z., Gerri, G. R. H., & Muñoz, I. I. (2015). As worlds collide: The role of marketing management in customer-to-customer interactions. *Journal of Business Research, 68*(1), 119–126.

Fitzgerald, S. (2019). Over-the-Top Video Services in India: Media Imperialism after Globalization. Media Indus. J. 6(1).

Grewal, D., Hulland, J., Kopalle, P. K., & Karahanna, E. (2020). The future of technology and marketing: A multidisciplinary perspective. *Journal of the Academy of Marketing Science, 48*(1), 1–8.

Mahendher, S., Sharma, A., Chhibber, P., & Hans, A. (2021). Impact of COVID-19 on digital entertainment industry. *UGC Care Journal, 44*, 148–161.

https://journals.sagepub.com/doi/full/10.1177/0972262921989118, accessed on June 10, 2021

https://www.indiatoday.in/magazine/news-makers/story/20210111-win-some-lose-some-1755080-2021-01-03, accessed on June 15, 2021

https://www.emerald.com/insight/content/doi/10.1108/IJPCC-07-2020-0083/full/html?skipTracking=true , accessed on June 15, 2021

https://archives.palarch.nl/index.php/jae/article/view/1662 , accessed on June 15, 2021

https://www.researchgate.net/publication/344561393_Covid-19_Conclusion_A_Media_And_Entertainment_Sector_Perspective_In_India, accessed on June 25, 2021

https://sambadenglish.com/the-rise-of-ott-platforms-in-india-and-the-fall-that-may-come-soon/, accessed on June 15, 2021

https://www.mid-day.com/lifestyle/infotainment/article/the-rise-of-ott-platforms-in-india-during-the-pandemic-23180042, accessed on June 19, 2021

https://www.researchgate.net/publication/341558182_Emergence_and_future_of_Over-the-top_OTT_video_services_in_India_an_analytical_research, accessed on July 5,2021

https://www.emerald.com/insight/content/doi/10.1108/IJPCC-07-2020-0083/full/html?skipTracking=true&utm_source=TrendMD&utm_medium=cpc&utm_campaign=International_Journal_of_Pervasive_Computing_and_Communications_TrendMD_0&WT.mc_id=Emerald_TrendMD_0, accessed on June 12,2021

https://www.globalpresshub.com/index.php/ABAARJ/article/view/1107, accessed on July 3,2021 https://www.researchgate.net/profile/Sheetal-Mahendher/publication/350063792_IMPACT_OF_COVID, accessed on June 15,2021

http://researchhub.org.in/researchhub/admin/uploadedImage/reserch/1614976018.pdf accessed on June 30, 2021

https://scholar.archive.org/work/rqx5uyhaynazxoxwp42j5lrrvu/access/wayback/https://www.ijcmph.com/index.php/ijcmph/article/download/8203/5011, accessed on July 2, 2021

https://www.amity.edu/gwalior/jccc/pdf/dec_09.pdf, accessed on June 27, 2021

https://www.researchgate.net/profile/Sunitha-S-2/publication/344561393_Covid-19_Conclusion_A_Media_And_Entertainment_Sector_Perspective_In_India/links/5f80483f92851c14bcb9397c/Covid-19-Conclusion-A-Media-And-Entertainment-Sector-Perspective-In-India.pdf, accessed on June 22, 2021

Johny, J., & Alukal, P. (2018). Video on demand industry: Challenges and opportunities in the Indian Market. *International Journal of Innovative Science and Research Technology, 3*(5), 598–612.

Moochhala, Q. (2018). The Future of Online OTT Entertainment Services in India.

Sujata, J., Sohag, S., Tanu, D., Chintan, D., Shubham, P., and Sumit, G. (2015). Impact of over-the-top (OTT) services on telecom service providers. Indian J Sci Technol. 8(S4):145–160.

Tong, S. R., Du, S. T., Chen, L. W., Chen, S., and Yeh, E. (2015). A peer-to-peer streaming CDN for supporting OTT video broadcast service in mobile networks. In *2015 IEEE International Conference on Consumer Electronics- Taiwan* (260–261). IEEE.

Udovita, P. V. M. V. D. (2020). Conceptual review on dimensions of digital transformation in modern era. *International Journal of Scientific and Research Publications, 10*(2), 520–529.

Yun, J. T., Segijn, C. M., Pearson, S., Malthouse, E. C., Konstan, J. A., & Shankar, V. (2020). Challenges and future directions of computational advertising measurement systems. *Journal of Advertising, 49*(4), 446–458.

12 An empirical analysis of women entrepreneurship—An insight into opportunities and challenges

Simeon S. Simon and Utkarssha Marathe

St Francis Institute of Management and Research, Mumbai, India

Abstract

The purpose of this research is to investigate new opportunities encouraging women entrepreneurs to start their own businesses and to explore the various barriers encountered by them during their business journey. Women entrepreneurship is all about women empowerment, this study would help women recognise the oncoming challenges in their businesses and can help them foresee and come up with appropriate solutions. It is important to study women entrepreneurs in modern times and there is a need to carry out appropriate research concerning various problems faced by women entrepreneurs in our country. This study paves the way to explore what opportunities lay ahead for women entrepreneurs. Such a study encourages women to start their own businesses and improve their social and economic standing. The information that will be obtained from this research will serve as guidelines for future businesses, enhance women's personalities, identify their motivational factors, challenges and opportunities women would encounter in the future, and the requirements of ideal characters of women entrepreneurs, in a more precise manner. With the findings from the research, the profile of women entrepreneurs and the aspiring candidates whose ambition is to become future entrepreneurs could be well defined with a new level of understanding.

Depending on the purpose of the study and the nature of the phenomenon, the descriptive design has been undertaken, and quantitative research has been used to make use of survey questionnaires to collect primary data from women entrepreneurs in Mumbai city and convenient sampling has been used in sample design. The empirics were collected by structured questionnaires. The questionnaire measures the opinion of respondents on various factors of entrepreneurial opportunities, challenges, and development in Mumbai city. This research undertook regression analysis showing a perfect positive relationship between the independent and dependent variables, which explains the level of impact due to political, environmental, and financial challenges encountered by women entrepreneurs.

Indian women entrepreneurship is becoming one of the fastest-growing sectors, where women can enter and thrive in various business activities. Most women are capable of taking risks, introducing innovations, and managing their businesses with their creative experiences. Whether it is a small enterprise or a big organisation, women can very well build up their entrepreneurial skills and run their businesses efficiently. This study brings out the opportune factors for women to enter new business sectors, exposing the challenges they would face during their business journey, giving them a scope to foresee, explore, and manage confidently such obstacles in the future.

Keywords: Remedial measures to enhance women entrepreneurship, women entrepreneurial challenges, women entrepreneurial opportunities

Introduction

Women entrepreneurship has been a subject of debate in the recent past, but there is a visible growth of women leadership in entrepreneurial businesses. Today, a lot of corporate firms have women leaders, efficiently managing the big corporate companies. There has been a wide recognition and acceptance of female managers, leaders, etc. in the corporate sectors over the last few years. It has been seen that women entrepreneurs are immensely supporting economic development by creating new jobs and by improving GDP. According to research studies it has been seen that from the year 2000, there has been a consistent change in the jobs of women—they are getting into more professional jobs and are working in corporate sectors as well. Women represent almost one-half of the world's population having significant ability and capacity; however, it is evident that they are being underutilised towards the economic development of the nation. The Indian scenario is not an exception in this context. Although small businesses owned by women are traditionally focusing on the fashion industry and boutiques, now women entrepreneurs are entering manufacturing, production, logistics, food, catering, and other services sectors. Women-owned businesses evidently contribute to various economies of the world. According to the survey of 2019, it is seen that 13.76% of businesses are owned by women entrepreneurs, which is a significant increase from the last decade. The government of India offers a helping hand to women entrepreneurs in diverse forms. The government has introduced Bhartiya Mahila Bank Business Loan, Mudra Yojana Scheme, etc. to financially support women entrepreneurs.

The emergence of women on the economic scene as marketers is showing a significant development, which motivates them towards securing a distinguished and deserving place in society. As a matter of fact, the role of women in national development is a crucial one. Women are playing an important role in the vital economic progress of developing countries. With an increase in the number of women getting educated, there is a considerable awareness among women to be self-employed and gradually the role of women in our society is changing. The entry of women into organised business sectors as entrepreneurs is a recent development. However, women have been contributing to the production process since the evolution of cottage industries. Women have all along participated in outdoor occupations, namely agricultural and other allied activities. There have been many professional working women, who have used their educational skills to become doctors, teachers, hairdressers, fashion designers, etc. However, it should be realised that they also need to play a crucial role in future economic growth and development.

There are various challenges and hurdles these women entrepreneurs have to encounter. Research data and surveys show that there still exists gender inequality. According to a survey done in 2020, it has been seen that women run 13% of small businesses. The general challenges are insufficient financial resources and lack of credit resources. In some places in India, society is yet to accept women entrepreneurs as their leaders.

With all the demotivating factors from society, women are still managing to run the business entity. Some studies have shown that the women-run businesses are making promising contributions to economic development, national competitiveness, and effective network trade by bringing out innovative products into the national market. As per the findings of the research study, women entrepreneurs have established the ability to build and maintain long-term relationships and develop networks for effective communication between the organisations, being aware of the environmental needs, and always supporting and improving cultural differences. Most of the top leading brands in India are owned and run by female CEOs. They always strive to overcome challenges and explore opportunities to accomplish their objectives.

All over the world, it is evident that women entrepreneurship is contributing towards the establishment of a stable environment leading to healthy well-being amongst the communities and helping them to give economic opportunities for unprivileged groups including women, low wage earners, and minorities. Another important contribution to society is the creation of wealth and giving employment opportunities. In India, it is found out that many women are still illiterate, unemployed, and exist in poor living conditions. These situations do not prevent them from participating in local economies and becoming entrepreneurs. Small enterprises offer them a chance to improve their lives by creating new jobs. The participation of women in economic development in India contributes to a more human, cooperative, balanced, and pleasant work environment in women-led enterprises, in which individual development is engraved.

Background study

Entrepreneurship is something that gives an opportunity to introduce and market the products and services in an international or national market. It refers to the concept of developing and managing a business entity in order to gain profits by taking various risks in a win-win situation. Entrepreneurship generally involves risk beyond what is normally experienced in starting a business, which may include some factors for instance economic, political, environmental, social, cultural, etc. It is the process of discovering new ways to combine resources and generate a product or a service. To gain profit for the firm, the entrepreneur must ensure that his product has a greater market value than the others, generated elsewhere by using the same resources. It is a multi-level and complex phenomenon that has gained importance in the world economy. It is seen that entrepreneurship has contributed to the global economy by offering jobs to millions, by mobilizing public wealth; there has also been significant growth in the GDP.

One of the entrepreneur's jobs is to manage and look for the right time to launch products and to keep a positive approach towards the growth of an enterprise. Entrepreneurs need to create something distinct, something innovative, something creative that changes or alters the product value. Regardless of the firm size, big or small, they can take part in entrepreneurship opportunities. The opportunity to become an entrepreneur requires four criteria. First, there must be new opportunities or situations where the resources can be used to generate profit for the company. Second, different kind of people should be involved, such as those who can recognise a new opportunity and the other who can make the resources useful for the new opportunity. Third part is where the entrepreneur must be ready to take some risks. Fourth, the entrepreneurial process requires stability and communication between organisation of people and resources.

Entrepreneurship has been showing a big gender gap and this industry has been dominated by male members for many decades now. However, this has changed in the last few years as now women entrepreneurship has started to be recognised. They have created new job opportunities and new career paths for themselves. Firstly, empowering women and motivating them to start their own business, and innovating new brands has made a major impact on economic development. To make our economy stronger we need to focus on creative ways to expand our economic and social development.

Role of women entrepreneurship

Women entrepreneurs are those women who innovate, initiate, or adopt a business activity. They run their businesses by owning at least 51% of the capital. Women's entrepreneurship has been recognised during the last decade with the introduction of new jobs. They offer different novel ideas, jobs and solutions to the management, organisation, and business problems. Not only do they start their own business, but they are also working as managers in various companies. Women entrepreneurship is not only about starting their own business but it's all about women empowerment. Many top firms have female managers and CEOs who make big decisions for the company. In this era of globalisation, Indian women are playing a magnificent role in the progress of the country and trying to increase the economy and raise their income. Previously, women used to work in the agricultural sector or in small industries, but now they are interested in starting their own small businesses. They are not just earning money, but they are also trying to save money and run their families. In urban areas, especially in developing countries, Indian women are actively participating in two sectors – organised and unorganised. Women are working in both private and public sectors and in some cases, they are running their own firm.

The government has also understood the importance of women's entrepreneurship and has introduced various initiatives and schemes. There is The Bhartiya Mahila Bank which was introduced to provide financial support to underprivileged women wanting to start their own business. Also, there is Dena Shakti Scheme where women have been sanctioned loans of up to 20 lakhs and many more.

Although 1/3rd of the business sector is owned by women, there are various other challenges they have to face in their businesses, for instance being dominated by the male population in the sector. But women entrepreneurs are still growing in numbers, making India one of the 20 top countries that have growing women entrepreneurship. Opportunities are also seen in this sector for women. They are trying to join computer business, confectionary business, general items business, vegetables or fruits business, stationery shops, printing press, the newspaper business, publication business, writing books, mobile shop holders, coaching institutions, tea stalls, medical stores, hospital business, automobile business, etc. There is a great change in women's thinking patterns and culture. In India, they are not afraid of taking risks. They come forward taking loans from private or government sectors. They feel secure, creative, self-confident, happy, busy, and economically independent. If we want more women entrepreneurs in Indian society, the needs of women entrepreneurs should be fulfilled by their family members and the government. If there is no gender difference found in the workplace, they can work in a better way.

Major women entrepreneurship activities

Major women entrepreneurial activities in Mumbai are retail-oriented and some of them are engaged in manufacturing and production. Mumbai city is known for start-ups and has seen many successful ones. Small to large-scale industries are functioning successfully in Mumbai. People even have some businesses functioning from their home where the topmost one is to provide tiffin services. Mumbai is also headquarters to a lot of financial institutions such as Bombay stock exchange, reserve bank of India, national stock exchange. The city is also known for various other big Indian companies such as the Tata group, Reliance group, Aditya Birla group, Hindustan Petroleum as also goods industries namely Hindustan Unilever, Proctor and Gamble, Godrej products, Nivea and much more. Other than this the city has generated 3.8 billion $ of revenue from its tourism sector as per the reports in 2016 and supported 7.3% of its total employment.

Women entrepreneurs in Mumbai are from various industries, ranging from food to fashion, they are trying to slowly penetrate all the industries. There are many notable women entrepreneurs in Mumbai—Falguni Nayar, owner of Nykaa founded in 2008, created the beauty and wellness e-commerce platform, for buying online beauty products. The company value is estimated to be 1.2 billion, known as the most trusted brand in the beauty sector. The owner of Mumum Co Farah Nathani Menzies, founded the company in 2017, with an aim to provide food—highly nutritious and organic with no preservatives—has a value worth 35 Million. Another well-known owner of entrepreneur business is Malini Agrawal, owner of Miss Malini entertainment. She is an influencer, an author and a reporter for the entertainment business, the net worth of the company is 1 to 5 billion. Except for these big businesses, they are women who own small or even household businesses. There is a woman running a business of Gujarati foods from her house, selling on the platform of Swiggy, Zomato as well as from her own sources, the company is known as Gujju ben ka Nashta, it is a sensation on the internet. Other than these women are now ruling the fashion sector and have their own boutiques and even have their own designer label.

COVID-19 and its impact on entrepreneurs

COVID-19 has devastated many lives, societies, and economies all around the world. COVID-19, being a pandemic, has created a huge shift not only in human-itarian aspects but also in economic and social aspects. It has affected all types of businesses, from small to big, as a result of which many companies have suffered severe losses during this pandemic. The economy around the world has been very disruptive. The Indian economy sank down to 3.1% according to the ministry of statistics and it was mainly due to the pandemic. Almost every sector in India has been badly affected as domestic demand and exports have fallen rapidly, although some sectors such as pharma, home delivery sites, online retailing have not been impacted that much.

According to a survey over 80% of small businesses have had a negative impact and it is believed that it will take years to recover. The pandemic has affected the imports and exports of the country, which in return has affected small to large-scale industries. According to a survey, the Indian imports and exports have fallen to approx. A total of 10% as compared to 2019. Export of jewellery had dropped to 98.74% and export of leather products had fallen up to 92%. Big Indian brands such as BHEL, Tata Motors, UltraTech Cement, Grasim Industries, and L&T, etc., have shut down their operations or reduced their services significantly.

Aviation and tourism industries have been dealing with severe cash flow issues, laying off 70% of their total workforce. The beauty sector has also seen a major drop for due to the constant lockdown they are unable to run their businesses and beauty shops. Businesses have seen a major financial dropdown; they were even unable to pay off the salaries and have seen a major setback. The retail industry has almost hit rock bottom. Small in-house catering services have also seen financial breakdowns. Event management companies have also been hit severely, which in turn, has affected the suppliers and vendors, along with travel agencies putting them in an adverse effect.

It was noticed that due to constant lockdown, small-scale industries have been severely impacted. In urban areas as well, small firms have been affected due to this pandemic. According to a survey done, nearly 46% of businesses that were permanently closed had no intention of starting another business, 27.8% of businesses were neutral on restarting, and 26.4% were positive about starting a new business. It was shocking to know that almost 5% of the businesses shut down permanently and had no intention to even restart the firm. Enterprises have seen a major loss and have shut down completely, some of the companies have laid off people due to lack of capital. Mumbai city has also been under lockdown since March 2020, the government relaxed some measures in the city for some months but again due to the increase of patients the city had to go under lockdown. This affected a lot of small-scale businesses. Restaurants, hotels, beauty salons and parlours, malls, movie theatres, etc. were partially opened or were even completely closed since last year. This has not only affected the businesses but has affected the economy in general. The government should incorporate some initiatives to help the business to revamp and restart. There should be education training for re-launching small sector businesses. The business needs financial support along with some technological advancements and skilled employees. The business entrepreneurs should also apply techniques to survive this pandemic, organisations need to understand the present external environment, for which they need to conduct PESTLE analysis. Technology-related changes need to be properly addressed and assessed. Based on the internal and external analysis, the business entities should use SWOT analysis to correctly identify its strengths, weaknesses, opportunities, and threats.

Objectives

To investigate the factors encouraging women entrepreneurs to start their own businesses

To explore the barriers encountered by women entrepreneurs

To examine new opportunities in the business sector for women entrepreneurs

Research design

Research design performs the strategy to carry out research that defines a concise and logical plan to overcome the given question by collecting, interpreting, analysing, and discussing the data to find out the conclusion. The following research comprises two types of data that is primary data and secondary data. Primary data was collected by the researcher from the main source directly. In this research the primary data was collected from the targeted audience—the women entrepreneurs-working in Mumbai by a questionnaire floated on a google form. Secondary data was collected from the information collected by other researchers. The sampling technique used in the following research was convenience sampling. Convenience sampling is one of the non-probability sampling methods. It is one of the easiest methods of sampling as it is based on the availability of the target audience and on their willingness to take part. Convenience sampling is a method that involves getting the participants where they are conveniently available. The type of research used for this research is descriptive research. It is the method that describes the population and situation that is being studied. It generally focuses on answering the 'what' of the research instead of 'why' in the research. Descriptive research is also called observational research, as in this method not a single variable is affected or influenced during the process. Descriptive research is a quantitative method, it collects information from the targeted audience and analyses it statistically. The target audience for this research is women who run their own businesses of any nature and size. The targeted respondents are women entrepreneurs only based in Mumbai city. The sample size of this survey is 50 respondents. 50 women entrepreneurs have responded, and the response rate is 100%. A questionnaire is a type of research instrument that allows us to collect first-hand information to prepare primary data. It has a series of questions that cover a mix of closed-ended and open-ended questions. It is a very convenient way to collect answers from a large audience in a very short period. It is very important to design a questionnaire so that the responses are accurate, and the results are concluded appropriately.

Significant data analysis

Political problems faced by women entrepreneurs while running a business

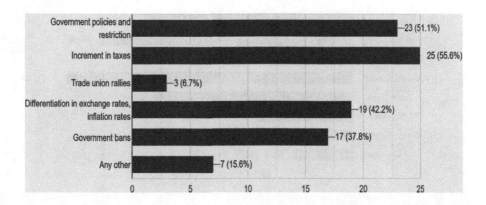

Environmental and social challenges faced by women entrepreneurs while running a business

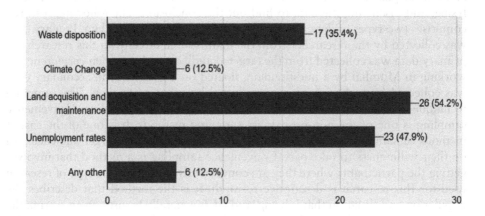

Respondents opinion on Financial problems faced by women entrepreneurs

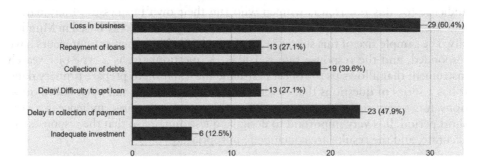

Respondents opinion on entrepreneurial opportunities or growth sector

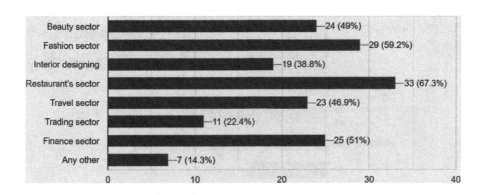

Challenges faced by women entrepreneurs during COVID-19 pandemic

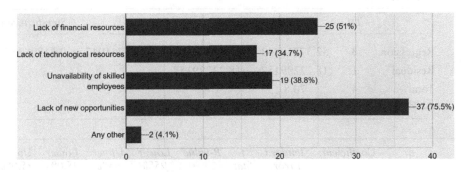

Tool used: Multiple regression method: The use of multiple regression here in this study is highly remarkable to estimate the degree of relationship between various challenges encountered by women entrepreneurs and its level of impact due to such challenges. Multiple regression is used to find a relationship between the independent and dependent variables. It can be used for more than one variable and helps us to understand whether the result is appropriate or not. Here in this study, multiple regression is used to find a relationship between the independent variables such as political challenges, environmental challenges, and financial challenges and its dependent variable—the level impact of such challenges.

Political	Environmental	Financial	Y(impact)
23	17	29	2
25	6	13	11
19	26	19	8
17	23	13	4
7	6	23	1

Regression statistics

Regression statistics	
Multiple R	0.903371299
R Square	0.816079703
Adjusted R square	0.264318814
Standard error	4.889748312
Observations	5

ANOVA

	Df	*SS*	*MS*	*F*	*Significance F*
Regression	3	52.57710843	17.52570281	0.961741047	0.617062273
Residual	1	18.22289157	18.22289157		
Total	4	70.8			
ANOVA					

	Coefficients	*Standard Error*	*t Stat*	*P-value*	*Lower 95%*	*Upper 95%*	*Lower 95.0%*	*Upper 95.0%*
Intercept	6.84	9.53	0.72	0.60	–114.25	127.93	–114.25	127.93
Political	0.34	0.31	1.08	0.47	–3.64	4.32	–3.64	4.32
Environmental	–0.06	0.23	–0.25	0.85	–3.01	2.90	–3.01	2.90
Financial	–0.36	0.32	–1.13	0.46	–4.37	3.66	–4.37	3.66

Null Hypothesis, H0 = B1 = B2 = B3 = 0, There is no relationship between independent and dependent variables.

Alternate Hypothesis, H1 = at least 1 B1 ≠ 0, There is the relationship between independent and dependent variables.

Multiple regression = 0.90, which shows a perfect positive relationship between the independent and dependant variables, which explains the level of impact due to political, environmental, and financial challenges encountered by women entrepreneurs.

The table shows that the multiple regression coefficient is 0.90 and it measures the degree of relationship between the actual values and the predicted values of the impact of challenges because the predicted values are obtained as a linear combination of political, environmental, and financial challenges. The co-efficient value of 0.90 indicates that the relationship between the level of impact experienced by the entrepreneurs and the various challenges causing the impact such as politics, environment, and Finance is very strong and positive.

The Table shows that the coefficient of determination R-square measures the goodness of fit of the estimated sample regression plane in terms of the proportion of the variation in the dependent variables explained by the fitted sample regression equation. Thus, the value of R-square is 0.81, which simply means that about 0.81 % of the variation in the impact level of various challenges, which is explained by the estimated SRP that uses the factors of various challenges due to 'political, environmental and financial' as the independent variables and R-square value is significant at 1% percent level.

Discussion on findings

There are positive and significant linkages between age and business performance of entrepreneurs in developing countries. This can be understood from the context that married women with children are faced with more responsibilities. It was evident from this research that most women entrepreneurs are above 45 years of age with the lowest age group starting a business being below the age of 25 and most of them are married entrepreneurs. In this research, 36% of the women entrepreneurs are unmarried and running their own business and the remaining are married entrepreneurs. Education is presumably related to knowledge, skills, motivation, self-confidence, problem-solving ability, commitment, and discipline. The research shows that 58% of respondents are educated up to graduation and above, but then, many women entrepreneurs have a very basic education. The effect of previous entrepreneurial experience normally has a positive impact on business performance. This research found out that 36% of women were working women before they started their own business, and a large number of them were housewives. The research shows almost 25% of women had no experience before starting their business. They learn and grow while doing the business. Women entrepreneurs start new businesses due to dissatisfaction with their previous jobs as a major motivating factor. 36% of women run their small enterprises in their homes or they own a small shop with 510 employees, while 26% of women have business activities such as grocery shops, or everyday essentials or vegetable shops. The research reveals that many women entrepreneurs are running service businesses like pharmacies, medical clinics, food services, beauty parlours or an interior design and architecture firm, fashion and designing, bakery and grocery shops, and in the textile area. The research shows that while launching a new firm, women entrepreneurs will take 16 months. A total of 66% of women have a turnover of 0 to 20 lakhs annually. This shows they are financially independent while 28% of them had 20 to 40 lakhs of turnover. The research shows that 75.5% of women use their own savings or assets to start a business. 40.8% had to take a loan from some financial institution as a source to start their business. There are various challenges faced by women entrepreneurs while in a business. Most political challenges faced by women entrepreneurs are high taxes imposed by the government. The government restrictions were major challenges during the ongoing pandemic when the lockdown was imposed. Land acquisition and maintenance have also been big challenges faced by women entrepreneurs. The ongoing employment rates have also been a social issue while running a business. Financial problems have been a challenge for everyone in entrepreneurial businesses. Women entrepreneurs have majorly faced losses in their business and delay in the collection of bill payments. The difficulty in getting a loan has also been a problem. Women entrepreneurs experience discriminating treatment in society and strong competition from male domination. The above challenges demotivate women entrepreneurs while they are running a business. The COVID-19 pandemic has been one of the worst curses impacting their businesses all around the world. Mumbai city has also been affected badly and has been in lockdown for more than a year. Major challenges women must face are lack of new opportunities, the lack of financial resources, and lack of skilled employees along with technological resources. Most women are of the opinion that there are growth opportunities in the restaurant sector, fashion sector, and finance sector. Women entrepreneurs have a strong opinion that they can grow their businesses in beauty, travel, and tourism sectors. Mumbai city appears to have grown significantly in catering and food services. The finance sector and automobile sectors also seem to have grown with future opportunities.

Opportunities for women entrepreneurs in Mumbai: Women entrepreneurship has seen an increase not only in India but all over the world. Earlier there used to be only 10% of women entrepreneurs and now they are doubling up slowly year by year, which is an outcome of ongoing initiatives to empower women in the entrepreneurship sector. There are several opportunities in Mumbai for women to enter the field of entrepreneurship. Many women have started small businesses, which they run from their own houses due to various factors. Some of the opportunities in 2021 concerning women are to enter the field of digital marketing, advertising, blogging, and website development. They can be powerful social media influencers, and social media is one of the majorly growing industries along with food-related businesses. The food industry has not been overly affected in COVID-19, although restaurants are closed, but the government has allowed delivery of products. Since homemade cakes and bakery items are in high demand, there are many small businesses where women are selling bakery items from their homes. COVID-19 has made it difficult to work but has also opened many new opportunities. Now that online education has observed a sudden surge, women can now sit at home and give online lectures all over the country. Along with that, since people are concentrating more on health and wellness, they are in search of immunity suppliers, and vitamins, etc., as these products are in high demand during COVID-19.

Challenges faced by women entrepreneurs: Women entrepreneurs have faced many challenges, struggles, hindrances while running their own firms. Entering a business venture has not been such an easy task for the women as they had to face many difficulties to get success. Some of the challenges faced by women entrepreneurs are given below.

Limited financial access: Financial shortage or low capital has been one of the major setbacks for many entrepreneurs. Women face a big challenge when it comes to capital investment. In some cases, women are supported by family members but most of the time they must use their own savings or borrow from friends or take out a loan. To collect capital for starting a firm has been a big issue for women entrepreneurs. They also face financial problems while dealing with raw materials, collection of payments, inventory charges, etc.

Lack of managerial skills: When it comes to entering a market, women get a little scared while dealing with certain issues. This is due to a lack of support from society and they are also deprived of required training and education related to marketing of products strategically. Women experience low self-confidence when it comes to marketing a product which is due to a lack of experience in the business area.

Dealing with the middleman: Dealing with the middleman is mostly dealing with the suppliers, retailers, and vendors. They also suffer from limited access to contacts, although women are good at maintaining relations, still, they have a low business network as compared to men. There are very few middlemen who don't want to make business dealings with women. They struggle with getting quality and low-price raw materials easily. As a woman, it becomes difficult for them to keep a business network with these middlemen, sometimes they are not trusted or are ill-treated or are even cheated on the daily prices for the resources of raw materials

Lack of societal support: The societal norms and traditions sometimes create an obstacle for women entrepreneurs. Caste and religious hindrances are seen in the rural area. Women also get less support by society and are even trusted less as compared to men. Sometimes the family also doesn't support the women when they go out and run a business. All this makes it difficult for women to run a business.

Political challenges: There are various political challenges faced by women. Increment in taxes every year is one of the top challenges faced by entrepreneurs. Nowadays many businesses are under lockdown due to the pandemic, which has created a lot of intricacies for the growth of enterprises. Some of the other challenges are government bans, union rallies, employee strikes, trade union strikes, inflation, government restrictions, and changes in the exchange rate.

Dealing with the male-dominated sector: Business industries have seen male domination for a long time. Women are not trusted in the business sectors, while they are still under-estimated for their marketing ability, risk-bearing ability, and self-confidence. They must cope with the stiff competition around them and stand out in this male-dominated sector.

Lack of new opportunities: Even after long years of experience as business entrepreneurs, women are still not trusted by society. They are looked down upon when it comes to delivering products, manufacturing items, etc. This eventually leads to lack of new opportunities offered to women entrepreneurs.

Lack of education: It has been seen that the female literacy rates are low as compared to that of men. Women are deprived of education and this can be due to various reasons, it can be partly due to early marriage, partly due to household responsibilities, and partly due to poverty. Due to lack of proper education, most women entrepreneurs find it difficult to cope up with the development of new technology, new techniques of production, new marketing strategies, networking with stakeholders, and other governmental agencies.

Work imbalance: Balancing work and family gets difficult to manage. . Women in India are expected to do more on their part, they are supposed to attend to all the domestic work, to look after the children, and other family members, too. They are always expected to take care of most of the family responsibilities. This kind of situation makes it difficult for women entrepreneurs to manage their work and family life together.

Low risk-taking ability: Women entrepreneurs generally lack self-confidence; this is primarily due to a lack of motivation and support given to them by society and their families. This low motivation makes them take little risk and rather play on the safer side. There should be a risk-bearing ability in every entrepreneur to run his/her business successfully. But due to an emotional side and soft personality, sometimes women get demotivated or scared to take the risks required in critical situations. Lack of proper education and training also reduces their ability to bear the risk involved in running an enterprise.

Mobility constraints: Occupation traveling has been a great obstacle for women entrepreneurs. Especially in India women's mobility is limited and has become a problem due to traditional values and limited driving skills.

Lack of technological skills: Nowadays a lot of work is dependent on the Internet and it requires technical skills and facilities. Due to lack of education and training women face problems dealing with technology.

Land acquisition and maintenance: It has been seen that women entrepreneurs have a problem acquiring land for their business. This is due to less trust shown in them by society. There are many more entrepreneurial challenges for women running their own businesses. Some of them are stiff competition by the male sector, lack of self-confidence, lack of motivation, lack of political network, etc. In Mumbai, female entrepreneurs are gradually changing the situation. More and more women are going out for work whether it be service or running one's own businesses.

To make women's entrepreneurship more successful there are various measures that could be undertaken. The government should organise training programs to develop professional competencies in managerial, leadership, marketing, financial, production process, profit planning, account keeping, and other budgeting skills. This will encourage women to undertake businesses. Women should also attend training programs, seminars, workshops, and conferences. Educational institutes should tie-up with various government and non-government agencies to assist mainly in entrepreneurship development. Government should start women's education awareness for the underprivileged females around Mumbai. The awareness programs through digital media can help and promote women entrepreneurs all around.

Remedial measures to enhance women entrepreneurship in India

Women entrepreneurs encounter multiple challenges in India and such challenges need to be addressed precisely. The government could play an important role by formulating appropriate policies and plans that motivate women entrepreneurs. The government must review the existing regulatory framework and make necessary modifications. Women's education and course curriculum should be such that women should be motivated towards entrepreneurship. Course curriculum should be designed to impart both theoretical and practical aspects to acquire the entrepreneurial skill sets required by women entrepreneurs. Higher educational support, incentives, and advanced training programs towards the development of management and leadership skills among women should be given top priority. The government should set up polytechnics and vocational/industrial institutes, especially for women. Appropriate vocational training and motivational campaigns in setting up new enterprises need to be emphasised and implemented. Government should support young entrepreneurs by creating appropriate infrastructure, incubation, and business development facilities to nurture and cherish new and small businesses by supporting them in their early stages of development. The startups and new venture businesses should have access to the resources—required raw materials, water, electricity, serviceable roads, telecommunication, telephones, electronic media, and postal services which are all crucial for business start-up, development, and performance and in addition to the expert advisors, mentors, administrative support, office equipment, training, and/or potential investors. The government must support women entrepreneurs, through microfinancing, by offering bank loans for new projects and required infrastructure such as land allotment and other machinery assets. Tax discounts, special allowances, incentives, and other motivational awards could be established, and many other administrative barriers are removed to encourage women's participation. Women entrepreneurs should have every kind of access to information concerning entrepreneurship so that they can grow faster;

having access to social networks, can play a crucial role in mobilising the resources, people, and technology faster.

Impact of women entrepreneurship and future scope

Women entrepreneurship has been a challenging one along with a lot of barriers and opportunities, but a large number of women are still able to explore opportunities to start their own businesses. Some women are motivated to run their businesses, some have the ambition to pursue, and some have a household responsibility. Especially in Mumbai people have a hidden entrepreneurial spirit that has helped open many small businesses from pottery to leather, from food to fashion, from baking to education institutions, etc. As per the survey in 2020, there are 58.5 million entrepreneurs in India, and out of that 8.08 million of those are women entrepreneurs. The number may be low but still, it has increased from 2019. Increments in women's entrepreneurship have been seen from last year onwards. In 2014 women entrepreneurs in India were 10.17% and in 2020 it has been increased to 13.36%. The growth may be slow and steady, but women entrepreneurs are willing to take risks and go forward.

There are various factors that influence women to own and run a business unit. Economic independence is one of the major factors influencing women. They want to be financially stable and have enough income to take care of themselves and their family. A major reason is they have entrepreneurial drive and ambition to start their own business. They have the capability and passion to use their creative mind according to the requirements of the environment. This also gives them self-identity, satisfaction and builds their self-confidence. This is seen as one of the motivating factors for women to become entrepreneurs. They deserve self-respect and have a desire to be recognised. Some women have strong support from their family members which motivates them to do what they want to do to be successful entrepreneurs. The push factors are those elements that show the necessity, such as insufficient family income, death of the bread earner of the family, dissatisfaction with the current job, difficulty to find the job they love, etc. Whereas the pull factors are those which attract the person, such as, financial independence, self-fulfilment, entrepreneurial ambition, desire for wealth and power, societal status, and a strong need for achievement.

Conclusion

With the objective of the research to investigate the challenges and opportunities for women entrepreneurs in Mumbai, the research has found out various challenges women face while running their businesses. These include limited financial access, lack of managerial skills, dealing with the middleman, lack of societal support, political challenges, dealing with male-dominated sector, lack of new opportunities, lack of education, balancing work and family life, low risk-taking ability, mobility constraints, lack of technological skills, land acquisition, maintenance and so on. It is high time that women entrepreneurs grew with societal and family support managing their challenges. It is seen that women entrepreneurs in Mumbai are gradually increasing in number and are setting their foot in various industries such as fashion, architecture, engineering, medical, travel and tourism, food industry, finance industry, and many more. The government schemes, incentives, and subsidies have stimulated and provided support measures to women entrepreneurs. With the increasing number of women getting an education, there are considerable opportunities among women to be self-employed, taking the pioneering role in society. Women entrepreneurs' role in economic development is also being witnessed significantly and steps are being taken slowly to promote women entrepreneurship. Although during COVID-19, there is fluctuation in the economy, but then, new opportunities are also opening. Women entrepreneurs are trying to seize every opportunity coming their way while they face all-around challenges.

References

https://www.researchgate.net/publication/316481936_Women_Entrepreneurs_In_India_Challenges_And_Opportunities

https://pestrust.edu.in/pesiams/project-reports/M.Com%20project%20report%202019-20/Rakshitha%20N.S%20-%20PC181217.pdf

4ResearchPaper-WomenEntrepreneursinIndia-OpportunitiesandChallenges.pdf

http://www.iosrjournals.org/iosr-jbm/papers/Conf.NCRTCT%E2%80%9919/Series-2/11.%2034-36.pdf

http://www.iosrjournals.org/iosr-jbm/papers/ies-mcrc-ibrc/volume-3/RC-34.pdf

https://core.ac.uk/download/pdf/11822087.pdf

shodhganga.inflibnet.ac.in

https://www.frontiersin.org/articles/10.3389/fpsyg.2020.01557/full

https://journal-jger.springeropen.com/articles/10.1186/s40497-016-0055-x

https://amity.edu/UserFiles/admaa/db0c0Paper%204.pdf

https://theknowledgereview.com/women-entrepreneurship-challenges-opportunities/

http://ijrar.com/upload_issue/ijrar_issue_1244.pdf

https://www.trp.org.in/issues/a-study-on-women-entrepreneurship-opportunities-and-challenges

https://www.researchgate.net/publication/339017006_RURAL_WOMEN_ENTREPRENEURSHIP_IN_INDIA_CHALLENGES_OPPORTUNITIES_AND_MOTIVATIONAL_FACTORS

https://www.orfonline.org/research/women-entrepreneurs-in-india-what-is-holding-them-back-55852/

https://www.bain.com/contentassets/dd3604b612d84aa48a0b120f0b589532/report_powering_the_economy_with_her_-_women_entrepreneurship_in-india.pdf

13 Day-of-week-effect in stock market of India: A case study of sectoral indices

Ruchita Verma[1], Dhanraj Sharma[1] and Heavendeep Singh[2]

[1]Assistant Professor, Central University of Punjab, India

[2]Research Scholar, Central University of Punjab, India

Abstract

As the main focus of traders or investors is to earn a higher return from the stock market, if there is any type of anomalies in the market they try to exploit it. This paper is trying to investigate day-of-the-week-effect in sectoral indices of NSE (Nifty). We are using the latest 10 years of data for study purposes. It also includes the major event of the COVID-19 pandemic and market crash and also V shape recovery of the market. Data are collected from the NSE official website from1st January 2011 to 30th June 2021 of daily closing values of the indices. We convert the daily closing value into daily returns. We are using the purposive sampling method for data collection. Samples are selected based on the availability of data of indices for the whole period of study (out of 15 indices, 9 indices are selected as samples). For analysis purposes, we are employing Dummy variable regression. We regress days on daily returns. The results show significant Monday returns in four indices, significant Thursday returns in one index and significant Friday returns in 1index out of nine indices. These results are important for traders and investors as their anomalies can be exploited by the traders and investors for better returns on investment. SEBI, the regulatory body of the Indian stock market, can also use this result to study the reason behind these inefficiencies and take corrective action to make the market more efficient.

Keywords: anomalies, Day of the week effect, Indian stock market, sector indices & dummy regression

Introduction

Efficient market hypothesis (EMH) has different forms of market hypothesis: 1. Weak form of market hypothesis, 2. semi strong form of market hypothesis, 3. the strong form of market hypothesis is based on the availability of relevant information. In the weak form of the market, the hypothesis assumed that the stock price moves randomly. It follows the random walk model. The price of the stock shows all past information in stock price so it is impossible to beat the market return using the technical analysis (Bodie et al. 2007) hence, technical analysis is useless. In semi-strong forms, stock prices show not only past information but also show the information that is available publicly so no one can beat market return using fundamental analysis (Bodie et al. 2007). In strong forms of the market no one can beat market return using fundamental or technical analysis (Brealey et al.1999), insider traders with all information cannot beat the market because all information available for free for all. EHM says that the stock price shows all the information that is available in the market, all the information private or public available for free for all. So it is impossible to beat the market in anyway. But researchers keep on working on finding the anomalies that exist in the market and by exploiting these anomalies the trader and investor can earn supernormal profit out of that. Agrawal and Tendon (1994) and Ariel (1984) did research related to anomalies in the stock market & found the empirical evidence against the EMH.

Different types of anomalies were investigated in different markets by different researchers like; Size anomalies, Momentum Anomalies, Calendar anomalies, Financial anomalies, and Technical anomalies. In a market where size anomalies exist small size companies beat the return of the big companies. In financial anomalies a company with different financial characteristics likes to beat the market return like low P/B ratio, low PE ratio, value, high dividend Graham and Dodd (1934), Fama (1991), Goodman and Peavy (1983) and Fama and French (1988). In a market where momentum anomalies exist, buying those stocks which are performing well in the shorter period using the momentum strategy and short (taking short position) in the looser stocks in shorter period which performed badly in the short period will give better returns. Due to momentum the traders can earn better than the market returns Hons and Tonks (2001). In a market where technical anomalies exist using different Support and resistant, moving average and other technical techniques for example when the short-term moving average (14 days moving average) cut and move above the long term moving average (mostly 200 days moving average) than trader take long position or buying decision and when the short term moving average cut and go below long term moving average, trader decide to short sell the stock and try to beat market returns (Brock 1992; Lakonishok et al. 1992). In a market where calendar anomalies exist, trader or investor can beat market return by investing at the particular time-of-day, day-of-week (DOW) or month-of-year. If the calendar anomalies exist in the market. There are also other calendar anomalies that researcher found like Halloween effect and Monsoon effect which shows returns are significant different for a different seasons in some markets. Turn of the month effect is also one type of calendar anomalies, in this anomalies the returns were found significant different for the turn of the month's days (mostly some last trading days of month previous & starting trading days of the next month taken as turn of the month days) than rest of the days of the months, Santa Claus rally effect, in which December days till Christmas returns are different compared to the rest of the days of the year. In the day of week effect the market gives exceptional negative or positive returns on a particular day compared to other DOW, so the researcher tries to find this opportunity for the traders and investors to get better returns by exploiting these opportunities.

This paper is divided into five parts including 1. Introduction of the topic 2. Literature review of previous studies 3. Research Methodology used for this study 4. Result and finding of the study and 5. Conclusion of the study.

Literature review

Researchers have done many kinds of research related to EMH and found empirical results to prove market inefficiency. Ahmed and Boutheina (2017) examined the day-of-week DOW effect in the Tunisian stock market where he found positive

Friday returns in the market. Abalala and Sollis. (2015) examined the Saudi Arabia stock market. In this market Islamic calendar is followed which means the week starts from Saturday not from Monday and a study found significant positive returns on the start of the week that is, Saturday. Al-Khazali (2008) did not find any day-of-the-week effect in the UAE stock exchange.

Some researchers did not limit them to study one market but they went further and examined more stock exchanges of different countries. Rossi and Gunardi (2018) examined four different countries of Europe. The study found Monday effect in one stock market out of the four stock markets. Zhang et al. 2017 studied the 25 different stock markets of different countries and also found the DOW effect in some countries. Singh (2014) studied the Asian stock exchange in China, Brazil, Russia, and India. The study found a negative return in China stock exchange on Tuesday. Doyle and Chen (2009) investigated the 8 different stock markets and did not find any DOW effect. All these studies use market major indices return as their variable for the study. Some studied not just one anomaly in the stock market but more anomalies at the same time. Mohanty (2018) examined the Indian stock market with other anomalies like the day of week effect and month of the year (MOY) effect in size, sector, and style related. The study found DOW and MOY effects. Singh (2014) investigated DOW and MOY effect in Asian markets. Amarnani and Vaidya (2014) studied the DOW effect in the Indian stock market and turn of the month effect (TOM). Compton et al(2013) analysed DOW and TOM effect in the Russian market. Khaled and Keef (2012) investigated DOW, TOM, MOY effect in 13 different countries. Worthington (2010) checked DOW, TOM, MOY effect in the Australian stock market.

Study did not remain limited to stock market related to the DOW effect, they studied this effect in other markets as well. Kumar and Pathak (2016) examined the DOW effect in the currency market of India and found positive returns on the first three DOW starting from Monday compared to Thursday. Compton et al (2013) analysed the DOW effect in the Russian bond market and not found any anomaly. Washer et al. (2011) was interested in examining the DOW effect in corporate and treasury paper market and found the Tuesday effect in the market. Swinkels and Van Vlie (2012) did a study related to inter-relation among the different calendar anomalies and check the profitably of the different calendar anomalies in the US stock market. Khaled and Keef (2012) examined RIET index and RIET stock index related anomalies in 13 countries and found stock indices behaving the same but the stock index behaves more efficiently.

In India, studies were done by Mohanty (2018) that examined across the size, style and sector-related DOW, MOY effect and found the DOW effect across the size, sector, and style. Kumar and Pathak (2016) examined the currency market and found a negative return on Thursday. The DOW effect examined by Aziz and Ansari (2015) in this study found positive Monday and Wednesday effect. Srinivasan and Kalaivani (2013) also found positive Monday and Wednesday effects. Different types of calendar anomalies were studied by Amarnani and Vaidya (2014) and did not find any evidence of the DOW effect. As most of the studies focused on a market-main index as a sample not many studies considered sectoral indices for analysis of the DOW effect, but this paper is focused on the sectoral aspect so that any anomalies that are found can be exploited by the trader and investor to beat the market return and earn supernormal profit from that.

Objective & hypothesis

The main objective of this study is to investigate the DOW effect in the Indian stock market across the selected sector. The hypothesis of the study is as follows:

H0: There is no significant difference in returns of a different DOW across the selected sector indices.

H1: There is a significant difference in returns of a different DOW across the selected sector indices.

Research methodology

Data and study period

The data are collected from NSE official website for study. The closing price of each index is collected. The period of the study is 1 January 2010 to 30 June 2021 for all the selected indices that are presented in Table 1. This period also includes the stock market crash due to the COVID-19 pandemic and V shape recovery of the market after the crash. This study includes a total of 2598 trading days (515 Monday, 522 Tuesday, 521 Wednesday, 515 Thursday, 512 Friday, 9 Saturday and 3 Sunday).

Sample profile

Table 13.1 is showing the characteristics of all the sector indices of the NSE. In column 1 we have 15 indices in the sectoral index list of NSE till 31 July 2021. Column 2 shows sector indices list all index titles. Column 3 shows the base year for valuation and value for that base year in the bracket, we have the oldest index base year as 1-JAN-1996 for NIFTY IT and NIFTY FMCG, latest base year as 30-DEC-2005 for NIFTY MEDIA, the base value is taken as 1000 for all index for that particular year. Column 4 shows the launch date of the indices, we have NIFTY FMCG as the oldest index with the launch date of 22-SEP-1996 and the newest Nifty Healthcare with launch date 18-NOV-2020. The 5^h column shows the indices that are taken as samples for the study or not, yes means taken as sample no means not taken as sample. Column 6 shows the number of companies that contained in the index; we have a maximum of 20 companies for 3 indices and a minimum of 10 companies for 5 indices. Column 7 shows the methodology used for the calculation value of the index where all indices use periodic Capped Free Float method. Column 8 shows index balancing time for the indices, all indices use the semi-annual index balancing approach. Column 9 shows Calculation Frequency for index, total 3 indices namely 1. Nifty Consumer Durables 2. Nifty Healthcare & 3. Nifty Oil & Gas are using EOD daily and remaining are using online daily.

We use NSE sectoral indices of the Indian stock market for study and non-probability techniques for selecting the sample. 15 total sectoral indices exist at NSE on the current date and we selected 9 indices out of 15 for these data available

Table 13.1 List of NSE sectoral indices along with characteristics of the index

Sr No.	Index code	The base year (value)	Launch date	Taken as sample	Number of companies in the index	Methodology	Index balancing	Calculation frequency
1	NIFTY BANK	01-Jan-00 (1000)	15-Sep-03	Yes	12	Periodic capped free float	Semi-annually	Online daily
2	NIFTY FMCG	01-Jan-96 (1000)	22-Sep-99	Yes	15	Periodic capped free float	Semi-annually	Online daily
3	NIFTY Pharma	01-Jan-01 (1000)	01-Jul-05	Yes	10	Periodic capped free float	Semi-annually	Online daily
4	NIFTY PSU Bank	01-Jan-04 (1000)	30-Aug-07	Yes	13	Periodic capped free float	Semi-annually	Online daily
5	NIFTY Realty	29-Dec-06 (1000)	30-Aug-07	Yes	10	Periodic capped free float	Semi-annually	Online daily
6	NIFTY Auto	01-Jan-04 (1000)	12-Jul-11	Yes	15	Periodic capped free float	Semi-annually	Online daily
7	NIFTY IT	01-Jan-96 (1000)	Unknown	Yes	10	Periodic capped free float	Semi-annually	Online daily
8	NIFTY Media	30-Dec-05 (1000)	19-Jul-11	Yes	10	Periodic capped free float	Semi-annually	Online daily
9	NIFTY Private Bank	01-Apr-05 (1000)	05-Jan-16	Yes	10	Periodic capped free float	Semi-annually	Online daily
10	Nifty Consumer Durables	01-Apr-05 (1000)	15-Jan-20	No	15	Periodic capped free float	Semi-annually	EOD daily
11	NIFTY Financial Services 25/50	01-Jan-04 (1000)	20-May-20	No	20	Periodic capped free float	Semi-annually	Online daily
12	Nifty Healthcare	01-Apr-05 (1000)	18-Nov-20	No	20	Periodic capped free float	Semi-annually	EOD daily
13	Nifty Oil & Gas	01-Apr-05 (1000)	15-Jan-20	No	15	Periodic capped free float	Semi-annually	EOD daily
14	NIFTY Financial Services	01-Jan-04 (1000)	07-Sep-11	No	20	Periodic capped free float	Semi-annually	Online daily
15	NIFTY Metal	01-Jan-04 (1000)	12-Jul-11	No	15	Periodic capped free float	Semi-annually	Online daily

Source: NSE official Website

for the whole study period. These are NIFTY BANK, NIFTY PRIVATE BANK, NIFTY PSU BANK, NIFTY AUTO, NIFTY PHARMA, NIFTY REALTY, NIFTY IT, NIFTY MEDIA, and NIFTY FMCG.

Methodology

We apply dummy variable regression for analysis purposes. First, we convert daily returns from the closing price of the indices. For this, the formula used is (closing price of today-closing price of the previous day/1*100). We calculated returns for all days of all indices. We calculate returns for all indices using the same method. After that, we apply dummy variable regression. Dummy variables are those days for which we assign 0. For that, if we want to check the Monday effect, we give 1 to Monday and 0 to other days and regress the return on days. Same for other days like for Tuesday effect we give 1 to Tuesday and 0 to other days and regress the equation. Returns are dependent variables and DOW are independent and dummy variables here. We apply the same method for dummy regression for each index one by one for nine indices.

Results and discussions

Descriptive statistics

Table 13.2 shows descriptive stats of the return of each index. We have indices in the first column, the number of observations for all selected indices, a third column showing the average return of all selected indices respectively, we have a standard deviation in the fourth column, minimum return on the fifth column, and maximum return on the sixth column. We have 2598 observations for all

Table 13.2 Descriptive statistics

Indices	N	Average	Standard deviation	Minimum	Maximum
NIFTY AUTO	2598	0.0453	1.3980	–13.8478	10.4063
NIFTY BANK	2598	0.0539	1.5762	–16.7340	10.5117
NIFTY FMCG	2598	0.0578	1.1069	–10.5954	8.3185
NIFTY IT	2598	0.0613	1.3372	–11.7418	9.3321
NIFTY MEDIA	2598	0.0158	1.5847	–16.3741	8.3745
NIFTY PHARMA	2598	0.0472	1.2291	–8.9269	10.3680
NIFTY PRIVATE BANK	2598	0.0641	1.5882	–17.8772	11.0548
NIFTY PSU BANK	2598	0.0007	2.1582	–13.1605	29.6265
NIFTY REALTY	598	0.0179	2.0885	–11.6044	8.4295

Source: Author's Computation

indices. We have the highest average return for NIFTY PRIVATE BANK with 0.0641% daily and the lowest average return 0.0007% daily for NIFTY PSU BANK. We have the highest standard deviation return for NIFTY PSU BANK with 2.158 and the lowest standard deviation of 1.1069 for NIFTY FMCG. We can see minimum one day return is –17.8772% for the NIFTY PRIVATE BANK. We can see maximum one day return is 29.6265% for NIFTY PSU BANK. As we can see during the crash most affected indices in one day was NIFTY PRIVATE BANK as banks represent the economy and get most affected during recovery and crash time as well.

Table 13.3 shows the average return of all days for all selected indices. In the first column, we have the number of days for the study of each day and total days of the study are shown. We have nine Saturdays and three Sundays in this study. Normally market remains open Monday to Friday but on special occasions like Diwali, markets remain open for some time as Muhurat trading no matter if it is a Sunday or a Saturday. In columns 311 we have sectoral indices average return for each day. A maximum return for NIFTY AUTO is 0.6452% for Sunday, for normal days we have a maximum of 0.1199% average return on Tuesday and a minimum average return of –0.0527% on Monday. Maximum return for NIFTY BANK is 0.1253% average return on Friday and a minimum average return of –0.0713% on Monday. We can see the sample from all the remaining indices from table 13.1.

Chart No. 13.1 shows average returns for all selected sectoral indices in graphical form from Monday to Friday, we are only using Monday to Friday returns in graphical presentation as for Saturday & Sunday we have few number of days. On X-axis we have days and on the y-axis, we have percentage returns. We can see negative returns in most indices on the case of Monday and positive returns on Wednesday in all indices. No doubt it shows negative returns on Monday and positive returns on Wednesday but we cannot conclude that it is a significant result for that we need to do a test of checking the static significance of the result.

Regression result

Table 13.4 is shows the regression result of the study. We have days in columns and in rows we have indices along with T-value, P-value and regression coefficient value of all the selected indices. Negative T-value and negative coefficient shows negative returns and positive values shows positive return and P-value shows the significance of the result. The P-value for all indices shows significant result if the value is less than 0.10 but more than 0.5 means results are significant at the 10% level of the significance and if the value is between .01 to .05 that means results are significant at 5% level and if the value is less than .01 than it means results are significant at 1% level of the significant. We find significant negative returns on Monday in Nifty Bank, Nifty Pharma & Nifty Private Bank at a 5% level of significance and in Nifty Auto at a 10% level of significance. A significant negative return on Thursday was found in Nifty IT at a 5% level of significance. A significant negative return on Friday was found in Nifty Pharma at a 10% level of significance.

Table 13.3 Average return for different sectoral indices

Number of days	DOW	Average return								
		NIFTY AUTO	NIFTY BANK	NIFTY FMCG	NIFTY IT	NIFTY media	NIFTY PHARMA	NIFTY PRIVATE BANK	NIFTY PSU BANK	NIFTY REALTY
515	MON	-0.0527	-0.0713	-0.0112	0.0543	-0.0641	-0.0600	-0.0683	-0.0565	-0.0701
522	TUE	0.1199	0.0818	0.0910	0.1209	0.0354	0.0629	0.1063	-0.0547	0.0031
521	WED	0.0396	0.0926	0.1032	0.1328	0.1064	0.0911	0.0918	0.1065	0.1360
515	THU	0.0361	0.0395	0.0613	-0.0522	0.0699	-0.0005	0.0698	-0.1162	0.0284
513	FRI	0.0808	0.1253	0.0538	0.0432	-0.0721	0.1316	0.1165	0.1249	0.0018
9	SAT	-0.0416	0.1216	-0.5660	0.2985	-0.2018	0.5197	0.2653	-0.1352	-0.6605
3	SUN	0.6452	0.0394	0.2340	0.3333	0.7282	0.4338	0.0646	0.3289	0.2380
2598	TOTAL	0.0453	0.0539	0.0578	0.0613	0.0155	0.0472	0.0641	0.0007	0.0179

Source: Author's Computation

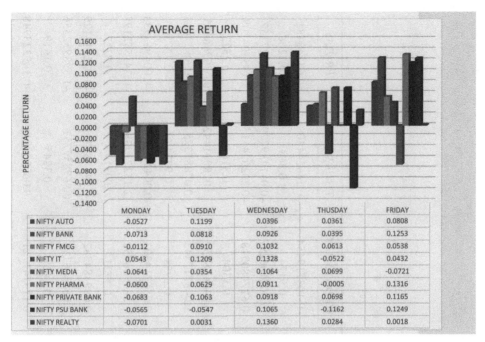

	MONDAY	TUESDAY	WEDNESDAY	THUSDAY	FRIDAY
■ NIFTY AUTO	-0.0527	0.1199	0.0396	0.0361	0.0808
■ NIFTY BANK	-0.0713	0.0818	0.0926	0.0395	0.1253
■ NIFTY FMCG	-0.0112	0.0910	0.1032	0.0613	0.0538
■ NIFTY IT	0.0543	0.1209	0.1328	-0.0522	0.0432
■ NIFTY MEDIA	-0.0641	0.0354	0.1064	0.0699	-0.0721
■ NIFTY PHARMA	-0.0600	0.0629	0.0911	-0.0005	0.1316
■ NIFTY PRIVATE BANK	-0.0683	0.1063	0.0918	0.0698	0.1165
■ NIFTY PSU BANK	-0.0565	-0.0547	0.1065	-0.1162	0.1249
■ NIFTY REALTY	-0.0701	0.0031	0.1360	0.0284	0.0018

Chart 13.1 Average return of each day for different sectoral indices
Source: Author's Computation

Conclusion

As we can found in literature that most of the studies were done related by considering the stock market major indices to check the efficiency of the market, very few studies were done related to sectoral related study so we in this study examined the day of the week effect by considering the sector-related indices and found the negative significant return on Monday in four indices out of nine indices and a positive return on Wednesday and Thursday in 1 index out of 9 indices. Our results are the same as in some study Mohanty (2018) in this they found anomalies across the sector. Amarnani and Vaidya (2014) study did not find DOW in their result; our results are contradictory to their result. At international level Abalala and Sollis. (2015) also found the Saturday returns significant in their studies, as the study conducted in Saudi stock market where the Islamic calendar is followed that means the Saturday is the first day of the week same as Monday is in most of the countries. In simple words the first day of the week returns were significant negative same as our result show as Monday results are significant negative.

As result show returns are negative on Monday in Nifty Bank, Nifty Pharma & Nifty Private Bank indices so as an investor it is not good to invest on trading day before Monday or take a long position in trading on Friday/ trading day before Monday in these indices. Results also show negative significant returns in NIFTY IT on Thursday. so as an investor it is not good to invest on trading day before Thursday or take a long position in trading on Wednesday/ trading day before

Table 13.4 Regression result for different sectoral indices

DAYS		MONDAY	TUESDAY	WEDNESDAY	THURSDAY	FRIDAY
NIFTY AUTO	T-stats	-1.777805357	1.363397296	-0.103719454	-0.16244406	0.64249481
	P-Values	0.0756*	0.1729	0.9174	0.868	0.5206
	Coefficients	-0.122262396	0.093312371	-0.007106297	-0.011439779	0.04427357
NIFTY BANK	T-stats	-2.014713712	0.451711593	0.627480918	-0.232024115	1.145304208
	P-Values	0.044**	0.6515	0.5304	0.8165	0.2522
	Coefficients	-0.156189834	0.03486761	0.048468259	-0.018001442	0.088966475
NIFTY FMCG	T-stats	-1.581512704	0.764935243	1.045717843	0.07887375	-0.090977011
	P-Values	0.1139	0.4444	0.2958	0.9371	0.9275
	Coefficients	-0.086123558	0.041460396	0.056714303	0.004297247	-0.004963933
NIFTY IT	T-stats	-0.132749605	1.139145367	1.365966732	-2.152779386	-0.341552198
	P-Values	0.8944	0.2547	0.1721	0.0314**	0.7327
	Coefficients	-0.008737431	0.074579927	0.089484382	-0.141567712	-0.022513129
NIFTY MEDIA	T-stats	-1.273514847	0.321321822	1.465366118	0.869857751	-1.39952356
	P-Values	0.2029	0.748	0.1429	0.3845	0.1619
	Coefficients	-0.099291128	0.024932909	0.113741721	0.06783081	-0.109223948

NIFTY PHARMA	T-stats	-2.211290398	0.327188236	0.911205546	-0.98410513	1.736145404
	P-Values	0.0271**	0.7435	0.3623	0.3252	0.0827*
	Coefficients	-0.133655377	0.019694154	0.054879145	-0.059526423	0.105128371
NIFTY PRIVATE BANK	T-stats	-2.113803866	0.679795067	0.446646714	0.090930248	0.834456981
	P-Values	0.0346**	0.4967	0.6552	0.9276	0.4041
	Coefficients	-0.165099821	0.052868139	0.034762735	0.007108255	0.065318709
NIFTY PSU BANK	T-stats	-0.671677901	-0.655952203	1.251189285	-1.372938822	1.455195361
	P-Values	0.5018	0.5119	0.211	0.1699	0.1457
	Coefficients	-0.071345846	-0.069323567	0.13229658	-0.145793761	0.154748394
NIFTY REALTY	T-stats	-1.069110036	-0.182140907	1.443613761	0.126208469	-0.195578136
	P-Values	0.2851	0.8555	0.149	0.8996	0.845
	Coefficients	-0.10987909	-0.018629117	0.147698517	0.012974045	-0.020134547

Source: Author's Computation

Note: In Table 2 *means 10 % of the level of significance, **means 5 % of the level of significance& ***means 1 % of the level of significance

Thursday in NIFTY IT. Trader and investor can take a long position on Thursday in NIFTY Pharma as results show returns are significant positive on Friday in NIFTY PHARMA. The probability of overall positive return will be higher if trader and investor have taken position according to this. They can earn higher returns compared to the market if anomalies remain in the market as previously was there in the market.

These results are helpful for the traders and investors to take investment decisions in a better way and help them to earn supernormal profit by investing at the right time in the right indices. At the same time, these results are helpful for the regulator of the market to see the inefficiency of the market and try to take steps for making the market more efficient. This study is taking indices of the only NSE of the Indian market for study purposes. It does not include the indices of other stock exchanges of the Indian stock market- indices like BSE sectoral indices. The results may vary in other stock exchanges. So it remains limited to NSE Sectoral indices. This study uses only those indices for which data is available for the study period. So the remaining six indices are not covered in this study, those are established in between the study period.

Further studies related to this problem can be done by taking into consideration other stock exchanges of the country and further can be expanded by taking into consideration the other countries of Asia, BRICS or on the basis of developed and developing stock exchange or in different market conditions as well, like bearish market and bullish market. Further study can also be conducted for finding the reason related to these anomalies in particular sectoral indices on a particular day. What is the factor that creates the anomalies in particular indices? Is it behaviour or other factors?

References

Abalala, T. and Sollis, R. (2015). The Saturday effect: an interesting anomaly in the Saudi stock market. Appl. Eco. 47(58):6317–6330.

Agrawal, A. and Tandon, K. (1994). Anomalies or illusions? Evidence from stock markets in eighteen countries. J Int Money Finance.. 13(1):83–106.

Ahmed, B. and Boutheina, R. (2017). Financial market anomalies: Evidence from Tunisia stock market. *Asian Journal of Empirical Research*, 7(9), 238–250.

Al-Khazali, O. M. (2008). The impact of thin trading on day-of-the-week effect. *Review of accounting and Finance*.

Amarnani, N. and Vaidya, P. (2014). Study of Calendar Anomalies in Indian Stock Markets. *Perspectives on Financial Markets and Systems-Market Efficiency, Behavioural Finance and Financial Inclusion,(Ahmedabad, Institute of Management, Nirma University)*.

Ariel, R. A. (1987). A monthly effect in stock returns. *Journal of financial economics*, 18(1):161–174.

Aziz, T. and Ansari, V. A. (2015). The day of the week effect: evidence from India. Afro-Asian J. Finance Account.5(2):99–112.

Bodie, Z. A. and Kane, A. J. Marcus (2007). Essentials of investments, 6th edition, McGraw-Hill / Irwin

Brealey, R. A. S. C. and Myers. A. J. Marcus. 1999. Fundamentals of corporate finance, 2nd Edition, McGraw-hill.

Brock, W., Lakonishok, J., and LeBaron, B. (1992). Simple technical trading rules and the stochastic properties of stock returns. finance. Finan. 47(5):1731–1764.

Compton, W., Kunkel, R. A., and Kuhlemeyer, G. (2013). Calendar anomalies in Russian stocks and bonds. Manag. Financ..

Doyle, J. R. and Chen, C. H. (2009). The wandering weekday effect in major stock markets. J. Bank Financ. 33(8):1388–1399.

Fama, E. F. (1991). Efficient markets II. J. Financ. 46(5):1575–1617.

Fama, E. F. and French, K. R. (1988). Dividend Yields and Expected Stock Returns. J. Financ. Eco. 22(1):3–25.

Goodman, D. A. and Peavy, J. W. (1983). Industry Relative Price-Earnings Ratios as Indicators of Investment Returns. Financ. Analy. J. 39(4):60–66.

Graham, B., Dodd, D. L. F., and Cottle, S. (1934). Security analysis (Vol. 452). New York: McGraw-Hill.

Hon, M. T. and Tonks, I. (2003). Momentum in the UK stock market. J. Multinat. Finan. Manag. 13(1):43–70.

Khaled, M. S. and Keef, S. P. (2012). Calendar anomalies in REITs: international evidence. J. Prop. Invest. Finance.

Satish Kumar Rajesh Pathak , (2016), "Do the calendar anomalies still exist? Evidence from Indian currency market", Managerial Finance. 42(2):136–150.

Lakonishok, J., Shleifer, A., Vishny, R. W., Hart, O., & Perry, G. L. (1992). The Structure and Performance of the Money Management Industry. Brookings Papers on Economic Activity. Microeconomics, 1992: 339–391. https://doi.org/10.2307/2534766

Mohanty, S. S. (2018). Calendar return seasonality across sectors, sizes and styles-evidence from the Indian equity markets. Afro-Asian J. Finance Account. 8(3):317–335.

Rossi, M. and Gunardi, A. (2018). Efficient market hypothesis and stock market anomalies: Empirical evidence in four European countries. J. Appl. Bus. Res. 34(1):183–192.

Singh, S. P. (2014). Stock market anomalies: Evidence from emerging BRIC markets. Vision. 18(1):23–28.

Srinivasan, P. and Kalaivani, M. (2013). Day-of-the-Week Effects in the Indian stock market. MPRA Paper, 46805.

Swinkels, L. ands Van Vliet, P. (2012). An anatomy of calendar effects. 'J. Asset Manag. 13(4):271–286.

Washer, K., Nippani, S., and Wingender, J. (2011). Day-of-the-week effect in the Canadian money market. Manager. Financ. 37(9):855.

Worthington, A. C. (2010). The decline of calendar seasonality in the Australian stock exchange, 1958–2005. Annals of Finance. 6(3):421–433.

Zhang, J., Lai, Y., and Lin, J. (2017). The day-of-the-week effects of stock markets in different countries. Financ. Res. Lett. 20:47–62.

14 Variable tradeoff between diversification and volatility on risk-averse approaches to crypto allocation for Indian retail investors

Ajay Agarwal

School of Computing, DIT University, Dehradun, India

Abstract

With the increase in the space of direct allocation and management accessibilities offered to the retail investors in India due to certain recent FinTech solutions, there is dysphoria around the market sentiment on cryptoasset allocations. Apart from higher volatility, the current investors' outlook on such crypto assets mirrors the same as it was prior for large-cap equity classes which carried significant risks. The transition of the current generation of retail investors from a risk-averse approach for capital appreciation through low- return investment classes like FDs and Bonds to diversification into diligent equity investments made through thematic strategies, it is accurate to conclude that investment interests in new asset classes can only be aided through tools that provide explainability and public-salient interpretability. Our paper aims to work on this existing lacuna, providing explainability-integrated benchmarks and parameters that can increase investor confidence for crypto diversification with attention to potential risks and behavioural fluctuations in the long run. This is achieved by creating a market sentiment index named CMMI that is validated against S&P Bitcoin Index, S&P Ethereum Index, and S&P Cryptocurrency MegaCap Index. We also extend our research to propose a methodology for creating thematic crypto-investment strategies that can benchmark against existing indices for equity and crypto asset classes.

Keywords: cryptocurrency, human-computer interaction, portfolio allocation

Introduction

Potential risks often succeed over possible long-term returns as the criteria that formulate the maxim on which most Indian retail investors centralise their investment strategy. It cannot be ignored, however, that there exists a certain trade off between risks and returns for investment in any asset class, and hence, the definition of potential risks for such retail investors is mostly constricted by the converging horizons of their market knowledge and due diligence for any asset allocation. Consequently, such investment strategies that are often passed on as heirloom from one generation to another that heavily centralize around risk-free investments like FDs and savings fail to appreciate wealth, if not in value, in the long run is staggered with market fluctuations.

The introduction of excessive spare time in the schedule of the earning strata in India due to the given crisis, and the exaggerated exposure captured by get-rich-quick schemes over the last year (examples are GameStop, DogeCoin, ITC, etc) has inflated expectations of returns and investment confidence amongst the younger generation. This has been reflected in the direct correlation observed between these passing months and the exponential increase in the number of new Demat accounts and crypto-wallets being curated for a new wave of investors. As identified by prior research, this phenomenon of the massive inflow of new retail investors in both equity and cryptomarkets has pushed the existing heirloom financial advice aside and has introduced new traits to the definition of the Indian retail investor – cautionary, independent, and risk tolerant.

Consequently, this has given rise to the exploration regarding new and higher value appreciation assets – cryptocurrency. Given the association of the cryptomarkets with vicious pump-and-dump schemes and get-rich-quick schemes with little approximation to market rationality, despite being cautionary and risk-tolerant, the current retail investor faces the dilemma of ease for investments, interpretability regarding market movements, and explainability regarding fundamental forces that drive the market on a macroeconomic level. This poses the need for creating a solution that addresses the lacunas faced in making the transition of current global and Indian crypto-investors from FOMO crypto investments to diligent crypto investments that allow possibilities of higher capital appreciation, hedging, and sustaining inflationary market sentiments.

But, before we proceed to understand the nuances of cryptomarkets and the intrinsic features that line up the moat to entry for investment in the given asset class, we first need to understand what is a cryptocurrency and how it is different from another fiat (alternatively, stable alternatives like Indian Rupee, United States Dollar, etc.). After the same, we shall pivot our discussion to understand what separates investment in Indian equity markets from that in cryptomarkets. Finally, we shall explore the basics of what is the financial portfolio allocation and optimisation problem and how the same is utilised for CoinKart to provide an entry-access in crypto investments for Indian retail traders.

Introduction to cryptocurrency

A cryptocurrency is a digital or virtual currency that is protected by encryption, making counterfeiting or double-spending practically impossible. Many cryptocurrencies are decentralised networks built on blockchain technology, which is a distributed ledger enforced by a network of computers. Cryptocurrencies are distinguished by the fact that they are generally not issued by any central authority, making them potentially impervious to government meddling or manipulation.

They essentially function as platforms that enable secure online payments denominated in terms of virtual 'tokens,' which are represented by internal system ledger entries. The term 'crypto' refers to the encryption methods and cryptographic techniques used to protect these entries, such as public-private key pairs, hashing functions, and elliptical curve encryption (Rauchs and Hileman, 2017).

Types of cryptocurrency

Cryptocurrencies are primarily based on blockchain technology. Since the advent of the same, various cryptocurrencies have been built, deployed, and earned their fair share of attention. However, despite the variable ranking, these newer alternatives enjoy, the first cryptocurrency was Bitcoin which was built on blockchain technology. Given its premier status and predominantly effective sautilisation of blockchain technology, the source code of Bitcoin (now, publicly available) is utilised to create alternative coins similar to the original Bitcoin. These new versions of Bitcoins could be termed 'alt-coins' derived from the word – 'alternative coins' (Ryan, 2015). Alt-coins are primarily forked versions or exact clones of Bitcoin with enough distinction to separate them from the market share of Bitcoin.

The massive success of Bitcoin was almost financially plagiarised in a non-ethical fashion by the establishment of coins like LiteCoin, Namecoin, Peercoin, etc. Later, modifications and improvements were made to the version of the technology that Bitcoin allowed for the creation of better alternatives and 'algorithmically-enhanced' versions of Bitcoin. These included the likes of Ethereum, Cardano, and EOS. (Ujan M., et al. 2016). To bring a financial perspective to this scenario, by the end of September 2021, the market share of all the cryptocurrencies in existence is more than 2 trillion US Dollars, with the contribution of Bitcoin alone at 47%. For providing a better understanding of the fluctuations in the cryptomarket share, its subsequent rise, and fall, and later, corresponding sustenance with Bitcoin maintaining its dominance, Figures 14.13 are provided. Figure 14.1 represents the total cryptocurrency market cap starting from April 28th 2013 till September 29th, 2021. It also shows the total market sacapitalisation of all cryptoassets which also includes crypto-tokens including stable coins.

Figure 14.2 represents the total cryptocurrency market sacapitalisation excluding Bitcoin. It also represents the total market sacapitalisation for cryptocurrency which also includes tokens and stable coins, excluding, however, the contribution of Bitcoin. In the terms of cryptoanalysts, a graphical representation for Bitcoin-exclusive market capisatalisation is a pivotal graph to measure and assess two things – 1. cryptomarkets in terms of raising new cryptocoins, and 2. variations of the total alternative crypto- currency market sacapitalisation.

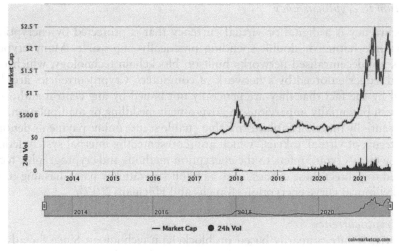

Figure 14.1 Total cryptocurrency market sacapitalisation from April 28th, 2013 to September 29th, 2021. Data courtesy CoinMarketCap
Source: www.coinmarketcap.com

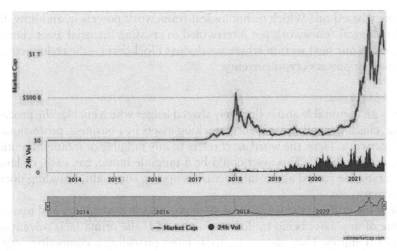

Figure 14.2 Total cryptocurrency market sacapitalisation (excluding Bitcoin) from April 28th, 2013 to September 29th, 2021. Data courtesy – CoinMarketCap
Source: www.coinmarketcap.com

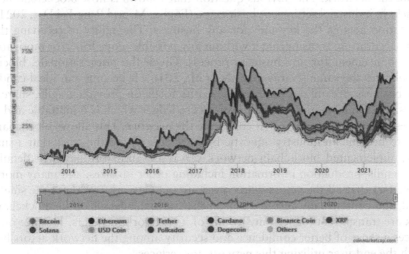

Figure 14.3 Individual market cap distribution of top 10 cryptoassets in market cap contribution from April 29th, 2013 to September 29th, 2021. Data courtesy – CoinMarketCap
Source: www.coinmarketcap.com

Finally Figure 14.3, as stated, represents the individual contributions of the largest crypto assets relative to the total cryptocurrency market sacapitalisation. Given the fact that Bitcoin (BTC) was the first cryptoasset, it continues to dominate its contribution in cryptomarket sacapitalisation (Chuen et al., 2017). This predominance by BTC also explains the cognitive likening for the asset amongst the public. In terms of cryptoanalysts, such tracked depictions of cryptoassets which include stable coins as well as crypto-tokens play a major role in tracking the progression of public sentiment for the cryptomarket and the assets traded, for years.

With all this above discussion regarding how cryptocurrency has been shaped as 'as – set-classes' of the future, it becomes imperative to question – What is cryptocurrency based on? Which technological framework powers it, and how did such a technological framework got intertwined in creating financial asset classes. This brings us to our next section where we discuss blockchain – the technological advancement that powers cryptocurrency.

Overview of blockchain

Blockchain is an immutable and collectively shared ledger which enables the process of recording, checking, and consequently tracking assets in a business, professional, or personal network. Here, the word *asset* refers to any tangible or intangible entity (Liu and Tsyvinski, 2021). This asset could be a tangible house, car, cash, or land, etc., or an intangible record about intellectual property, copyright, branding documents, trademark, etc.

The facility for utilising the leverage of virtually tracking, assessing, and managing the value of any asset being traded or purchased is the prima facia advantage that blockchain enjoys. This advantage, apart from providing a competitive edge, also reciprocates in its use cases for the industrial landscape. The same coerces in reducing costs and cutting risks involved in the administration and the actors which constitute the network. The obvious question that follows is how blockchain networks help in industrial settings or businesses. (Foglia, M. and Peng-Fei Dai, 2021).

Information acts as the key unit for any business. The agility in receiving the same and accuracy in transmitting it without any possible scope for error motivates further enhancement for any business process. Given the prior rationale, blockchain replicates the same (Narayanan, A. et al., 2016). It becomes an ideal candidate for business streamlines processes given its focus on providing agile, shared, and transparent information stored in the secure ledger which is immutable and is only accessible to the members that constitute the network. This allows blockchain network to become an industry agnostic business solution in the sense that a successfully, implemented blockchain network can track and store payment details, account details, production information including order invoices, and many more. Given the fact that all the actors who constitute the network can share the single, unbiased, and consensually agreed image of the truth, the details of the blockchain network are transparent for scrutiny by any of its network members. This not only introduces a sense of better confidence and security among the network actors but also with the end-user utilizing this network for services.

Operations frequently squander time and effort on redundant record keeping and third-party validations. Fraud and cyber attacks can exploit record-keeping systems. Data verification might be slowed by a lack of openness. And, with the advent of IoT, transaction volumes have skyrocketed. All of this slows business and depletes the bottom line, indicating the need for a better solution. Enter the blockchain. Immediately, one is greeted with a sense of greater trust, improved security, and enhanced efficiencies. As stated earlier and highlighted, blockchain acts analogous to a members-only network which allows the fact that only the members in the network can act as validators for the data being transacted through nodes within the network. As each transaction is updated, created, or destroyed, the chain of these ledgers accessible to all acts like a 'public' scrutinised ledger of what acts as the source truth. The possibility of defrauding and tampering with ledgers of the transaction, hence, becomes impossible, to say the least. As a consequence, every node in the network enjoys a better and greater magnitude of trust within the network (Raymaekers, 2015).

Create security becomes the second leverage that blockchain offers for business solutions. As all the legends are publicly available consensus on data accuracy becomes a consequence since all members within a network are required to validate any new transactions data made within the network.

Since each transaction within a network is stored permanently and cannot be changed thereafter, a greater sense of security is offered by blockchain with assessing and managing asset transactions in a business network. It must be noted that no transaction can be deleted even by the highest access member, which in the case of a business solution could even be a system administrator (Breidbach and Silviana, 2021).

The tertiary benefit offered by blockchain technology for business solutions is enhanced efficiency in time distribution for the validation of transactions. As established earlier, every ledger of transactions made within a network is distributed among all the members within the network, consequently leading to the elimination of redundancy and misuse of computational time. This enhanced efficiency is also facilitated by the concept of 'smart contract' which essentially means a set of predefined rules that are stored on a blockchain network and are executed instantaneously whenever a new transaction is made within the network. To understand better the concept of smart contracts, we can take the technical definition of what the term means. Smart contracts are simply schema-based programs that are stored on a blockchain network that run instantaneously whenever a new ledger of the transaction meets a set of existing rules. They primarily allow the automation of a sense of validation among all the participants within a network so that the transaction made recently can be validated as a legal one. Given the fact that these are new schema rules, it also enables lesser time sautilisation for computation of different node networks to validate a new ledger trans-action. These smart contracts could be programmed through a developer although nowadays many organisations that utilise blockchain framework for business solutions already provide an existing template or a web interface or any other possible GUI tool which could simplify processing, creation, modification, and further deployment of such smart contracts. In its most basic sense, a smart contract could be assumed as a set of if/then statements for a ledger of transactions. With this, we move ahead to the formulation of the process regarding how a blockchain network technologically functions.

Transactions within blockchain networks

As stated earlier each blockchain network has a set of nodes where every ledger of the transaction is publicly distributed for permanent validation. Let's consider a scenario where a new transaction of any asset is made in such a network. As each transaction occurs or a new transaction is made, the details for the same are stored in a block of what could be named as metadata for the given transaction. To a greater extent, these blocks indicate the flow or the movement of the asset being traded, be it tangible or intangible, within a network. If we take a scenario where a blockchain network is formed within a food processing industry, a new transaction

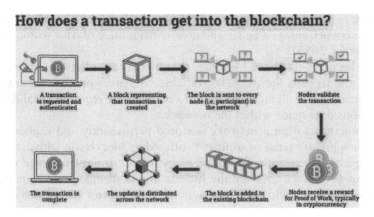

Figure 14.4 The above figure represents the schematic process that takes place whenever a new transaction is added and validated in a blockchain network
Source: www.coinmarketcap.com

in such a scenario would form a new block of data which would consequently contain conditions regarding what food is being stored, who bought the food, its price, where the purchase was made, and even description regarding the temperature of the food shipment when received or delivered.

The second step takes place after a new block is created for a new transaction which is a part of the blockchain network where the newly formed block is connected to the ones before and after it. Note that in a blockchain network each block of metadata is involved in forming a long publicly distributed chain of ledger. It essentially means that a chain of such nature represents the flow of acid within different nodes of the network. In a practical sense, it means that the ownership of the acid changes from one person to another as time progresses. This new block, therefore, confirms and validates the exact timestamp and position within the chain when search a new transaction is made within the network. This is because each block that forms the chain is securely linked with the prior and the post block consequently preventing insertion, modification, alteration, and/or deletion of any existing block.

Finally, we move to the last step that forms the process of what we know as blockchain. Since all the ledgers of transactions that constitute this chain of blocks are irreversible in nature we can say that such a chain of blocks forms what we know today as blockchain. The addition of a new block within a blockchain, in some sense, increases the security of the entire blockchain, validates the previous block, and validates the immutability of the entire blockchain for all the nodes that form a part of the network. A simple diagram to represent what the process of adding a new transaction in a blockchain looks like has been represented in Figure 14.4.

One might note in the above diagram that the term proof of work has been mentioned. Simply speaking, and reiterating from what has been mentioned before, every time a new transaction is made within the blockchain business network it needs to be validated by all the members within that network. This validation process is performed using schematic rules called smart contracts that are nothing but what we mean by proof of work. It is this proof of work-based consensus mechanism that prevents possible hijacking of a blockchain network by external attackers. It must be noted however that the process of validating a transaction within a huge blockchain network requires extensive computational power and the chances of a simple desktop computer being fortunate enough to be able to validate an entire blockchain transaction of Bitcoin is less than one in a trillion.

By this point in time, we have completed our understanding of what we know about cryptocurrency, how it functions on the blockchain, and finally how crypto markets have evolved over the past decade. We shall now focus our attention on understanding how crypto markets in the context of India have performed over the last year when compared with the equity class markets of India.

Lessons from lockdown – A study of Indian equity and crypto markets
Markets of every asset class have some degree of volatility that cannot be avoided. Historically, market crashes caused panic and reduced activity. Let's compare how the markets in India behaved over the last 18 months for the equity and cryptoasset class respectively.

Stance and trend of equity market
Equity markets witnessed a stable trend over the last 18 months, which has been depicted in Figure 14.5. Unexpectedly, this time the crisis led to a new wave of Indian retail investors into the market. What helped this new wave of retail investors in the equity market? The crucial three factors that enabled this new wave include a) free time during lockdown, b) access to innovative FinTech solutions, and c) low bank deposit rates. As stated earlier, Figure 14.5 represents the weekly additions to the Demat accounts opened in India's top leading brokerage firm – Zerodha over the last 18 months when compared against the performance of the Nifty 50 equity-class index . While correlation doesn't imply causation, the fact that

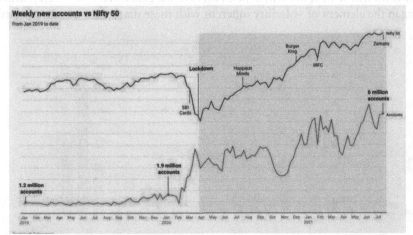

Figure 14.5 Weekly new account addition for Zerodha brokerage firm when compared against the performance of Nifty 50 equity index over the last 18 months of nationwide lockdown
Source: www.twitter.com/Nithin0dha

such a correlation exists is astonishing. A contextual analysis of such a correlation provides hints that might indicate factors for possible causation. Over the last 18 months what we recall as a period of nationwide lockdown with strict closure of all trade and activity, it became rather obvious that the repercussions of such excruciating measures would be reflected in the performance of the market's performance. As expected, the equity market crashed which in turn led to widespread investor panic and reduced buyer and seller activity.

But this crisis that the equity market faced led to a wave of young and dynamic retail investors who were in a search to buy stocks that were on sale. These young retail investors added access time to their hands due to the imposed lockdown and their efforts were indirectly supported by low deposit rates maintained by various Indian banks during this period. Once this younger wave of first-time retail investors entered markets and booked significant profits in a short period, they realised the possible potential of these looming markets during this time frame. Word of mouth spread which gathered the interest of the peers, friends, and family members to enter the market with a sense of confidence, and passion to take the logical risk.

Consequently, the markets outperformed even in these times of crisis and failed to lose momentum. As a result, such a correlation was naturally expected, along with a possible reason for causation.

However, this correlation trend wasn't an isolated picture for the platform Zerodha. Rather, a similar trend was witnessed when we take into consideration the opening of new Demat accounts (both on NSDL and CDSL) over the last 10 years, including this lockdown period. This comparative visualisation between the volume of new Demat accounts opened against the performance of the Nifty index has been depicted in Figure 14.6.

What we can conclude regarding equity markets of India from these graphs analysing two-time spans, the previous decade and the previous year, establishes the following observation – public confidence in the markets is dictated by the trends in the market indices which, in turn, depend on revenue generated from such markets factoring in the element of volatility inherent with these markets. The more volatile

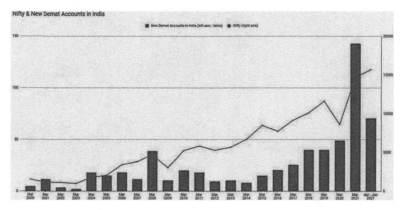

Figure 14.6 The above figure depicts the comparative correlation between the addition of new Demat accounts (both NSDL and CDSL) against the performance of the Nifty 50 equity index over the last two decades
Source: www.twitter.com/Nithin0dha

the market is, the higher the revenue is, consequentially leading to better performance of the market indices.

This leads to the question of whether a similar stance was observed by the Indian crypto markets, which forms the point of discussion for our next section.

Stance and trend of crypto markets

While to say that the crypto markets in India performed similarly to the Indian Equity markets over the last year would constitute falsehood, however, it cannot be denied that the landscape of Indian cryptocurrency investment did become clearer with great strides made over the past year. While the sentiment for entering the crypto market and considering the same as an alternative and lucrative asset class is consistently rising, financial institutions, regulatory authorities, and RBI are yet to objectively clear their stance on the same.

31st May 2021 was a historic day in the Indian Crypto Market. This day became historic due to the RBI circular issued that clarified distinctively – Banks cannot stop people from investing in virtual currencies (also known as cryptocurrency). This cleared a major pathway for retail investors to invest in cryptoassets. CoinDCX, the leading crypto unicorn in India, also reported 340% Y-o-Y growth of user sign-ups between the 25.50 years on the platform during the pandemic.

The problems with crypto investments

As stated earlier, the Indian retail investor is a risk-averse individual. Given the historically misguided image of crypto markets as a 'risky-gamble' even in countries like the USA, it was not surprising to realise a lack of interest in cryptoasset portfolio diversification for Indian retail investors. However, it wasn't the tarnished image that was to blame. Primarily, we list down a few possible problems with the Indian crypto currency asset investment which has been validated by prior research. These problems include–

1. Risk-averse tendencies - Indian retail investors are primarily risk-averse with a bias toward less volatile asset classes.
2. Tarnished image – The image on crypto investment has been contaminated by the possible interest of the public in pump-dump schemes. Exaggerated media expo- sure on get-rich-quick schemes led by DogeCoin, BTC,etc.
3. Herd behaviour – This dictates the reason behind crypto diversification for new investors. Investment routes are primarily led by fear of missing out especially when the market is in the bullrun.
4. Unknown terrain – While the crypto markets have existed for decades, the new found interest in the same has deemed this cryptoasset terrain as unexplored and a path less trodden. This problem is further exacerbated by scattered and un- verified information disseminated as knowledge to new investors.
5. Industrial Solution Lacuna – While there exist many cryptobokerages to carry out crypto-specific transactions and crypto exchanges to trade cryptoassets, the absence of any solution to guide a new investor to make the right crypto purchases leads to appalling attrition of public confidence in the cryptomarkets. Lack of focus on public-salient interpretability of the cryptocurrency asset class dictates current industrial solutions

CoinKart – Solution suite targeted for contextual problems

CoinKart as a FinTech solution offers an almost demographic-agnostic industrial advantage for the Indian retail investors to include crypto allocations in their financial portfolio for long-run gains. This is achieved through various capacities that CoinKart as a platform offers the user –

1. CoinKart provides thematic crypto-investment baskets that reduce investors' need to perform cryptocurrency due diligence for making sectoral investments
2. Each Coinkart can be compared with S&P Bitcoin Index, S&P Ethereum Index, and S&P Cryptocurrency MegaCap Index for checking potential hedging possibilities in existing equity portfolios
3. CoinKarts also provides parameter-based implementations for popular equity in- vestment strategies like Coffee Can Investing, Naked Trader, ESG, etc.
4. Apart from sectoral and strategy-based themes, CoinKart also provides crypto investment carts based on market cap for given cryptocurrency in its carts titled – *Moon 250, Moon100.*
5. Alongside, CoinKart provides the retail trader to utilise its CryptoFunda – which is a fundamental analysis methodology for analysis of a given cryptocurrency
6. Lastly, CoinKart provides the retail trader the capacity to aid his/her investments using our algorithm-designed Crypto Market Sentiment Index (CMSI).

Solution differentiation – CoinKart's USP

At its onset, if one was to describe CoinKart, a perfect succinct summary could be – 'Indexed thematic Cryptocurrency Carts optimised using ML'. Primarily, CoinKart comprises three solutions – Coinkart, CMSI and cryptofunda. Each of these solutions is described below in brief:

1. Coinkart - Thematic cryptocurrency carts ML-optimised indexed against S&P Bitcoin Index, S&P Ethereum Index, and S&P Cryptocurrency MegaCapIndex
2. Cryptocurrency market sentiment index - Cryptocurrency Market Sentiment Index based on the observations made by the team independently regarding the crypto- currency market
3. Cryptofunda - A researched methodology for performing fundamental analysis of any cryptocurrency, along with equity-class similar investment strategies for cryptocurrency markets

Apart from the benefits offered through these three solutions, other benefits include –

1. Reduces investors' need to perform prior due diligence for making sectoral in- vestments
2. Indexed against three major global crypto indices – S&P Bitcoin Index, S&P Ethereum Index, and S&P Cryptocurrency MegaCapIndex
3. Each CoinKart is optimized and allocated using ML-based portfolio optimisation tools
4. Trade funds directly through web-solution on major Indian Cryptocurrency exchanges like Binanceetc.

Research and implementation methodology

Based on prior research conducted in similar FinTech solutions offered in equity markets and crypto markets for making strategic and informed decisions an approximate manifestation of the methodology that is to be followed has been visualised in Figure 14.7. Further corrections and additions shall be done in course of the research project.

System requirements

Currently, the following system requirements were identified for conduction of mentioned methodology –

1. RStudio and Python
2. MATLAB

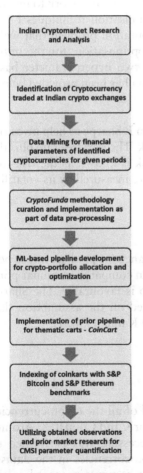

Figure 14.7 The above figure depicts the block diagram representing the flow of methodology for implementation of the CoinKart project

Also, prior knowledge of Markowitz Theory of Portfolio Selection, Metcalfe's Law, *etc.* is required along with familiarity in reading white papers of cryptocurrencies and general comfort in dealing with cryptomarket terminology.

Each chosen platform has its role in allowing the CoinKart pipeline to work. The role played by each of the softwares has been described below –

1. Rstudio: Used for performing CoinKart indexing and prior back-testing.
2. Python and PyFinance - Used for creating ML-pipelines in the context of CoinKart portfolio allocation and optimisation.
3. MATLAB - Used for displayed high-quality visualisation for certain strategies. Also, complements usage of R and Python.

For the first phase of the demo, we restrict ourselves to the basic implementation of Moon 4 using the Monte-Carlo simulation method for financial portfolio allocation and optimisation using chosen two parameters – Sharpe Ratio and Volatility (Jerome et al., 2003; Tarnopolski, 2017). Later, we shall extend our work to include more profound financial portfolio allocation and optimisation techniques based on multiple financial hyperparameters. Since the computation problem that we're tackling is that of financial portfolio allocation and optimisation, for the initial demonstration of the same for a CoinKart, we chose two hyperparameter baselines – Sharpe ratio and volatility, whose brief description has been provided below.

Sharpe ratio and volatility
The Sharpe ratio was created by Nobel Laureate William F. Sharpe to help investors comprehend the return on investment concerning its risk. The risk-free rate plus the average return earned per unit of volatility or total risk is known as the risk-free rate ratio. The price changes of an asset or a portfolio are measured by its volatility (Mesias and Kannan 2021).

Conceptual limitations of Sharpe ratio

The Sharpe ratio adjusts a portfolio's previous performance (or predicts future performance) to account for the investor's excess risk. When compared to similar portfolios or funds with lower returns, a high Sharpe ratio is favourable. The Sharpe ratio has several flaws, one of which is that it is based on the assumption that investment returns are regularly distributed Mesias and Kannan (2021).

Implementation modules with description

Primary data-mining of OHLC crytpodatasets

Two datasets were created. The first dataset comprised of all the cryptocurrencies traded on Indian Cryptocurrency exchanges – be it WasirX and CoinDCX. Around 187 cryptocurrencies were collected. Manual pre-processing was performed to assign a 'thematic' category for each of the 180 cryptocurrencies in the dataset based on the study of each cryptocurrency's white paper, community records, websites, and other publicly available data. Figure 14.8 and Figure 14.9 represent the screenshots of the dataset at its extreme lengths.

Figure 14.8 The above screenshot is taken from the first dataset that contains a thematic association of the 187 collected cryptocurrencies traded in Indian Crypto Exchanges

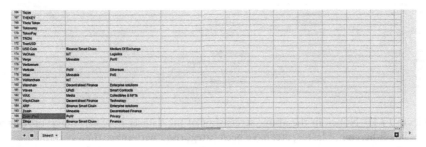

Figure 14.9 Notice in the above screenshot that all the 187 cryptocurrencies are thematically associated with either one or the other category

Some cryptocurrencies were even associated with more than two thematic categories, as depicted in Figure 14.10 where a snapshot of the dataset includes mentions of such cryptocurrencies.

Finally, the second dataset comprised of OHLC (Open-High-Low-Close) data along with other market-capitalisation-related details for the 187 identified, different cryptocurrencies traded in India. This dataset would form the base or the source data for performing financial portfolio allocation and optimisation later, along with formulation of CoinKarts like Moon 4, Moon 5, etc. which are CoinKarts based primarily on market capitalisation. Figure 14.11 shows the header of the same dataset.

Consequently, the historical prices of the cryptocurrencies mentioned in the two datasets for each day were extracted through Yfinance. Implementation for the dataset mining through Yfinance has been depicted in Figure 14.12.

The optimisation pipeline progresses with pre-processing function definition curation for calculating daily return and mean daily return, along with covariance matrix, depiction of the same has been shown in Figure 14.13 and Figure 14.14 respectively.

With this, we proceed further in our pipeline, where we declare a function for portfolio optimisation (n=10000) and Sharpe ratio calculation for each random portfolio based on the Monte-Carlo method. For displaying the optimal results, both local optimal i.e., portfolio with highest Sharpe ratio, and global optimal i.e.,

	A	B	C	D	E
40	CyberMiles	E Commerce	Cosmos Ecosystem		
41	Dai	Ethereum	Binance smart chain	Decentralised Finance	
42	Dash	DAO	Hybrid (PoS & PoW)		
43	Decentraland	Ethereum	Gaming & Collectibles		
44	Decred	DAO	Hybrid (PoS & PoW)		
45	Dent	Ethereum	Mobile Data Market		
46	Dentacoin	Ethereum	Health		
47	DigiByte	IoT	PoW		
48	Digitex	Ethereum	Centralised Exchange		
49	DigixDAO	Ethereum	Stablecoin - Asset Backed		
50	Dogecoin	Meme	Binance smart chain	PoW	
51	Dragonchain	Ethereum	Enterprise solutions		
52	Dropil	Ethereum	Smart Contracts	Untracked Listing	
53	Dynamic Trading Rights	Ethereum	Marketplace		
54	Eidoo (pNetwork)	Ethereum	Decentralised Finance	DAO	
55	Elastos	Ethereum	DPoS	Distributed Computing	
56	Electroneum	Finance			
57	Emercoin	Distributed Services	Hybrid (PoS & PoW)		
58	Endor Protocol	Ethereum	Business AI		
59	Enigma	Ethereum	Privacy		
60	Enjin Coin	Ethereum	Gaming & Collectibles		
61	EOS	Binance smart chain	decentralised finance		
62	Etheera	Ethereum			
63	Ethereum Classic	Mineable	Binance smart chain		
64	Ethereum	Ethereum	Coinbase venture portfolio	Decentralised application	
65	Everipedia	Ethereum	EOS		
66	Factom	Enterprise	decentralised finance		
67	FunFair	Ethereum	decentralised gaming		
68	Fusion		financial service		
69	Gas	Ethereum	Smart contracts		

+ ▦ Sheet1 ▾

Figure 14.10 Notice in the above screenshot of the dataset how certain cryptocurrencies like Ethereum, Elastos, etc. have been categorised with more than two themes

	slug	symbol	name	date	ranknow	open	high	low	close	volume	market	close_ratio	spread
2	bitcoin	BTC	Bitcoin	28-04-2013	1	135.3	135.98	132.1	134.21	0	1.45E+09	0.5438	3.88
3	bitcoin	BTC	Bitcoin	29-04-2013	1	134.44	147.49	134	144.54	0	1.6E+09	0.7813	13.49
4	bitcoin	BTC	Bitcoin	30-04-2013	1	144	146.93	134.05	139	0	1.54E+09	0.3843	12.88
5	bitcoin	BTC	Bitcoin	01-05-2013	1	139	139.89	107.72	116.99	0	1.3E+09	0.2802	32.17
6	bitcoin	BTC	Bitcoin	02-05-2013	1	116.38	125.6	92.28	105.21	0	1.17E+09	0.3881	33.32
7	bitcoin	BTC	Bitcoin	03-05-2013	1	106.25	108.13	79.1	97.75	0	1.09E+09	0.6424	29.03
8	bitcoin	BTC	Bitcoin	04-05-2013	1	98.1	115	92.5	112.5	0	1.25E+09	0.8889	22.5
9	bitcoin	BTC	Bitcoin	05-05-2013	1	112.9	118.8	107.14	115.91	0	1.29E+09	0.7521	11.66
10	bitcoin	BTC	Bitcoin	06-05-2013	1	115.98	124.66	106.64	112.3	0	1.25E+09	0.3141	18.02
11	bitcoin	BTC	Bitcoin	07-05-2013	1	112.25	113.44	97.7	111.5	0	1.24E+09	0.8767	15.74
12	bitcoin	BTC	Bitcoin	08-05-2013	1	109.6	115.78	109.6	113.57	0	1.26E+09	0.6424	6.18
13	bitcoin	BTC	Bitcoin	09-05-2013	1	113.2	113.46	109.26	112.67	0	1.25E+09	0.8119	4.2
14	bitcoin	BTC	Bitcoin	10-05-2013	1	112.8	122	111.55	117.2	0	1.31E+09	0.5407	10.45
15	bitcoin	BTC	Bitcoin	11-05-2013	1	117.7	118.68	113.01	115.24	0	1.28E+09	0.3933	5.67
16	bitcoin	BTC	Bitcoin	12-05-2013	1	115.64	117.45	113.43	115	0	1.28E+09	0.3905	4.02
17	bitcoin	BTC	Bitcoin	13-05-2013	1	114.82	118.7	114.5	117.98	0	1.32E+09	0.8286	4.2
18	bitcoin	BTC	Bitcoin	14-05-2013	1	117.98	119.8	110.25	111.5	0	1.24E+09	0.1309	9.55
19	bitcoin	BTC	Bitcoin	15-05-2013	1	111.4	115.81	103.5	114.22	0	1.27E+09	0.8708	12.31
20	bitcoin	BTC	Bitcoin	16-05-2013	1	114.22	118.76	112.2	118.76	0	1.33E+09	1	6.56
21	bitcoin	BTC	Bitcoin	17-05-2013	1	118.21	125.3	116.57	123.01	0	1.37E+09	0.7377	8.73
22	bitcoin	BTC	Bitcoin	18-05-2013	1	123.5	125.25	122.3	123.5	0	1.38E+09	0.4068	2.95
23	bitcoin	BTC	Bitcoin	19-05-2013	1	123.21	124.5	119.57	121.99	0	1.36E+09	0.4909	4.93

crypto-markets - Copy

Ready

Figure 14.11 The above screenshot depicts the OHLC crypto datasets that contain OHLC financial data (open price, high price, low price, and close price) along with the crypto market volume, close-ratio, spread, etc

portfolio with the lowest volatility, the function was defined for the same respectively. Finally, the results are plotted on a return-volatility graph with the red star indicating portfolio with highest Sharpe Ratio and green star for lowest volatility. Function declaration for the same visualisation and the execution of the same has been depicted in Figure 14.15.

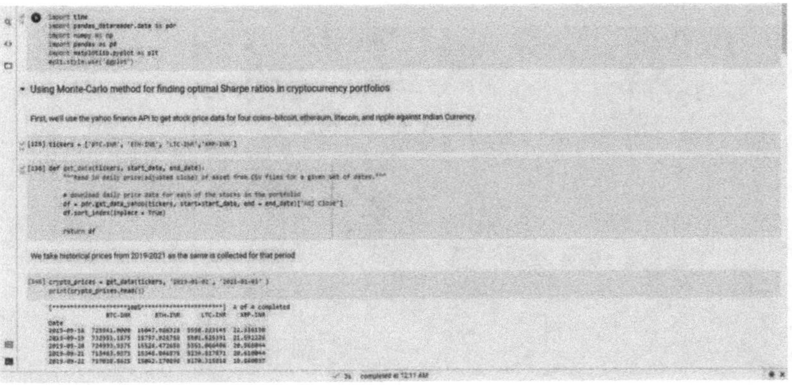

Figure 14.12 The above screenshot depicts the cell definition and function that allow for mining OHLC crypto data using Yfinance API

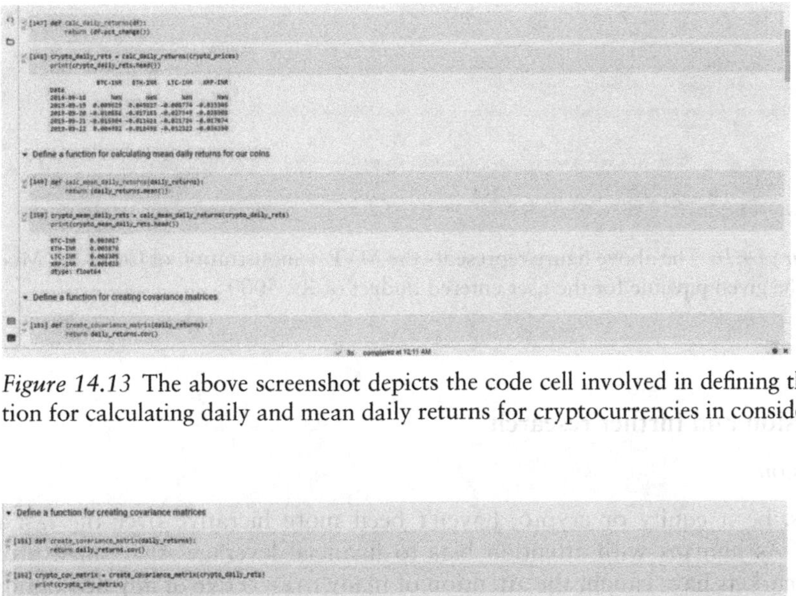

Figure 14.13 The above screenshot depicts the code cell involved in defining the function for calculating daily and mean daily returns for cryptocurrencies in consideration

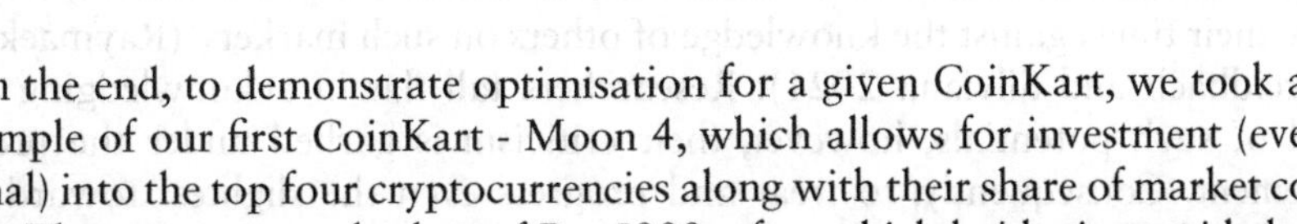

Figure 14.14 The above screenshot depicts the code cell involved in defining the function for calculating the covariance matrix

In the end, to demonstrate optimisation for a given CoinKart, we took a simple example of our first CoinKart - Moon 4, which allows for investment (even, fractional) into the top four cryptocurrencies along with their share of market contribution. The user enters a budget of Rs. 5000, after which he/she is provided with the corresponding allocation that is to be made by him/her based on the portfolio with the lowest volatility. Implementation for the same has been shown in Figure 14.16.

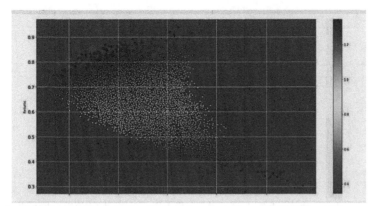

Figure 14.15 The above figure represents the plot of returns against volatility for all the randomly sampled 10,000 portfolios with local optimum marked with a red star and the global optimum marked with a green star

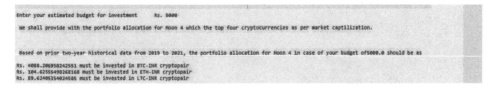

Figure 14.16 The above figure represents the MVP demonstration of CoinKart Moon 4 on the given pipeline for the user entered budget of Rs. 5000

Conclusion and further research

Conclusion

Markets, be it equity or crypto, haven't been more lucrative over the last few months. As humans with attention bias to financial leverages that smell profits, crypto markets have caught the attention of many irrespective of any demographic variable. However, the sentiment for such potential leverages is cut short due to the divided and partitioned landscape that cryptomarkets exist in. Every day as new subclasses of cryptoassets like NFTs, Tokens, etc. are brought into deployment, it becomes obvious and rather imperative to be clouded by the choices. While some seek the route of instant investment for the sake of FOMO satiation, others exchange their time against the knowledge of others on such markets (Raymaekers 2015; Breidbach and Silviana 2021). Researchers fall flat in acknowledging the potential of such potentials, however, their criticism is garbed under the previous statement. Consequently, to treat and progress even the slightest toward an unclouded and divided future of crypto investments accessible to all, CoinKart as a solution is proposed to the beneficiaries already a part of this network and the gatekeepers who wish to enter the network of crypto investments.

Further research roadmap

The whole research project is divided into three phases.

Phase 1. Thematic association of collected cryptocoins and testing basic crypto portfolio allocation and optimisation for any given CoinKart to act as MVP for the project

Phase 2. Hyperparameter tuning for portfolio allocation and optimisation using advanced financial parameters, along with formulation of CryptoFunda – crypto investment fundamental analysis methodology. In this phase, we also expand the definition of CoinKarts from 'thematic-baskets' to 'equity-investment strategy analogous' baskets.

Phase 3. Deployment of pipeline with the front end web application for attempts at increasing abstraction level. Further, possibilities for connecting the pipeline with crypto wallets using Binance API would be explored. Finally, based on each individual's understanding of the cryptomarket domain, the definition of CMSI is formulated.

With this, we conclude by calling out Figure 14.17 that represents our possible method- ology for implementing the goals for Phase 2.

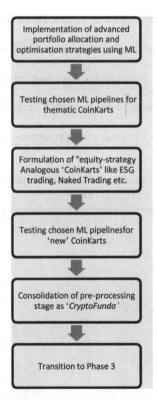

Figure 14.17 The above figure represents the roadmap for Phase 2

Acknowledgement

I would like to acknowledge the following people from my institute DIT University for their continued support in building the next FinTech revolutionary product (CoinKart) – Dr. Pradeep Singh Rawat, Aduet Dabral, Aman Bisht, and Aditi Bist

References

Breidbach, C. F. and Silviana, T. (2021). Betting on Bitcoin: How social collectives shape cryptocurrency markets. J. Bus. Res. 122:311–320.

Chuen, K., LEE, D, Li, G., and Yu, W. (2017). The Journal of Alternative Investments; London. 20(3):16–40.

Foglia, M. and Peng-Fei Dai (2021). Ubiquitous uncertainties: spillovers across economic policy uncertainty and cryptocurrency uncertainty indices. Journal of Asian Business and Economic Studies (2021).

Jerome, B. D., Garcia, R., and Marcel, R. (2003). A Monte Carlo method for optimal portfolios. J. Finan. 58(1):401–446.

https://www.euromoney.com/learning/blockchain-explained/how-transactions-get-into- the-blockchain

https://twitter.com/Nithin0dha

https://www.ibm.com/in-en/topics/what-is-blockchain

Liu, Y., and Tsyvinski, A. (2021). Risks and returns of cryptocurrency. Rev. Finan. Stu. 34(6):2689–2727.

Mesias, A. and Kannan, S. (2021). Pricing Exotic Derivatives for Cryptocurrency As- sets-A Monte Carlo Perspective. Available at SSRN 3862655.

Narayanan, A., et al. (2016). Bitcoin and cryptocurrency technologies: a comprehensive intro- duction. Princeton University Press, United States.

Rauchs, M. and Hileman, G. (2017). Global cryptocurrency benchmarking study. Cambridge Centre for Alternative Finance. 33 33113.

Raymaekers, W. (2015). Cryptocurrency Bitcoin: Disruption, challenges and opportuni- ties. J. Pay. Strat. Sys. 9(1):30–46.

Ryan F. (2015). An analysis of the cryptocurrency industry.

Tarnopolski, M. (2017). Modeling the price of Bitcoin with geometric fractional Brownian motion: a Monte Carlo approach. arXiv preprint arXiv:1707.03746.

Ujan M., et al. (2016). A brief survey of cryptocurrency systems. 14th annual conference on privacy, security and trust (PST). IEEE.

15 Impact of the COVID-19 pandemic on volatility spillover across sectors in the US markets

Syed Ahzam Tariq

Undergraduate Researcher, Birla Institute of Technology and Science, Pilani, India

Abstract

The coronavirus pandemic has brought about a great change in investor behaviour and has had an irreversible impact on stock markets across the world. Financial markets are highly prone to various crises which make exploring the COVID-19 induced shock all the very important. The present research tries to investigate the change in volatility spillover due to the pandemic across the prominent sectors of the US markets – information technology, consumer discretionary, healthcare, consumer staples, and industrials using the DCC-GARCH model. Volatility gives us a good measure of the risk faced by a stock, index, or a sector and it is relevant to investors to understand the transmission of this volatility across sectors to make good investment decisions during a crisis.

Keywords: COVID-19 pandemic, DCC-GARCH, S&P 500, Volatility spillover effect

Introduction and literature review

The COVID-19 pandemic is having a major impact on the financial markets across the globe and across various sectors. Some sectors have been positively impacted by the pandemic and others negatively. This makes the study of performance of sectors very important especially during a crisis as the COVID-19 pandemic.

Financial markets today are more connected than ever, and stock markets react swiftly to COVID-19 confirmed cases as well as fatalities as explored by Ashraf (2020) which makes it very essential to understand the relationship between various sectors of the US markets and how the COVID-19 pandemic has affected that relationship. Financial markets have become prone to policy changes regarding the pandemic as identified by Zhang and Hu (2020) and have experienced increased volatility which makes it more important to identify the impact of COVID-19 on volatility spillover across sectors.

Black swan events such as pandemics lead to a panic-selling response from the investors as explored by Burch (2016). Recent studies on impact of COVID-19 pandemic on financial markets have shown very insightful results. Baker (2020) concluded that COVID-19 had a far more devastating impact on the US markets than by other diseases earlier. Driss and Garcin (2020) showed that the Asian markets were more affected than the European markets. Yarovaya et al. (2020) argued that Islamic bonds showed the properties of a safe haven during COVID-19.

It has been the first time that a pandemic has struck the world when we are equipped with econometric tools to understand its impact and what lies ahead but it is not the first time that a crisis has struck us. In financial literature, voluminous studies have been devoted to spillover impact due to various financial crises in the past. Dufrenot (2014) explored effect of 2008 global financial crisis on the volatility of Indian markets. Spillover effects of 2008 financial crisis were analysed for the Latin American markets by Hwang (2014). Alotaibi and Mishra (2015) explored global and regional volatility spillovers to GCC markets. A similar study was undertaken by Kang and Uddin (2019) for the ASEAN markets.

This study aims to apply the methodology developed by Diebold and Yilmaz (2012) and construct volatility spillover indices using a DCC-GARCH framework to model the relationship between the various sectors of the US markets. This study analyses the relationship between the information technology, consumer staples, consumer discretionary, healthcare and industrials sectors of the S&P 500. This study is unique in its way as it is for the first time that the impact of the COVID-19 pandemic on volatility spillovers across sectors is being analysed for the US markets.

Methodology

Data

The study analyses the volatility spillover across top five sectors of the US markets – Information technology, Consumer Staples, Consumer Discretionary, Industrials and Healthcare. For the pre-COVID-19 period, market data from 01-Jan-2018 to 31-Dec-2019 is considered and for the COVID-19 period, market data from 01-Jan-2020 to 31-Dec-2021 is analysed. All the market data has been sourced from Yahoo Finance. This market data is then used to calculate daily returns as shown in Figure 15.1 and Figure 15.2. Summary of various statistical parameters of the data set is mentioned in Table 15.1.

Compatibility tests

Several tests are performed to ascertain the applicability of the DCC-GARCH (1,1) model on the data set. Two tests – ADF and PP are performed to ascertain the stationarity of data sets. After confirmation of the stationarity of the data set, ARCH effect is determined in the data sets. Only after the confirmation of the ARCH effects, GARCH can be applied to obtain meaningful results.

The data sets were found to be stationary and exhibited ARCH effects and thus is suitable for the application of DCC-GARCH (1,1) model.

DCC-GARCH model

The DCC-GARCH (1,1) model in a nutshell estimates time-varying variances and co-variances in a system of multiple time-series. The model used in this paper is represented as follows:

$$x_t = \mu_t + \varepsilon_t \tag{1}$$

$$\varepsilon = H_t^{1/2}\varepsilon_t \tag{2}$$

$$H_t = D_t R_t D_t \tag{3}$$

where $\varepsilon_t \sim N(0,H_t), \mu_t \sim N(0,I)$

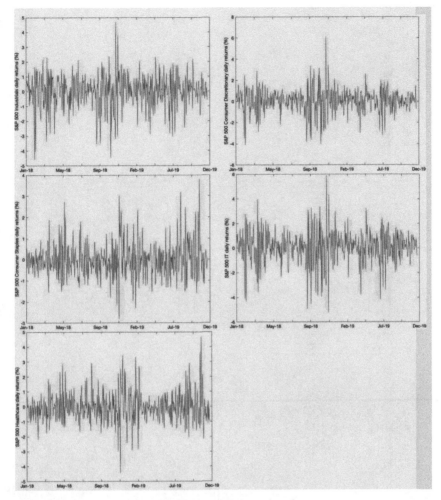

Figure 15.1 (a)–(e) Daily returns before COVID-19 pandemic
Source: Data sourced from Yahoo finance

where μ_t and ε_t are mX1 dimensional vectors representing mean and standardized error terms, respectively. Moreover, R_t and D_t are mXm dimensional matrices representing DCC and time-varying conditional variances.

In order to compute dynamic conditional correlation, following steps are required:

Step1: First of all, Generalized Forecast Error Variance Decomposition (GFEVD) is calculated that represents the pairwise directional connectedness from j to i. This is calculated by:

$$\psi_{ij,t}^{\sim g}(J) = \frac{\sum_{t=1}^{J-1}\psi_{ij,t}^{2,g}}{\sum_{j=1}^{N}\sum_{t=1}^{J-1}\psi_{ij,t}^{2,g}} \tag{4}$$

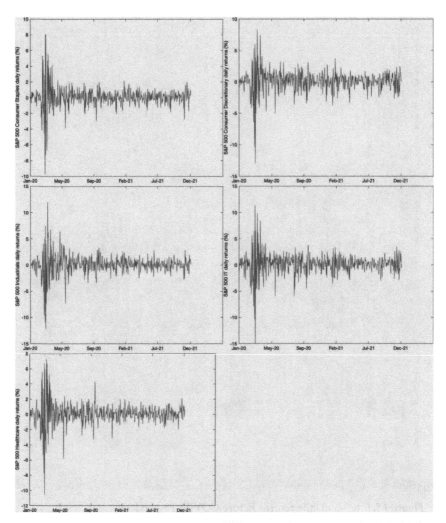

Figure 15.2 (a)–(e) Daily returns during COVID-19 pandemic
Source: Data sourced from Yahoo finance

where $\sum_{j=1}^{N} \psi_{ij,t}^{\tilde{} g}(J) = 1$ and $\sum_{i,j=1}^{N} \psi_{ij,t}^{\tilde{} g}(J) = m$. The numerator in the expression represents the effect of the ith shock whereas the denominator represents the effect of all the shocks.

Step 2: Total directional connectedness is computed which measures how much shock in i is transmitted to all other variables taken into consideration. It is calculated as:

$$C_{i \rightarrow j,t}^{g}(K) = \frac{\sum_{j=1,i!=j}^{m} \psi_{ij,t}^{\tilde{} g}(K)}{\sum_{j=1}^{m} \psi_{ij,t}^{\tilde{} g}(K)} \tag{5}$$

Table 15.1 Summary statistics of market data

	Mean	Variance	Skewness	Kurtosis
Before COVID–19				
IT	0.066	1.798	–0.484	2.294
Consumer discretionary	0.038	1.249	–0.267	3.155
Consumer staples	–0.014	0.661	0.698	2.111
Industrials	0.012	1.228	–0.653	2.217
Healthcare	–0.035	0.981	0.593	2.638
During COVID–19				
IT	0.126	4.074	–0.685	11.047
Consumer discretionary	0.096	2.910	–1.244	11.103
Consumer staples	0.044	1.813	–0.340	14.302
Industrials	0.049	3.646	–0.664	10.739
Healthcare	0.065	2.170	–0.450	11.040

Source: Self-Calculated

Step 3: As a next step, total directional connectedness from others is computed which represents the influence which a variable *i* has on the analysed variables. It is calculated as follows:

$$C^g_{i \leftarrow j,t}(K) = \frac{\sum_{j=1,i!=j}^{m} \psi^{-g}_{ij,t}(K)}{\sum_{j=1}^{m} \psi^{-g}_{ij,t}(K)} \tag{6}$$

Step 4: As the last step of constructing a dynamic connectedness table, we find the net directional connectedness as follows:

$$C^g_t(K) = C^g_{i \rightarrow j,t}(K) - C^g_{i \leftarrow j,t}(K) \tag{7}$$

The dynamic connectedness correlation tables constructed for both the pre-COVID and during-COVID scenario is presented in Table 2.

Results and conclusion

The net directional connectedness represents the impact of one variable as it is net of the shock received and transmitted to a variable. The results of the DCC table imply that the information technology the consumer discretionary sector are the main transmitters of shock and that the Healthcare and consumer staples are the receivers of the shocks. Moreover, an interesting observation is that the Healthcare sector was a transmitter of shock in the pre-COVID period but has now become a receiver of shocks. Information technology has always been a transmitter of shocks and consumer staples has always been a receiver of shocks and the COVID-19

Table 15.2 Average connectedness table

	Consumer discretionary	Consumer staples	Industrials	Information technology	Healthcare	FROM
Before COVID-19						
Consumer discretionary	40.39	0.19	24.03	35.19	0.21	59.61
Consumer staples	0.88	67.38	0.91	1.54	29.28	32.62
Industrials	22.38	0.17	48.48	28.71	0.26	51.52
Information technology	24.99	0.16	21.83	52.77	0.25	47.23
Healthcare	0.52	16.80	0.37	0.51	81.79	18.21
Contribution to others	48.77	17.31	47.13	65.96	30.00	209.18
Net directional connectedness	−10.84	−15.30	−4.38	18.73	11.79	–
During COVID-19						
Consumer discretionary	43.23	5.02	13.73	30.43	7.59	56.77
Consumer staples	15.46	28.33	20.73	19.60	15.89	71.67
Industrials	16.94	8.37	47.44	17.26	9.99	52.56
Information technology	25.41	5.31	11.57	48.25	9.46	51.75
Healthcare	5.52	10.59	16.34	23.23	34.32	65.68
Contribution to others	73.33	29.29	62.36	90.51	42.92	298.42
Net directional connectedness	16.56	−42.38	9.80	38.77	−22.75	–

Source: Self-Calculated

pandemic had no effect on their state, though the magnitude of their net directional connectedness has been affected. The industrials sector was the least impacted by the COVID-19 pandemic when considering the magnitude of the difference in net connectedness between Pre-COVID and during-COVID periods.

Law makers should consider the volatility spillover across sectors to form strategies to watch capital flows and support the financial performance of stock markets during such a catastrophic event as suggested by Jebran (2017). Akhtaruzzaman et al. (2020) suggested that liquidity should be provided by the government in such scenarios to support the markets. The existence of volatility spillover suggests that there is little room for diversification of investments, so investors should reallocate their investments among financially interconnected countries by increasing the importance (weight) of less integrated stock markets with minimum spillover effects as suggested by Gulzar et al. (2019)

A further step of this research could be to increase the number of sectors being considered. Moreover, this study should be performed on other markets as well to understand whether these results were only US-specific or other markets also show similar results. This will help us identify market behaviour during the times of crisis. Such results could be of great importance while making investment decision during uncertain times.

Acknowledgements

The author expresses his gratitude towards David Gebauer for his econometric tool which helped him verify the results.

Declaration of competing interests

The author declares that he has no known competing financial interests or personal relationships that could have appeared to influence the work reported in this paper.

References

Alotaibi, A. R. and Mishra, A. V. (2015). Global and regional volatility spillovers to GCC stock markets. Int. Economic. Modelling. 45:38–49. Elsevier BV. https://doi.org/10.1016/j.econmod.2014.10.052

Akhtaruzzaman, M., Boubaker, S., and Sensoy, A. (2021). Financial contagion during COVID-19 crisis. Int. Financ. Res. Lett. 38:101604. Elsevier BV. https://doi.org/10.1016/j.frl.2020.101604

Ammy-Driss, A. and Matthieu, G. (2020). Efficiency of the financial markets during the COVID-19 crisis: Time-varying parameters of fractional stable dynamics. *arXiv* arXiv:2007.10727

Ashraf, B. N. (2020). Stock markets' reaction to COVID-19: Cases or fatalities? In Research in Int. Bus. Financ. 54: 101249. Elsevier BV. https://doi.org/10.1016/j.ribaf.2020.101249

Baker, S., Bloom, N., Davis, S., Kost, K., Sammon, M., and Viratyosin, T. (2020). The Unprecedented Stock Market Impact of COVID-19. National Bureau of Economic Research. https://doi.org/10.3386/w26945

Burch, T. R., Emery, D. R., and Fuerst, M. E. (2016). Who Moves Markets in a Sudden Marketwide Crisis? Evidence from 9/11. Int. J. Financ. Quantitat. Analy. 51(2): 463–487). Cambridge University Press (CUP). https://doi.org/1

Dufrénot, G. and Keddad, B. (2014). Spillover effects of the 2008 global financial crisis on the volatility of the Indian equity markets: Coupling or uncoupling? A study on sector-based data. Int. Rev.Financ. Anal. 33:17–3.

Gulzar, S., Mujtaba Kayani, G., Xiaofeng, H., Ayub, U., and Rafique, A. (2019). Financial cointegration and spillover effect of global financial crisis: a study of emerging Asian financial markets. In Economic Research-Ekonomska Istraživanja (Vol. 32, Issue

Hwang, J. K. (2014). Spillover Effects of the 2008 Financial Crisis in Latin America Stock Markets. Int. Adv. Econ. Res. 20:311–324. https://doi.org/10.1007/s11294-014-9472-1

Jebran, K., Chen, S., Ullah, I., and Mirza, S. S. (2017). Does volatility spillover among stock markets varies from normal to turbulent periods? Evidence from emerging markets of Asia. Int. J. Financ. Data Sci. 3(1–4): 20–23.

Kang, S. H., Uddin, G. S., Troster, V., and Yoon, S. M. (2019). Directional spillover effects between ASEAN and world stock markets. Int. J. Multinat. Financ. Manag. 52–53: 100592. Elsevier BV. https://doi.org/10.1016/j.mulfin.201

Yousfi, M., Ben Zaied, Y., Ben Cheikh, N., Ben Lahouel, B., and Bouzgarrou, H. (2021). Effects of the COVID-19 pandemic on the US stock market and uncertainty: A comparative assessment between the first and second waves. In Technological Forecasting and Soc

Yarovaya, L., Ahmed, H. E., and Shawkat, M. H. (2020). Searching for Safe Havens during the COVID-19 Pandemic: Determinants of Spillovers between Islamic and Conventional Financial Markets. Available online: https://papers.ssrn.com/ sol3/papers

Zhang, D., Hu, M., and Ji, Q. (2020). Financial markets under the global pandemic of COVID-19. Int. Financ. Res. Lett. 36: 101528. Elsevier BV. https://doi.org/10.1016/j.frl.2020.101528

16 A study on risk return relationship of Indian equity markets

Sankar Thappa

Associate Professor, Department of Management, Rajiv Gandhi University, (Central University), Doimukh, Arunachal Pradesh, India

Abstract

The use of money or funds with the anticipation of future income or capital appreciation is considered as an investment. 'An investment is a commitment of funds made in the expectation of some significant rate of return,' according to Fischer and Jordan. If the investment is done properly, the return will be proportional to the risk taken on by the investor. Return and risk are the two most important influencing factors in the investment decision-making process. The investment return is the increase in the value of the initial investment after taxation. The risk of not achieving the expected return on investment is referred to as risk. Investors can participate in the capital market on both the primary and secondary markets. The two primary capital market instruments are equity and debt. The secondary market is where equity securities issued in the primary market are posted for trading and liquidation. Investors use the secondary market to make investment decisions and to revise those decisions. To put it in other words, they buy, hold, and sell it. The Bombay Stock Exchange (BSE) and the National Stock Exchange (NSE) are the two most important secondary markets in India (NSE). In line of all this, the current article attempts to examine the risk-return relationship of Indian equity markets. The paper is trying to assess the performance of Indian Equity Market in terms of return-risk relationship. It also trying to compare and know which index is performing better from the perspective of investor.

Keywords: BSE, index, NSE, return, risk

Introduction

The use of money or funds with the anticipation of future income or capital appreciation is considered as an investment. 'An investment is a commitment of funds made in the expectation of some significant rate of return,' according to Fischer and Jordan. If the investment is done properly, the return will be proportional to the risk taken on by the investor. Return and risk are the two most important influencing factors in the investment decision-making process. The Investment Return is the increase in the value of the initial investment after taxation. The risk of not achieving the expected return on investment is referred to as risk. Investors can participate in the capital market on both the primary and secondary markets. The two primary capital market instruments are equity and debt. The secondary market is where equity securities issued in the primary market are posted for trading and liquidation. Investors use the secondary market to make investment decisions and to revise those decisions. To put it in other words, they buy, hold, and sell it. The

Bombay Stock Exchange (BSE) and the National Stock Exchange (NSE) are the two most important secondary markets in India (NSE).

Literature review

Sharma et al., (2012) examines the risk return behavior of the stocks listed in the stock exchanges of South Asia. The study was aimed at finding out the return and risk associated over time using the descriptive statistics. They find that there is a high return and reasonable risk involved in those Asian countries. Poornima and Swathiga (2017 – their study of relationship between risk and return analysis is based on capital asset pricing model. Their study is limited to two sectors (automobile and IT) listed in NSE where the automobile companies have performed better and increased growth in the MARKET compared to IT sector. Kandel (2018), in his paper, analyses the risk and return on common stock investment of Nepalese stock market and is focused on common stock of two commercial banks listed in Nepal stock exchange Limited. Investors have varying perceptions toward risk and enterprising activities. They invest in those opportunities which have certain degree of risk associated with it. This research study found that there is a positive relationship between risk and return. Mallikarjunappa and Shaini (2016) conducted a study on comparative analysis of risk and return with reference to stocks of CNX Bank Nifty. This study analyses the risk and returns in the banking sector. They compare the performance of the 12 listed banks in the Nifty Bank Index.

Objectives

- To appraise the performance of Indian Equity Market in the context of risk-return relationship
- To judge which Indian market index is performing better from the viewpoint of investor.

Methodology

This study is based purely on secondary data. The BSE SENSEX and NSE NIFTY are taken as sample market index for the study. The data for a period of 10 years have been taken for the study from 2010–11 to 2019–20. All the data required for the study have been taken from BSE and NSE websites.

The daily closing price of selected market indices are converted into daily return series using the formula given below:

$$R_t = \log \frac{P_t}{P_{t-1}}$$

Where:
R_t = *Daily log return on market index for time t*
Pt = *Closing price at time 't'*
P_{t-1} = *Corresponding price in the period at time t − 1*

Sample: The BSE Sensex and NSE NIFTY are taken as sample market index for the study.

Sources of data

This study is purely based on secondary data. The BSE SENSEX and NSE NIFTY are taken as sample market index for the study. The data for a period of 10 years have been taken for the study from 2010–11 to 2019–20. All the data required for the study have been taken from BSE and NSE official websites and related literature published in the Books, Journals etc.

Period of study: The study period is from 2010–11 to 2019–20.

Techniques for the analysis

In order to measure the risk and return of BSE Sensex and NSE Nifty the important variables – mean return, standard deviation variance and coefficient of variations are used in this study. ANOVA is conducted to test the hypothesis in the study. The hypotheses are tested at 5% level of significance.

Hypothesis

H_0: There exists no significant relationship between return of BSE SENSEX and NSE NIFTY for the period 2010-11 through 2019-20.

H1: There exists significant relationship between return of BSE SENSEX and NSE NIFTY for the period 2010-11 through 2019-20.

Results and discussions

Table 16.1 shows the details of the variables used to calculate the risk and return; the risk and return of NSE NIFTY have been presented in the Table 16.1. According to the table, the index yielded the highest mean return in 2014–2015 and the lowest return in 2019–2020. The standard deviation of risk is highest in the year 2019–2020, indicating the highest risk level. In the year 2017–2018, the lowest risk level is shown. The coefficient of variation depicts that in the year 2012–2013, NIFTY recorded the maximum return per unit of standard deviation.

Table 16.2 shows the details of the variables used to calculate the risk and return of the BSE SENSEX. As per the table, the index yielded the highest mean return in 2014–2015 and the lowest return in 2019–2020. The standard deviation of risk is highest in the year 2019–2020, indicating the highest risk level. In the year 2017–2018, the lowest risk level is shown. In the year 2010–2011, the Co-efficient of variation indicates that the BSE Sensex provided the highest return per unit of standard deviation.

The returns of BSE SENSEX and NSE NIFTY are being shown by Figure 16.3. This shows the direction of returns of both the indices moved together very strongly.

Table 16.3 shows the results of the ANOVA between the BSE SENSEX and the NSE NIFTY returns. The table's p-value indicates that the sample indices' returns have a significant relationship. As a result, the null hypothesis (H0) is rejected, while the alternate hypothesis (H1) is accepted, indicating that there was a significant relationship between the BSE Sensex and the NSE Nifty returns.

Table 16.1 Risk–return variables of NSE Nifty for the period from 201011 to 2019–20

	2010–11	2011–12	2012–13	2013–14	2014–15	2015–16	2016–17	2017–18	2018–19	2019–20
MEAN	0.038635	−0.038497	0.026743	0.064599	0.096596	−0.042604	0.070216	0.036972	0.052437	−0.139989
MAX	3.483363	3.554587	2.714052	3.737970	2.943554	3.311503	2.37117	1.884477	2.297375	6.414547
MIN	−3.264761	−4.168886	−2.258330	−4.168548	−3.042205	−6.097258	−2.728136	−2.353914	−2.704354	−13.90375
STDEV	1.119883	1.297409	0.817279	1.145066	0.864865	1.091786	0.785794	0.629277	0.783401	1.738366
VAR	1.254138	1.68327	0.667945	1.311176	0.747991	1.191997	0.617472	0.39599	0.613717	3.021916
CV	28.98623	−33.7016	30.560483	17.72575	8.953425	−25.6264	11.1911	17.02037	14.93985	−12.4179

Source: www.nseindia.com

Table 16.2 Risk–return variables of BSE SENSEX for the period 2010–2011 through 2019–2020

	2010–2011	2011–2012	2012–2013	2013–2014	2014–2015	2015–2016	2016–2017	2017–2018	2018–2019	2019–2020
MEAN	0.037333	−0.044198	0.030164	0.068461	0.090724	−0.044307	0.064317	0.039738	0.061103	−0.112581
MAX	3.436245	3.518089	2.670895	3.703417	2.868370	3.323639	2.249610	1.817229	2.131259	6.746831
MIN	−3.049154	−4.212875	−2191015	−4.053732	−3.118485	−6.119712	−2.572483	−2.366941	−2.278212	−14.10174
STDEV	1.105952	1.284477	0.794543	1.101627	0.868761	1.079797	0.769313	0.627415	0.764897	1.777985
VAR	1.22313	1.649881	0.631299	1.213582	0.754746	1.165962	0.591842	0.39365	0.585067	3.161231
CV	29.62398	−29.0619	26.34077	16.09131	9.575867	−24.3708	11.96127	15.78879	12.51816	−15.7929

Source: www.bseindia.com

Table 16.3 ANOVA results (between the returns of BSE SENSEX and NSE NIFTY

ANOVA						
Source of variation	SS	df	MS	F	P-value	F crit
Between groups	1.06445E-05	9	1.18272E-06	19.96861	2.97226E-05	3.0203829
Within groups	5.92288E-07	10	5.92288E-08			
Total	1.12367E-05	19				

Source: www.bseindia.com, www.nseindia.com

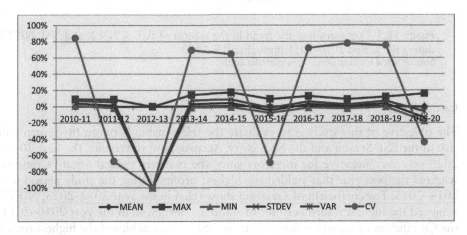

Figure 16.1 The trend in return and risk variables of NSE Nifty for the period 2010–11 through 2019–20
Source: www.nseindia.com

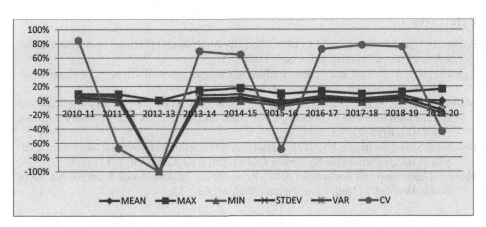

Figure 16.2 The trend in return and risk variables of BSE SENSEX for the period 2010–2011 through 2019–2020
Source: www.bseindia.com

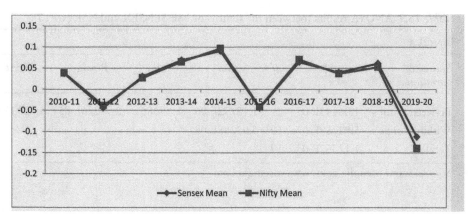

Figure 16.3 Comparison of the trend in the returns of BSE SENSEX and NSE NIFTY during the period 2010–2011 through 2019–2020
Source: www.bseindia.com, www.nseindia.com

Conclusion

The objective of this study is to evaluate the relationship between the return and risk of the BSE Sensex and the NSE Nifty. According to the results, the year 2019–2020 was very negative for investors since the markets yielded negative returns, whereas the best year that yielded the highest profits during the study period was 2014–2015. The coefficient of variation shows that in the year 2012–2013, NIFTY achieved the highest return per unit of standard deviation. In the year 2010–2011, the Co-efficient of variation shows that the BSE Sensex achieved the highest return per unit of standard deviation. This analysis has attempted to understand market performance in order to help investors in making good investment decision.

References

Fischer, D. E. and Jordan Ronald J. (1994). Security Analysis and portfolio management, fifth edition. Prentice Hall of India, New Delhi.

Kandel L. R. (2018). Risk and Return Analysis of Commercial Banks of Nepal with reference to NABIL and NIBIL. *Pravahe J. - J. Manag.* 24(1):109–119.

Mallikarjunappa, T. and Shaini, N. (2016). A study on Comparative Analysis of Risk and Return with reference to stocks of CNX Bank Nifty. *Int. J. Sci. Res. Modern Education (IJSRME).* I(I):737–743.

Poornima, S. and Swathiga, P. (2017). A study on relationship between risk and return analysis of selected stocks on NSE using CAPM. *Int. J. Appl. Res.* 3(7): 375–378.

Sharma, Gagandeep and Bodla B.S. (2012). Rewards and Risks in Stock Markets: A Case of South Asia. *Int. J. Appl. Econ. Financ. Stud.* 6(2):37–52.